POLITICAL JUDGMENT

RONALD BEINER

POLITICAL
JUDGMENT

THE UNIVERSITY OF CHICAGO PRESS

· TO MY PARENTS ·

The University of Chicago Press, Chicago 60637
Methuen & Co. Ltd., London EC4P 4EE

© 1983 by Ronald Beiner

All rights reserved. Published 1983
Printed in Great Britain by the
University Press, Cambridge

92 91 90 89 88 87 86 85 84 83   54321

ISBN 0 226 04164 6 (cloth)
     0 226 04165 4 (paper)

LCN 83 – 50829

If language is to be a means of communication
there must be agreement not only in definitions
but also (queer as this may sound) in judgments.
Wittgenstein, *Philosophical Investigations*,
para. 242

... our human experience of the world, for
which we rely on our faculty of judgment ....
Hans-Georg Gadamer, *Truth and Method*,
p. 496

Contents

Foreword

The obvious is so often ignored. Basic assumptions are the most difficult to identify and criticize. The familiar is notoriously hard to characterize and simplicity of exposition is far more difficult to achieve than conventional sophistication. I have often thought that any fool can give a seminar or write a monograph but that it takes a very special kind of person to give a first year lecture or to write an introductory book. But Dr Beiner has every right to quote a dictum of Wittgenstein's from the *Philosophical Investigations*: 'The aspects of things that are most important for us are hidden because of their simplicity and familiarity. One is unable to notice something because it is always before one's eyes.'

Political judgment is everywhere. We praise it as a skill or a virtue or we deplore its absence – as when people show bad political judgment or, even worse, seek to deny that they are making political judgments at all, perhaps believing that they are merely applying rules ('the advocacy of disarmament is an inherently contentious purpose which, therefore, cannot be "charitable"') or are taking expert advice in some liberal–bureaucratic realm above politics ('no single, common examination paper can assess the wide ability levels of all children at 16'). Every classic political thinker mentions it, but while some mention it more than others – Aristotle, Spinoza, Hobbes, Hume, Burke and

Godwin notably – yet even they have done so only in passing. The concept is everywhere but it has no literature. Often what is written about seems more to follow scholarly fashion than to stem from any general, thoughtful attempt to appraise what is important, what needs elucidation if we are to understand better the condition we are in and what we may do about it or within it. Most political thinking is now about political thinking. A few years ago, for instance, I was trying to think in a simple-minded way about what were basic or recurring socialist values. 'Liberty, equality, fraternity' seemed an obvious answer or starting point; but it was immediately obvious that while there is a vast literature of books and articles, some speaking to the world but mostly to each other, on 'liberty' and on 'equality', there were few references to 'fraternity', though the word is everywhere. I am sure that Dr Beiner would think that I confused the concept of 'fraternity' with that of 'friendship' or 'mutual trust', which Aristotle regards as prime conditions for citizenship, indeed for political activity at all. Perhaps so, but while both 'fraternity' and 'friendship' occur or are assumed in nearly all major political writings, they have not been examined on their own.

Similarly with 'political judgment', ubiquitous but undefined. Dr Beiner came to this through an interest in Hannah Arendt, indeed he wrote his Oxford doctoral dissertation on 'Hannah Arendt and Political Judgment'. I had the good fortune to be asked to act as external examiner to the thesis about which I enthusiastically complained that it was really two outstanding theses: one on Arendt's political philosophy and the other on 'political judgment', comparing her treatment of the concept to that of Aristotle, Kant and Gadamer. This book is not a thesis, but it arose from the half on judgment. Rarely have I been more eager to urge that something should be published and read, and read by general intellectuals even more than by students of politics: it challenges them not equally, but more.

Arendt's work, however, is central to the argument (work whose importance is at last beginning to be appreciated in this country). 'Judging' was to have been the final section of a trilogy, *The Life of the Mind*, of which only *Thinking* and *Willing* were completed. Only the title page with two epigrams was found in her typewriter at her death. Ronald Beiner has recently edited for the University of Chicago Press her *Lectures on Kant's Political Philosophy*, lectures that professed to find in his *Critique of Judgment* an implicit theory of political judgment superior to that more obviously found in his *Critique of Practical Reason*, and he has added a lengthy interpretive essay on Arendt's actual fragmentary and probable developed views on 'judgment'. Kant held in his *Critique* that an aesthetic judgment is inherently social, making reference to a common or shared world, to what appears in public to all who judge; and it neither invokes private whim nor some external, absolute standard. The act of judging implies a commitment to communicate the judgment and to persuade, and this attempt to persuade is not then external to the judgment but is its very *raison d'être* – an activity valuable in itself whether or not the persuasion is successful. Similarly Arendt saw *political* judgment as a social activity, but (committed to speech, freedom and publicity) valuable in itself, to be praised (becomes the apparent paradox) irrespective of consequences. She wishes, no less, to rescue Aristotle and the classical political tradition from the gloss put upon it by nineteenth-century utilitarianism and encouraged by Kant's *Critique of Practical Reason*: that true actions are useful actions. Good judgments (the spectator) and good actions (the actor), she maintained, remain good whether or not they are defeated. *Victrix causa deis placuit, sed victa Catoni* was one of the epigrams found in her dead typewriter: 'The victorious cause pleased the gods, but the defeated one pleases Cato.'

Yet this book, while arising from Arendt, just as Arendt's prior concern with judgment took her back to but beyond Kant, is wholly original and, moreover, important. It is important both philosophically and politically. Philosophically it shows that the methods of the analytical tradition of British philosophy can be applied to the substantive questions of the Continental tradition of Arendt's teachers, Jaspers and Heidegger. Somehow, coming from McGill in Canada (though that is no explanation), Beiner refuses to take sides between Anglo-Saxon and Continental philosophy, but uses the methods of one to elucidate the great questions of the other – in a manner perhaps somewhat reminiscent of his fellow Canadian and sometime teacher, Charles Taylor. Politically it is important because:

> The purpose of inquiring into the nature of judgment is to disclose a mental faculty by which we situate ourselves in the political world without relying upon explicit rules and methods, and thus to

open up a space of deliberation that is being closed ever more tightly in technocratic societies. In respect of this faculty, the dignity of the common citizen suffers no derogation. Here the expert can claim no special privileges. If the faculty of judging is a general aptitude that is shared by all citizens, and if the exercise of this faculty is a sufficient qualification for active participation in political life, we have a basis for reclaiming the privilege of responsibility that has been prized from us on grounds of specialized competence. Ultimately, what is sought in this study is a re-definition of citizenship.

Quite literally people have been encouraged to distrust their own judgment, or, to speak more strictly, the judgments that they can come to form through mutual discussion and debate. Politics (and defence, say) are too complicated matters, it is said, for any but expert judgment. And yet the very nature of politics involves the inter-action of people (realistically, rulers and ruled; idealistically, equals) and the interaction of knowledge and opinion, not either alone. To see politics, as the behaviourists would have us do, as an objective world of 'power', 'interests' or 'rules' is mistaken: politics is something inherent to the wonderfully human intersubjectivities of language, debate, deliberation and judgment. To make an analysis of 'political judgment' a central concern has at least this in common with Rous-seau's concept of the 'general will': that it can be found to some degree or at some level in everyone.

This is not to suggest that Dr Beiner's book is not, while never technical, very demanding. It will not be understood by most of those who write or read political commentary. Yet its conclusion is popular: political judgment is an inherently human quality, related to what some call (again a concept rarely analysed) 'common sense'. And political judgment and common sense are everywhere being either scorned or undermined, often undermined by those intellectuals who profess to be defending it.

I felt some hesitancy when asked by the publishers to introduce this book because I have learned more from it than I knew myself about Arendt and Kant, let alone Gadamer and Habermas. It has led me to re-read Aristotle. It made me aware of the philosophical inadequacy, despite the rhetorical power, of my own *In Defence of Politics*. Perhaps that is all I should say, except that a book like this lifts one from the short-term political pessimism into which most of us have fallen or feel close to falling. For it is not merely a powerful restatement of the primary importance of political *thinking*, but it shows the precise content of a concept so overwhelmingly important yet so easy to dismiss as banal. And even if things were hopeless for a humane humanity, we should act politically and we should exercise the best judgment that we can.

Bernard Crick
Birkbeck College
University of London

Preface

This essay attempts to sketch the outlines of a political philosophy. A political philosophy defines in some way the essence of the political. The political philosophy that begins to find expression here sees the essence of the political not in the phenomena of power or interest or rule or most of the other concerns that dominate present political life, but rather, locates the essence of politics in language, deliberation, and judgment. Political experience, as a specific mode of being in the world, is constituted by speech, by the capacity of human beings to humanize their world through communication, discourse, and talk about what is shared and thus available for intersubjective judgment. This theoretical perspective is developed by means of an exploration of the concept of judgment.

This definition of the essence of political experience is to a fair extent counter-intuitive, for we all in some sense take politics to be about relations of power, domination, pursuit of interests, and the struggle to prevail over others. The purpose of this inquiry is to suggest a very different theoretical horizon for thinking about politics: it seeks a very different basis for delimiting the bounds of the political. It is a fact today that absolutely fundamental questions of human existence go undiscussed and unspoken, are not subject to deliberation or debate, are simply absent from the realm of general public discourse and speech: the meaning of modern technology, in its full implications; irreversible changes in our relation to nature; a dissolving of the bounded identity of human communities that has taken on the character of an inexorable process; the overwhelming sense of helplessness in the face of ethical and social developments that seem to surpass any human control; the impotence we all feel when confronted with developments that are rapidly changing the total condition of man on earth. Which present-day political leaders, political movements, parties, and ideologies come close to addressing issues that touch the real agenda of political concern? What does it mean for our nature as political beings that such matters go largely undiscussed and unspoken within the prevailing guidelines of contemporary political discourse? In the face of this enormous fatality of our moral and political life, questions of liberalism and individual rights, modes of distribution and economic organization, trade-offs between freedom and equality or between efficiency and justice, and most of the other staples of political conflict pale into insignificance as regards the realization or non-realization of our political essence. Again, attention to the nature and function of the faculty of judgment may serve to reopen fundamental questions about what makes us political beings, and how to recover a dimension of political existence that seems to be absent so long as supreme issues of social life on this planet are not made subject to public discourse, dialogue, and common deliberation.

In a political world that is everywhere dominated by technological imperatives, where the intrusion of technology and technological ways of thinking into every sphere of life, even the most private and intimate, continues to gather pace, and where everything – cultural experience, religion, sexuality – is, accordingly, reshaped in uncomprehended ways, the simple exercise of reflective judgment comes increasingly to be regarded as outmoded. There seems to be neither place nor status for the power of ordinary human judgment, that is, for a capacity for making sense of the things around us that is unaccountable in, and cannot be submitted to, the terms of technical rationality. It is in this context that we must renew efforts to define once again the meaning of citizenship, and to clarify for ourselves what it could mean to be citizens in such a world.

Let me restate, more boldly still (and at some risk of sounding overwrought), the claim that sets the context for this investigation of the nature of judgment: if we cannot even humanize by talk (in a public setting) the sorts of global transformations of the conditions of our existence that are now taking place, the invocation of 'liberal politics' is nothing but a sham. For such 'liberal politics' cannot give substance to that which alone can qualify the political sphere of existence as authentically political: namely speech. In these circumstances, it seems to me, the presumption of liberal politics cannot help but betray its groundlessness, and the only choice left open to us is to endeavour to rethink in a fundamental way the essence of politics and its relationship to language. My hope is that an analysis of the capacity of human judgment can make a constructive contribution to such efforts.

*

I wish to express deep thanks to friends and teachers in Montreal, friends and teachers at Oxford, and friends and colleagues in Southampton, who, by their encouragement and criticism, helped to shape and stimulate my thoughts on this subject. Among my teachers, I owe a special debt of gratitude to Charles Taylor and Alan Montefiore, who helped me to clarify and develop many of these ideas. I would also like to thank Bernard Crick and Zbigniew Pelczynski, who originally suggested I write this book; and I am grateful to Bernard Crick, Alan Montefiore, and Tom Sorell for their comments on the manuscript. Finally, I would like to thank the University of Chicago Press for allowing me to draw upon material from my interpretive essay in Hannah Arendt's *Lectures on Kant's Political Philosophy*, and Oxford University Press for permission to reprint extracts from *The Critique of Judgment* by Immanuel Kant, translated by James Creed Meredith (1952).

What is political judgment?

WHY WE SHOULD INQUIRE

The dominant implicit consciousness of contemporary political societies seems locked into a peculiar bind. On the one hand, rationality is exclusively identified with rule-governed behaviour, where the rules by which we are guided can be explicitly specified and made available for scrutiny according to strict canons of rational method. On the other hand, questions of ethical norms and political ends are assumed to be beyond rational scrutiny: here we retreat into a jealously guarded subjectivity where any questioning of our choices or priorities is regarded as a form of moral trespass, an intrusion into the realm of privileged individual 'values and preferences', or an imposition of our own individual 'values and preferences'. Consequently, the monopoly of political intelligence is handed over to experts, administrators, and political technicians who coordinate the rules of administration and decision-making that accord with the reigning canons of method, rational procedure, and expertise. This monopoly goes unquestioned because the exercise of political rationality is assumed to be beyond the competence of the ordinary individual, whose proper sphere of competence is the choice of his own moral and social 'values'. Total political responsibility is ceded to the expert or administrator, provided that the individual's private sphere of values is not invaded.

Under these conditions, political reason is stymied from the outset. It is no wonder that for most of us political life has lost its urgency. Nor should it come as a surprise to us that, according to Jürgen Habermas' analysis in his book *Legitimation Crisis*, modern political systems are depleted of the very resources of moral and political legitimation that would alone make it possible for them to fulfil the expectations that they themselves generate. The types of fiscal, political, and ideological crisis analysed by Habermas all have their roots in the fact that ordinary political reasoning and deliberation has been drained of its legitimacy. Convinced that the administration of the political system is the prerogative of specially qualified experts and that the opinion of the ordinary citizen fails to satisfy the established canons of rationality, the would-be citizen retreats to his own private domain where political frustration and malaise well up. Pitched between the rigid demands of rule-governed method and the equally constraining stipulations of reigning subjectivity, the rational opinion of the common citizen fails to find its proper voice.

Inquiry into the power of human judgment offers a possible way out of this impasse. Judgment is a form of mental activity that is not bound to rules, is not subject to explicit specification of its mode of operation (unlike methodical rationality), and comes into play beyond the confines of rule-governed intelligence. At the same time, judgment is not without rule or reason, but rather, must strive for general validity. If subjectivity could not be transcended, at least in principle, the rendering of judgments would be an entirely vain activity of asserting claims that could never be vindicated. For there to be the mere possibility of valid judgments, there must exist a way of breaking the twin stranglehold of methodical rules and arbitrary subjectivism.

Judgment allows us to comport ourselves to the world without dependence upon rules and methods, and allows us to defeat subjectivity by asserting claims that seek general assent. In this way political reason is liberated, and the common citizen can once again reappropriate the right of political responsibility and decision-making that had been monopolized by experts. If all human beings share a faculty of judgment that is sufficient for forming reasoned opinions about the political world, the monopoly of the expert and technocrat no longer possesses legitimacy. Political reason, from being a technical science, is restored to a practical science. As Hans-Georg Gadamer states in one of his essays: 'practical and political reason can only be realized and transmitted dialogically. I think, then, that the chief task of philosophy is to justify this way of reason and to defend practical and political reason against the domination of technology based on science.' Thus 'it vindicates again the noblest task of the citizen – decision-making according to one's own responsibility – instead of conceding that task to the expert'.[1] For many in the 1960s, it was the politicizing experience of the Vietnam War that schooled them in the active exercise of a faculty of critical judgment, and through the exercise of this faculty they came to participate in a new experience of political citizenship.

The purpose of inquiring into the nature of judgment is to disclose a mental faculty by which we situate ourselves in the political world without relying upon explicit rules and methods, and thus to open up a space of deliberation that is being closed ever more tightly in technocratic societies. In respect of this faculty, the dignity of the common citizen suffers no derogation. Here the expert can claim no special privileges. If the faculty of judging is a general aptitude that is shared by all citizens, and if the exercise of this faculty is a sufficient qualification for active participation in political life, we have a basis for reclaiming the privilege of responsibility that has been prized from us on grounds of specialized competence. Ultimately, what is sought in this study is a redefinition of citizenship.

Our topic, then, should be of concern to everyone, for it affects not just those with a specialist interest in politics but all of us whose lives are touched by politics, no less when political affairs seem most remote from our grasp. Politics removed from the sphere of common judgment is a perversion of the political, and as such, cannot help but manifest itself in political crisis. It is precisely because there is a deep-seated political crisis in the modern world that we are obliged to inquire into what is involved in judging and what makes it possible for us to exercise this faculty. Norman Jacobson writes:

> The sapping of authority has inevitably been accompanied by a crisis in judgment, for centuries thought somehow linked to 'common sense'. But what today may be regarded as 'common' amongst men, even those occupying the same geographic

boundaries and subject to the same laws and regulations? As for 'sense', the doubts cast by science upon what was once believed to 'make sense' have eroded the confidence of individuals and publics still further. Consequently, many of us cringe back from the precipice of judgment, for fear either of error or of fatal involvement in what we cannot even dimly comprehend. For such, political theory needs once again to become responsible. . . .[2]

Perhaps reflection upon this faculty – which has now fallen into crisis owing to the loss of authority of traditional standards of judgment – can contribute in some small way to the recovery of 'common sense', taken in the classical signification referred to by Jacobson.

THE CONCEPT OF JUDGMENT IN THE HISTORY OF POLITICAL PHILOSOPHY: BRIEF SURVEY

The theme of political judgment, historically considered, is a paradoxical one, for its presence within the western tradition of political thought is at one and the same time pervasive and elusive. The first recognition of a human faculty for judging particulars without the benefit of a universal rule goes back to Plato's dialogue, the *Statesman*. The theme of *phronesis* is developed extensively in Aristotle's work, and is transmitted to later thinkers both directly and via the political thought of Aquinas, who transposes into his own terms the Aristotelian analysis of moral life.[3] Among modern thinkers, we may mention Vico, who discusses prudence and eloquence in his essay *On the Study Methods of Our Time*; and Spinoza, who devotes chapter XX of the *Theologico-Political Treatise* and chapter III of the *Political Treatise* to a consideration of 'liberty of judgment'. Hobbes and Locke both had concepts of judgment: Hobbes devoted chapters 6–8 of part I of the *Leviathan* to examining the relationship between judgment and deliberation, and to distinguishing judgment from 'wit'; and Locke (*Essay Concerning Human Understanding*, II.XI; IV.XIV) regarded judgment as one of the two cognitive faculties of man, the other being knowledge. British thinkers of the eighteenth century, such as Shaftesbury, Hume, and Burke, devoted a great deal of reflection to the concepts of judgment, taste, and opinion. Finally, William Godwin, another notable empiricist philosopher, devoted a chapter of his *Enquiry Concerning Political Justice* (book II, chapter VI) to 'the Right of Private Judgement'. Bhikhu Parekh, in an essay on 'The nature of political philosophy', has proposed the very interesting hypothesis that judgment is primarily a category of idealist philosophy, and, accordingly, as idealism has declined, so too has interest in political judgment.[4] It would seem that Parekh here has in mind principally that sort of philosophical idealism which inspired Oakeshott.[5] However, the category of judgment was also a chief concern of the major empiricist philosophers, as we have just noted. To appreciate fully the centrality of the concepts of taste and judgment in eighteenth-century British empiricist thought, one may turn to Hume's essay 'Of the standard of taste', or to the Introductory Discourse 'On taste' added to Burke's *Philosophical Enquiry*, which could not have failed to influence Kant's aesthetic theory.

And yet, despite this repeated occurrence of the term 'judgment' throughout the tradition of western political thought, there is a sense in which the theme of political judgment has hitherto gone without explicit recognition. There is, strictly speaking, no 'literature' on the concept of political judgment, as there are for other leading political concepts, such as justice, property, freedom, rights, equality, power, rule of law, revolution, and numerous others (in spite of the fact that without the concept of judgment none of these others could possibly exist). Where the concept occurs it does so obliquely, introduced within more general inquiries rather than being pursued systematically for its own sake. Although Kant's *Critique of Judgment* is offered as a conceptualization of the capacity of judging as such, its applicability to politics is highly problematical, as we shall begin to explore in a later chapter. We look in vain for a comparably exhaustive analysis of *political* judgment proper, in the entire course of western political philosophy.[6]

The dearth of theoretical investigations of this all-important human faculty can only be accounted for by reference to Wittgenstein's dictum that 'the aspects of things that are most important for us are hidden because of their simplicity and familiarity. (One is unable to notice something – because it is always before one's eyes.)'[7] What is required is a Wittgensteinian-type inquiry ('assembling reminders') to draw our attention back to those things we all already know, but which escape our notice because the matter lies too close to us. Hannah Arendt, the political philosopher with whom we commence our inquiry in the next chapter, had intended to complete her final opus on *The Life of the Mind* with a treatise on *Judging*. However, she died before she was able even to start on the work, and we can merely speculate about where it would have led, on the basis of earlier writings and posthumously published lecture notes.[8] So the analysis of the nature of judging still awaits us, as a task for theory.

SCOPE OF THE INQUIRY

We are constantly forming judgments. Every perception, every observation, every situation of ourselves in the world, the very awareness of our own subjectivity, involves judging. The exercise of this faculty encompasses every aspect of our experience. How, then, can we prevent ourselves from being simply overwhelmed by the object of our inquiry, and sufficiently delimit the field of study?

To begin with, we may distinguish several different senses of the term judgment. Perhaps the most prominent philosophical connotation of the concept is judgment in the sense of logical judgment, which is an act of the mind by which we affirm or negate a proposition, e.g. 'all men are mortal'. (Judgment and proposition are often treated as synonymous in works of traditional logic.) Judgment is also used to denote a cognitive faculty, that is, a distinct sphere of mental operation. Finally, judgment may mean a quality of mind, in the sense in which we predicate of someone that they possess good or sound judgment, or when we say that we trust their judgment. In this study we are in large part concerned with this third sense of judgment, although we are at the same time concerned to determine whether and to what extent possession of such a quality of mind serves to disclose a distinct mental faculty.[9]

Leaving aside logical judgments, there remain a whole host of domains within which we can be said to exercise judgment: perceptual judgment ('This table is brown'); aesthetic judgment ('This painting is beautiful'); historical judgment ('This event was auspicious'); legal judgment ('This man is guilty'); hermeneutical judgment ('This interpretation of the text is justified'); moral judgment ('This is the right thing to do'; 'This is what it is to be virtuous'); and last but not least, political judgment ('This policy is just, or necessary, or advisable under the circumstances'). We do not mean to suggest that the divisions between these varieties of judgment are as tidy and determinate as they appear in our examples; nor do we imply that political judgment can be so simply and unequivocally segregated from all other domains of judgment. Quite the contrary, a rigorous specification of the distinguishing characteristics of political judgment is one of the leading challenges posed by the quest for a suitable theory of political judgment.

Even if we allow ourselves to bracket this enormous and unresolved question of the relationship between moral, aesthetic, historical, legal, hermeneutical, and political judgment, we are presented with still other pressing difficulties in trying to conceptualize judgment. Part of the 'grammar' of the concept leads us to think of judgment as something that *follows* the object of judgment, like a verdict. This is owing in large measure to the heavy *legal* associations of the term judgment (the rendering of a verdict by the judge or jury in a court of law). This implicit meaning is noted by Aquinas in his discussion of the development of the concept: 'The word judgment which in its original usage meant the right determination of what is just, has been stretched to cover the right determination on any matter whether theoretical or practical.'[10] Furthermore, when we consult the *OED* definition of judgment, we are struck by the preponderance of these legal connotations of the word, for instance, as it occurs in the concept of the Final Judgment, or the Day of Judgment. The unmistakable implication is that judgment is rendered when all is done, and the tally is complete.

However, another part of the concept's 'grammar' draws us in the opposite direction: judging is something we do when we seek to decide about a course of action, that is, in practical deliberation. This calls for *phronesis* or practical wisdom, the conditions of which are specified in a theory of prudence. Here the temporal direction of judgment is prospective rather than retrospective: it operates forward rather than backward in time. This contrast between judgment as a prospective and as a retrospective activity corresponds to another conceptual tension, between judgment as predicated of the agent and judgment as predicated of the spectator. The actor judges just as much as the spectator does – he considers, weighs alternatives, discriminates the various ways of describing criteria of action, and only *then* chooses – yet the connotations of the term judgment are rather different in these two cases. Although neither of these two aspects can be privileged over the other, they illustrate the duality inherent in the concept of judgment. These are some of the perplexities which confront us when we begin to analyse the concept, and merely suggest the kinds of difficulty that stand before us in attempting to clarify the meaning of judgment.

In every contact we have with the political world we are engaged in judgment. Judging is what we do when we read politics in our morning newspaper, when we discuss politics during family or friendly conversation, and when we watch politics on television. Judging is also what we as academics do when we try to keep abreast of the political developments in our world, or when we strive to appraise the course of modern political history. And finally, judging is what we are doing also when we *do* politics, that is, when we act in a public setting or assume public responsibilities for which we are held accountable. So the normal kind of contact that each of us – academics, political observers, and common citizens – has with politics is the opportunity to judge.

Examples of this range from the trivial to the not so trivial: we may note the rising or falling fortunes of a well-known politician; or we may remark upon the pronounced moral and public integrity of a new entrant into the political arena; or we may denounce the decision of a corporate stock-holders' meeting as yet another instance of the domination of the political process by a profit-minded ruling class. In each of these cases, varied as they may be, we witness the pronouncing of judgments, or we ourselves pronounce judgments. Similarly, we render judgment in deciding whether the monetarist policies of Mrs Thatcher's government are leading to the salvation or the ruin of British society, in deciding whether an urban guerrilla action is the act of an immoral terrorist or of an admirable freedom-fighter, in deciding whether American foreign policy is benevolent or malign (and in deciding what responses are called for, whether in thought or in action). Again, in all these cases, we enter into argument or self-deliberation in order to arrive at a correct judgment. We are simply asking: what does this consist in, what are its implications, and in what ways can knowledge of it contribute to our understanding of politics?

HOW TO PROCEED

Judgment is a natural capacity of human beings that can, potentially, be shared by all. It enables us to appraise particulars without dependence upon rules or rule-governed technique, and it involves release from the confines of private subjectivity since we can support our judgments with publicly adducible reasons or grounds. This raises two related sets of questions: first, if, in judging, I make a rational appeal that goes beyond mere subjectivity on the basis of adduced grounds that can be generally or universally acknowledged, what relation of community comes into play in the exercise of this faculty? How does the activity of judging relate me to my fellows, and by what authority can I appeal to and make claims upon a wider community of judgment? Second, if judging operates without the benefit of rules or explicit canons of methodical technique, what is the basis of the validity of our judgments, and from whence do they derive their legitimacy? How are valid judgments possible at all, and by what means do we justify the judgments that we make? These are Kantian questions, addressed by means of the transcendental method formulated in Kant's three *Critiques*.

Needless to say, we very often make judgments that are clouded, confused, ideologically distorted, or plainly unsound. But at the same time we are capable of recognizing these judgments to be such because we are also familiar with judgments that are reasonable or well-grounded. For instance, we can come to see, in retrospect, that earlier judgments of our own were hasty or premature or motivated by resentment and envy. It is possible for us to have a concept of deficient or distorted judgment only because of logically prior access to an ideal standard of adequate or fitting judgment. It is therefore important for us to clarify precisely what it is that constitutes a good judgment. Here we would do well to follow the Kantian procedure, which is to inquire into what are the conditions of the *possibility* of judgments possessing validity, what renders valid judgment *possible*. Aberrations can only be properly appraised by reference to this standard of possible validity.

This transcendental method of Kant's is in fact adopted by Jürgen Habermas in his recent work on 'communicational competence', in which he explores the notion of 'coming to an agreement', and how the counterfactual positing of an ideally achieved consent is built into the very structure of human rationality.[11] Stanley Cavell, in his essay 'Aesthetic problems of modern philosophy' (in *Must We Mean What We Say?*), also develops certain important insights from the *Critique of Judgment* concerning the process of claiming and winning acknowledgement for our judgments, and shows how Kant's account of aesthetic judgment can help to illuminate general features of human rationality.

Such attempts are of apparent relevance to the theory of political judgment that needs elaboration.

In the following chapter we shall look briefly at several contemporary works of political philosophy that may help to guide us in our inquiry. In them we hope to find clues for answering the questions that have been posed here: the nature of human judgment, the relationship between judgment and rational community, and the ways in which it is possible for us to ground the validity of our judgments.

T·W·O
Possible avenues of inquiry

Everyone is constantly making judgments, whether political, moral, aesthetic, or simply ordinary cognitive judgments (whether to describe something in this way or that). Yet very rarely has sustained reflection been devoted to the question of what it means for us to make judgments, what natural human endowment makes men capable of forming judgments, what renders it possible for our judgments to be valid, what is the ultimate basis of their validity, and, more specifically, what it is about the judging faculty that distinguishes man as a political being.

However, recent work in political philosophy has opened up a number of promising lines of inquiry for addressing such questions: Hannah Arendt claims that the faculty of judgment is 'the most political of man's mental abilities'. Arendt supports this claim in various of her works by developing certain themes and concepts from Kant's *Critique of Judgment*: the ideas of taste, 'enlarged mentality', *sensus communis*, disinterested reflection, and spectatorship. Hans-Georg Gadamer, in his important work *Truth and Method*, raises a set of critical objections to Kant's theory of aesthetic judgment, charging that Kant's highly formalized account of taste sheds the political and moral connotations of what had formerly been taken to be a social-moral faculty. Kant abstracts from the moral-political content once possessed by the idea of *sensus communis* (common sense), as we find it for instance in Shaftesbury. To make good these deficiencies in Kant, Gadamer seeks an alternative conceptualization of political judgment in Aristotle's account of *phronesis* (practical wisdom). Gadamer's Aristotelian critique of Kant poses a serious challenge to any attempt, along the lines proposed by Arendt, to model a theory of political judgment on the Kantian critique of aesthetic judgment. Meanwhile Jürgen Habermas, in part III of *Legitimation Crisis*, offers a theory of communicative ethics, based on the ideas of ideal speech situation, consensus theory of truth, and intersubjective validation of normative truth claims. Habermas, like Arendt, draws philosophical inspiration from Kant's critical philosophy, but, unlike Arendt, believes that moral judgment has a cognitive basis, and that practical discourse is oriented primarily to establishing truth.

In this chapter we shall try to sketch briefly each of these theories, in order to show how each of them, in conjunction and by critical interaction, can contribute to a fully rounded theory of political judgment.

ARENDT: POLITICS AND THE APPEAL TO KANTIAN AESTHETICS[1]

Politics is defined in the philosophical work of Hannah Arendt as an agency of disclosure. Rather than being characterized in terms of the purposes men pursue or the ends they achieve, political action is understood as constituting a realm of appearances in which human agents, acting together, disclose who they are and what they wish the world to look like. Politics is literally 'phenomenal': it opens up a space of appearances in which men can show themselves and show their deeds in public. To be without such a public space of appearances

> means to be deprived of reality, which, humanly and politically speaking, is the same as appearance. To men the reality of the world is guaranteed by the presence of others, by its appearing to all; 'for what appears to all, this we call Being' (Aristotle), and whatever lacks this appearance comes and passes away like a dream.[2]

In contrast to the activity of labour, which produces goods for consumption in satisfaction of natural bodily necessities, and the activity of work, which fabricates a durable world of use objects, political action, viewed phenomenologically, is an activity of collective self-disclosure: the performance of deeds and speeches in a public space specifically organized for public remembrance.

> [T]he Greeks always used such metaphors as flute-playing, dancing, healing, and seafaring to distinguish political from other activities, that is, . . . they drew their analogies from those arts in which virtuosity of performance is decisive. . . . The performing arts . . . have indeed a strong affinity with politics. Performing artists – dancers, play-actors, musicians, and the like – need an audience to show their virtuosity, just as acting men need the presence of others before whom they can appear; both need a publicly organized space for their 'work', and both depend upon others for the performance itself. . . . The Greek polis . . . provided men . . . with a kind of theatre where freedom could appear.[3]

It is through speech and action that men experience freedom. But this cannot be a solo performance, for it is only by acting in concert with our peers that there can be freedom, which for Arendt is in turn identical with the power generated by collective action. Freedom then becomes

> a worldly reality, tangible in words which can be heard, in deeds which can be seen, and in events which are talked about, remembered, and turned into stories before they are finally incorporated into the great storybook of human history. Whatever occurs in this space of appearances is political by definition. . . .[4]

Political action, alone among the worldly activities of man, offers a lasting source of meaning to human affairs, for the deeds and speeches of speaking and acting men can be gathered into a story that, when retold, allows their human intelligibility to become visible. Speaking and acting generate stories that give meaning to earthly existence stretched between birth and death. The essence of politics, in this view, is not to rule over others or to achieve instrumental objectives, but rather to join with others in collective deeds that win immortal remembrance. It is the words and deeds of political men, acting in concert in a public space, that Arendt believes holds the answer to the challenge of Silenus posed in Sophocles' play *Oedipus at Colonus* and restated by

Nietzsche in section 3 of *The Birth of Tragedy*: 'Not to be born prevails over all meaning uttered in words; by far the second-best for life, once it has appeared, is to go as swiftly as possible whence it came.'[5] Thus she writes at the very end of her book *On Revolution*: 'it was the polis, the space of men's free deeds and living words, which could endow life with splendour', it was this 'that enabled ordinary men, young and old, to bear life's burden'.[6]

In this world of appearances composed of the deeds of speaking and acting men we require a mental faculty by which to assimilate the phenomena of the public world and make sense of the stories of what men have done. It is the faculty of judgment that fits us into this world of phenomena and appearances, and makes it possible for us to find our proper place in it. It is precisely because the political world is defined by Arendt as a realm of phenomenal disclosure that the faculty of judging assumes such importance for her. It is for this reason that she says in her essay 'Thinking and moral considerations' that one may call the faculty of judgment with some justification 'the most political of man's mental abilities'.[7]

For the explication of this faculty Arendt turns to Kant. In Kant's critique of aesthetic judgment she discerns an account of 'appearances qua appearances', and therefore entertains the hope that the Kantian theory may help to elucidate the judging of political appearances. In fact, Arendt claims that the *Critique of Judgment* contains a hitherto unknown and unsuspected political philosophy. According to Arendt, Kant

> expounds two political philosophies which differ sharply from one another – the first being that which is generally accepted as such in his *Critique of Practical Reason* and the second that contained in his *Critique of Judgment*. That the first part of the latter is, in reality, a political philosophy is a fact that is seldom mentioned in works on Kant; on the other hand, it can, I think, be seen from all his political writings that for Kant himself the theme of 'judgment' carried more weight than that of 'practical reason'. In the *Critique of Judgment* freedom is portrayed as a predicate of the power of imagination and not of the will, and the power of imagination is linked most closely with that wider manner of thinking which is political thinking par excellence, because it enables us to 'put ourselves in the minds of other men'.[8]

The fact that this 'other' political philosophy has never before been recognized or appreciated (even by Kant himself!) Arendt attributes to the prejudices, as old as the tradition of western political philosophy itself, according to which politics is about rule or dominion, interest, instrumentality, and so forth. But in judgment we find none of this:

> We deal with a form of being together [shared judgment, community of taste] where no one rules and no one obeys. Where people persuade each other. . . . This is not to deny that interest and power and rule . . . are very important and even central political concepts. . . . The question is: Are they the fundamental concepts, or are they derived from the living-together that itself springs from a different source? (Company/Action).[9]

Arendt's view is that we are more likely to get at this other source by turning to a work whose explicit theme is 'appearances qua appearances' than by concentrating on the works that make up the established tradition of political philosophy:

> The *Critique of Judgment* is the only of [Kant's] great writings where his point of departure is the World and the senses and capabilities which made men (in the plural) fit to be inhabitants of it. This is perhaps not yet political philosophy, but it certainly is its condition *sine qua non*. If it could be found that in the capacities and regulative traffic and intercourse between men who are bound to each other by the common possession of a world (the earth) there exists an *a priori* principle, then it would be proved that man is essentially a political being.[10]

Among the writings published in her lifetime, Arendt's fullest account of judgment is contained in her essay 'The crisis in culture: its social and its political significance', included in *Between Past and Future*. Judgment is exercised by the spectator who apprehends cultural and political appearances. Culture, like politics, offers a space of display to things whose essence it is to appear: 'both [art and politics] are phenomena of the public world'.[11] The *Critique of Judgment* is appealed to, we are told, because in the first part, the 'Critique of aesthetic judgment', it offers 'an analytic of the beautiful primarily from the viewpoint of the judging spectator'.[12] This concern with the judging spectator follows directly from Arendt's definition of politics in terms of virtuosity or performance. The deeds of the actor are as in need of the judgment of the spectator as those of any other performer. Arendt begins her account of this idea of spectatorship by calling attention to the plurality presupposed in judgment, as opposed to the solitary nature of thought. She refers to the Kantian notion of 'enlarged mentality', which she elsewhere speaks of as 'representative thinking': 'thinking in the place of everybody else'.[13] This involves 'potential agreement with others', coming finally to some agreement.

Judgment, unlike logical reasoning, does not compel universal validity. Rather, it appeals to those judging persons 'present', those who are members of the public realm where the objects of judgment appear. Arendt appeals to the Aristotelian distinction between *phronesis* (practical wisdom) and *sophia* (theoretical wisdom): the latter strives to rise above common sense; the former is rooted in common sense, which 'discloses to us the nature of the world insofar as it is a common world', and 'enables man to orient himself in the public realm, in the common world'. This defence of common sense is a persistent theme of Arendt's work. Common sense means sharing a non-subjective and 'objective' (object-laden) world with others. 'Judging is one, if not the most, important activity in which this sharing-the-world-with-others comes to pass.'[14]

Part of the problem that has to be confronted here is the threat to judgment posed by the 'world-alienating' subjectivization of man in the modern age, whereby all public reality is thoroughly privatized and all truth claims are thoroughly relativized. Against this subjectivization 'no judgments could hold out: they were all reduced to the level of sensations, and ended on the level of the lowest of all sensations, the sensation of taste'. In this way, all judgments are degraded until they are on the same level as such matters of 'taste' as 'the preference for clam chowder over pea soup'.[15] Arendt credits Kant with having combated this degradation, and having dislodged the prejudice that judgments of taste lie outside the political realm (as well as outside the domain of reason). She claims that the alleged subjective arbitrariness of taste offended not Kant's aesthetic but his political sense. It was owing to his awareness of the public quality of beauty and the public relevance of beautiful things that Kant insisted that judgments of taste are open to discussion and subject to dispute.

In aesthetic no less than in political judgments, a decision is made, and although this decision is always determined by a certain subjectivity, by the simple fact that each person occupies a place of his own from which he looks upon and judges the world, it also derives from the fact that the world itself is an objective datum, something common to all its inhabitants. The activity of taste decides how this world, independent of its utility and our vital interests in it, is to look and sound, what men will see and what they will hear in it. Taste judges the world in its appearance and in its worldliness; its interest in the world is purely 'disinterested', and that means that neither the life interests of the individual nor the moral interests of the self are involved here. For judgments of taste, the world is the primary thing, not man, neither man's life nor his self.[16]

Judgment is contrasted with philosophical argument oriented towards truth. The latter, insisting upon demonstrable truth, seeks to *compel* agreement by a process of compelling proof. Judgments of taste, by contrast, are persuasive (like political opinions) – persuading 'in the hope of *coming* to an agreement with everyone else eventually'.

Culture and politics . . . belong together because it is not knowledge or truth which is at stake, but rather judgment and decision, the judicious exchange of opinion about the sphere of public life and the common world, and the decision what manner of action is to be taken in it, as well as to how it is to look henceforth, what kinds of things are to appear in it.[17]

These themes are further developed in her essay 'Truth and politics'. It is here that Arendt introduces her notion of the representative character of political thought:

I form an opinion by considering a given issue from different viewpoints, by making present to my mind the standpoints of those who are absent; that is, I represent them. This process of representation does not blindly adopt the actual views of those who stand somewhere else, and hence look upon the world from a different perspective; this is a question neither of empathy, as though I tried to be or to feel like somebody else, nor of counting noses and joining a majority but of being and thinking in my own identity where actually I am not. The more people's standpoints I have present in my mind while I am pondering a given issue, and the better I can imagine how I would feel and think if I were in their place, the stronger will be my capacity for representative thinking and the more valid my final conclusions, my opinion.[18]

This capacity, according to Arendt, is the Kantian 'enlarged mentality' which is the basis for man's ability to judge, although Kant, having recognized this capacity for impartial judgment, 'did not recognize the political and moral implications of his discovery'.[19] We try to *imagine* what it would be like to be somewhere else in thought, and 'the only condition for this exertion of the imagination is disinterestedness, the liberation from one's own private interests'.[20] This process of opinion formation, determined by those in whose places somebody thinks and uses his own mind, is such that 'a particular issue is forced into the open that it may show itself from all sides, in every possible perspective, until it is flooded and made transparent by the full light of human comprehension'.[21]

Arendt's discussion of taste in 'The crisis in culture' takes inspiration from Ciceronian humanism. Following Cicero, Arendt views the humanist as a non-specialist who 'exerts a faculty of judgment and taste which is beyond the coercion which each speciality imposes upon us'.[22] Such a humanism 'knows how to take care and preserve and admire the things of the world', for a cultivated man of taste is 'one who knows how to choose his company among men, among things, among thoughts, in the present as well as in the past'.[23] Taste 'decides not only how the world is to look, but also who belongs together in it'.[24] It defines a principle of belonging, is an expression of the company one keeps, and as such, like politics itself, is a matter of self-disclosure: 'By his manner of judging, the person discloses to an extent also himself, what kind of person he is, and this disclosure, which is involuntary, gains in validity to the degree that it has liberated itself from merely individual idiosyncrasies.'[25] Thus 'taste is the *political* capacity that truly humanizes the beautiful and creates a culture'.[26]

As we have seen, for Arendt politics is defined by phenomenality, as self-disclosure in a space of appearances. Political things, as Arendt conceives them, are phenomenally manifest: 'great things are self-evident, shine by themselves', the poet or historiographer merely *preserving* the glory that is already visible to all. Among the Greeks, 'great deeds and great words were, in their greatness, as real as a stone or a house, there to be seen and heard by everybody present. Greatness was easily recognizable.'[27] The phenomenality of politics is therefore analogous to the phenomenality of art:

> In order to become aware of appearances we first must be free to establish a certain distance between ourselves and the object, and the more important the sheer appearance of a thing is, the more distance it requires for its proper appreciation. This distance cannot arise unless we are in a position to forget ourselves, the cares and interests and urges of our lives, so that we will not seize what we admire but let it be as it is, in its appearance.[28]

Judgment discriminates among the appearances as they disclose themselves, and captures the full phenomenal richness of these appearances. Accordingly, the capacity of judgment for perceiving things as they are, that is, as they are phenomenally manifest, is closely related to the nature of politics as disclosure.[29] Judgment, as it were, confirms the being of that which has been disclosed. Thus it is in a very emphatic sense that human judgment always proceeds in a world of appearances.

GADAMER: HERMENEUTICS AND THE APPEAL TO ARISTOTELIAN ETHICS

Hans-Georg Gadamer, in his work *Truth and Method*, has established a new and important discipline: philosophical hermeneutics. Hermeneutics inquires into those spheres of human engagement where the activity of understanding and interpretation is primary. Traditional hermeneutics was associated with theology, and sought to discover rules for the interpretation of scriptural texts. Gadamer defines a much broader mandate for the discipline of hermeneutics.[30] Interpretation is called for not merely in the reading of texts, but more generally, in practical conduct and moral action. In deciding how to act well in a particular situation we draw upon an understanding of ourselves and our historical situation, of who we are and what ends we desire, and this necessarily entails an activity of interpretation. What we are interpreting is ourselves, and the past and present social worlds that make us what we are. Choices about how to act never arise in a vacuum, for in every context we already possess a pre-understanding of our historical identity and social relationships. This we get from our past, from the cultural and linguistic traditions that compose our historical identity. The cultural and historical tradition is the 'text' that we interpret in addressing problems of moral and social practice. This requires the exercise of a comprehensive faculty of taste which encompasses historical and moral judgment. Gadamer's basic endeavour is to uncover, at the philosophical level, the conditions of the possibility of this universal activity of interpretation, and to explain what makes aesthetic, historical, and linguistic understanding possible.

The traditional role of humanistic studies was to cultivate such self-understanding, so as to develop proper standards of good taste and good action in the concrete situations of life. However, Gadamer sees Kant's *Critique of Judgment* as marking a turning point in the history of the human sciences, radically transforming the traditional function of the humanities. Kant's effort to give to aesthetics a transcendental philosophical basis

> limited the idea of taste to an area in which, as a special principle of judgment, it could claim independent validity – and, by so doing, limited the concept of knowledge to the theoretical and practical use of reason. His transcendental purpose was fulfilled by the limited phenomenon of judgment of the beautiful (and sublime) and removed the more general experimental concept of taste and the activity of aesthetic judgment in the area of law and morality from the centre of philosophy. . . . [W]hat was here surrendered was that element in which literary and historical studies lived, and when they sought to set themselves up systematically under the name of 'human sciences' beside the natural sciences, it was the only possible source of their full self-understanding. Now Kant's transcendental analysis made it impossible to acknowledge the claim to truth of the tradition, to the cultivation and study of which they devoted themselves. But this meant that the unique method of the human sciences lost its justification.[31]

Prior to Kant, study of the humanities had as its guiding purpose the formation of moral character. Subsequently, there was a shift towards methodology, and the preoccupation was no longer with the truth claims exerted by art and history on our lives. Method, rather than the truth of cultural and historical existence, became the keystone.

In our exposition of Arendt's essay 'The crisis in culture' in the previous section, certain dominant concepts could be seen to emerge: culture, common sense, taste, judgment. It is these very same categories that Gadamer specifies, in the first part of *Truth and Method*, as constituting the foundation of the German classicist *Geisteswissenschaften* (cultural sciences or human sciences). This convergence is hardly fortuitous: both Arendt's vocabulary and the concepts analysed by Gadamer are rooted in Roman humanism, both derive equally from a Roman conception of the public. As Arendt expressly notes in 'The crisis in culture', 'humanism' is a specifically Roman creation.[32]

It is from the first part of Gadamer's *Truth and Method* that we may hope to get a proper understanding of the humanistic tradition that forms the context of Arendt's account of taste. As Gadamer explains, *Bildung* (culture, education), 'common sense', 'judgment', and 'taste' are the central concepts of the German classicist tradition of humanism, which took inspiration from antiquity and gave rise to the German *Geisteswissenschaften*. This constituted 'the atmosphere breathed by the human sciences of the nineteenth century'.[33] Gadamer traces the conception of *Geisteswissenschaften* back to Herder, to Hegel's notion of the *Bildung* of Spirit, and to Helmholtz's ideal of 'tact'. Gadamer also examines Vico's and Shaftesbury's reassertions of the humanistic tradition.[34] Both Vico, with his continuation of the rhetorical tradition of humanism, and Shaftesbury, with his influence upon the Scottish 'common sense' philosophy, help to revive and keep alive the ancient Roman idea of the *sensus communis*.

Thus far, Gadamer's concerns seem to match closely those of Arendt. However, Gadamer's evaluation of Kant is the very opposite of Arendt's. For Arendt, as we have seen, the third *Critique* reveals an unconscious political genius, whereas for Gadamer, Kant – along with the German Enlightenment generally – 'de-politicizes' the idea of *sensus communis* (as it occurs in Vico and Shaftesbury) which *already had* important political and moral connotations. Kant's formal and narrowed concept of judgment empties the older (Roman-rooted) conception of the very full moral-political content it formerly had. Kant, as it were, strips 'common sense' of the richness of its Roman meaning. *Sensus communis*, which had originally been understood as a general civic quality, carrying a Roman echo of suspicion towards the theoretical speculations of the philosophers, was taken by the German Enlightenment to denote a purely theoretical faculty.[35] Gadamer's basic challenge to Kant is stated as follows:

> The universality that is ascribed to the faculty of judgment is something by no means as common as Kant sees it. Judgment is not so much a faculty as a demand that has to be made of all. Everyone has enough 'sense of the common', i.e., judgment, that he can be expected to show a 'sense of the community', genuine moral and civic solidarity, but that means judgment of right and wrong, and a concern for the 'common good'. This is what makes Vico's reliance on the humanistic tradition so impressive for against the intellectualisation of the idea of the sense of the community, he holds firmly on to all the wealth of meaning that lived in the Roman tradition of this word. . . . Similarly, when Shaftesbury took up the idea it was . . . also a link with the political and social tradition of humanism. The sensus communis is an element of social and moral being. . . . By contrast, Kant's version of this idea in his *Kritik der Urteilskraft* has quite a different emphasis. There is no longer any systematic place for the basic moral sense of the concept. As we know, he developed his moral philosophy in downright opposition to the doctrine of 'moral feeling' that has been worked out in English philosophy. Thus he totally excluded the idea of sensus communis from moral philosophy.[36]

Kant 'intellectualizes' the *sensus communis*, 'aestheticizes' the faculty of taste that had formerly been understood as a social-moral faculty, narrowly circumscribes and delimits the range of these concepts, including judgment, and generally abstracts these concepts from all relationships of community. At the same time, Kant drives a wedge between aesthetic and moral theory, and divorces taste from knowledge. With this separation of aesthetics and knowledge, 'cultivation' ceases to count as a prerequisite of science, with the consequence that the *Geisteswissenschaften* lose their humanistic roots, their foundation in Roman humanism. However, Gadamer does recognize that Kant had his own special, transcendental reasons for altering this relationship between aesthetics and morality, between taste and knowledge (and between art and truth), and that the ramifications it was to have for the human sciences were beyond Kant's control. Kant is certainly aware of the broader social function of taste, but he consigns it to 'The methodology of taste', which is a mere appendix to the 'Critique of aesthetic judgment', and he also treats it in certain chapters of his *Anthropology*.[37] It does not form a part of the transcendental inquiry into taste.

For Arendt it was precisely the fact that Kant concerned himself with as politically charged an idea as judgment that evidenced the latent political dimension of his work. Gadamer exactly inverts this conclusion: Kant emasculated 'judgment' and 'taste' of the heavy political and social import they traditionally had, turning them into strictly delimited, *merely* 'aesthetic' concepts, which in turn involved serious repercussions for the post-Kantian methodology of the human sciences. The Kantian legacy undermines the humanistic culture in which the concepts of judgment, taste, and common sense have their true grounding.

The sections of *Truth and Method* that are most relevant for our purposes are: first part, I, 1, (b): 'Leading humanistic concepts'; second part, II, 2, in particular (b): 'The hermeneutic relevance of Aristotle'; second part, II, 3, (b): 'The concept of experience'; and supplement I: 'Hermeneutics and historicism', on Aristotle. As against the subjectivism wrought by romantic hermeneutics, Gadamer makes appeal to Aristotle (specifically, the emphasis on 'ethos' of Aristotelian ethics). Also, to the post-Kantian 'aesthetics of genius' and the cult of 'experience', Gadamer counterposes the salutary influence of Hegelian aesthetics and the conception of hermeneutics it implies.

It is not at all coincidental that both Gadamer and Arendt concern themselves with judgment, with taste, and with 'common sense'. Both thinkers derive their essential inspiration from Heidegger. One of Heidegger's major accomplishments is his de-subjectivization of aesthetics. Both Arendt and Gadamer share this impulse, and Gadamer, especially, bases his hermeneutics on Heidegger's re-establishment of the foundation of aesthetics upon a new basis, namely his idea of the 'truth' of art developed in 'The origin of the work of art'. It therefore becomes necessary to deny the 'autonomy' of art (what Gadamer labels 'aesthetic differentiation', the 'abstraction' of aesthetic consciousness), so that beauty is asserted to be a matter, not of private satisfaction, but of public quality. Art and beauty, rather than being aesthetically divorced from truth, from reality, from the world, assume responsibility towards the public realm, and issue in the public meaning of a culture.[38] Gadamer notes that aesthetics was given a subjective basis by Kant for particular transcendental purposes – namely, to provide *a priori* conditions for the possibility of beauty. But it is because of the grave consequences this has – extraneous to Kant's own preoccupations – in the human sciences that Gadamer must urge the transfer from a subjective to an objective basis for aesthetics (Hegel, and, along a different path, Heidegger).

Judgment is crucial for Gadamer because it concerns the relationship between universal and particular – and this, in turn, has to do with 'application', the lack of a concern with which he diagnoses as a major deficiency of romantic hermeneutics. This is why Gadamer sees it to be important to resurrect judgment as a humanistic category guiding the *Geisteswissenschaften* – namely, to restore to the human sciences the hermeneutic role of 'application'. As for application itself, the weighing of the dialectical relationship between universal principle and particular judgment, it is explicated with reference to Aristotelian *phronesis*.[39]

At the end of his essay 'Hermeneutics and historicism', Gadamer points out that a universalist theory of the good, such as Plato provided with his 'idea of the good', lessens the need for judgment (or Aristotelian *phronesis*), and diminishes the status of judgment. It is precisely because we do not have access to an absolute universal under which we need only subsume particulars that Gadamer seeks instruction from Aristotelian ethics. It is this that renders the problem of 'application' (relating particular to universal) so problematical, requiring delicate hermeneutic judgment. It is because we do not have available to us an infallible natural law that merely wants means of implementing that a painstaking process of judgment or *phronesis* in the Aristotelian sense, the careful weighing of given particulars, is required of us. Platonic *politike techne*, in direct contrast to Aristotelian *politike phronesis*, renders ethics unproblematical by oversimplifying the dialectical relationship between universal and particular. It is only when we are confronted by the demands of action in the context of a particular set of circumstances that we get a true understanding of what our ends really are, and reassess these ends in relation to a new understanding of our life as a whole. Action in the particular circumstances of life is a continuing dialogue between what we think our life is about, and the particularities of moral and practical exigency.

Gadamer opposes the reduction of judgment to mere subsumption of particulars under a universal, and one of the main intentions of his analysis of hermeneutics is to foster this appreciation of judgment as involving more than mere subsumption. Here Gadamer accords special attention to theological hermeneutics and legal hermeneutics, for both of these focus, in a particularly acute way, on the problem of the particular and the universal. The problem is how to apply the universal to a particular situation without the benefit of a rule for guiding this application: in legal hermeneutics, how to apply the law in the context of a particular legal case; in theological hermeneutics, how to apply the written word of scripture to particular pastoral situations, deriving spiritual lessons that are applicable to given contexts. Application of a law or teaching is not like affixing a pre-given label to a pre-differentiated particular, but rather, involves a highly demanding hermeneutic discipline. The interpretation of legal or scriptural texts presupposes the culturally acquired attributes of taste, cultivation, and ethical habituation, and it is these qualifications of sound judgment that receive their classical elucidation in Aristotle's exemplary analysis of *ethos*.

Arendt is similarly concerned with judgment as a faculty that provides more than merely rules for the subsumption of particular cases, but she believes that Kant is a sufficient guide for comprehending this faculty. Gadamer, as we have seen, offers critical doubts about Kant's legacy, and suggests that perhaps Aristotle is the better guide. Arendt, as we saw in the last section, does concede that Kant was unaware of 'the moral and political implications' of his aesthetics.[40] But this obliges us to inquire further into what accounts for this lack of awareness, and whether it impugns the authority of Kant's account. The issue posed by Gadamer, then, is whether it is Kant or Aristotle who offers sounder guidance on the nature of judgment. This question shall direct our reflections in following chapters.

HABERMAS: AN ETHICS OF COMMUNICATION

In a published lecture 'On the German-Jewish heritage', Jürgen Habermas pays tribute to Hannah Arendt's 'rediscovery of Kant's analysis of *Urteilskraft* or judgment for a theory of rationality' as an 'achievement of fundamental importance'.[41] He describes it as 'a first approach to a concept of communicative rationality which is built into speech and action itself', and as such, points in the direction of 'a project of an ethics of communication which connects practical reason to the idea of a universal discourse'.[42] Regardless of whether or not this is an accurate characterization of Arendt's theory of judging, it is certainly a fair statement of Habermas' own theoretical project.

The outlines of this project are sketched in part III of Habermas' book *Legitimation Crisis*, 'On the logic of legitimation problems'. Habermas' book is a study of the tendencies to economic crisis, rationality crisis, legitimation crisis, and motivation crisis within advanced capitalist societies. The basic problem is that late capitalist political systems are systematically incapable of satisfying the types of expectation aroused in their members, cannot rationally justify their fiscal-administrative activities to those who are the recipients of those activities, cannot command the political and ideological resources needed to win the steady allegiance of the citizens, and fail to elicit the socio-cultural motivations (such as the work ethic) necessary to keep the whole system working. In short, advanced capitalism exhibits pronounced symptoms of multiple crisis tendencies, and the function of critical social theory is to chart these tendencies in their systematic rather than merely contingent forms. Habermas thinks that the basis for inquiring into why a society comes to suffer from such 'legitimation deficits', expressed in motivation crisis where 'meaning' becomes a scarce resource, is through an investigation of the relation between legitimation and truth, and of whether a given social system can vindicate the truth claims implicit in its demand for legitimacy. (By contrast, Weberian social science prescribes empirical inquiry into legitimacy that abstracts from truth.) This inquiry presupposes 'a universal morality, which can be traced back to fundamental norms of rational speech'. This universal morality establishes its systematic superiority to competing ethics through 'the discursive redemption of its claim to validity'.[43] If meaning and legitimacy are scarce resources, this is ultimately because modern societies fail to meet the rational standards of this universal morality and cannot make good their constitutive truth claims.

Habermas believes that for the grounding of this rational morality it is not necessary to rehabilitate traditional or modern natural law (he is not convinced by any substantive theories of human nature, whether empirical or metaphysical).[44] Rather, he thinks that this job can be done by an inquiry into formal conditions of discourse as such: 'Recourse to the fundamental norms of rational speech which we presuppose in every discourse (including practical discourse) is sufficient.'[45] Philosophy is no longer a source of world-views, which means, among other things, that there can no longer be metaphysical foundations for ethics. Consequently, morality 'is formalized and detached from substantive interpretations. Practical reason can no longer be founded in the transcendental subject. Communicative ethics appeals now only to fundamental norms of rational speech, an ultimate "fact of reason".'[46] The problem then is how such a formalistic *Sprachethik* can still generate normative force sufficient to orient action. Despite Habermas' critique of Kantian-inspired forms of non-cognitivism, such as prescriptivism, his own theory remains basically Kantian.

Habermas seeks to defend a cognitivist account of practical questions which upholds the truth of norms arrived at by argumentation supported by reasons. By truth is meant a consensus of rational subjects established through free and unconstrained communication. Habermas rejects all forms of emotivism, decisionism, and non-cognitivism in ethics; his aim is to show that normative validity claims have a cognitive basis in counterfactual suppositions that the claims 'could be discursively redeemed – that is, grounded in the consensus of the participants through argumentation'.[47] The idea of rationally motivated agreement about norms presupposes a 'communication community of those affected, who as participants in a practical discourse test the validity claims of norms and, to the extent that they accept them with reasons, arrive at the conviction that in the given circumstances the proposed norms are "right"'.[48]

Moral argumentation exemplifies a form of rational justification that goes beyond processes of inference based on strict deductive reasoning. Whatever is capable of convincing participants in a discourse where the only aim is to discover the truth of the matter and where no fundamental norms of rational speech are violated, constitutes rational grounds for the recognition of validity claims. Habermas defines discourse as 'that form of communication that is removed from contexts of experience and action' for the express purpose of truth-seeking and the testing of validity claims. In discourse, validity claims are 'bracketed' so that they become 'the exclusive object of discussion'.[49] There are no restrictions at all on the scope of discussion, provided that the only goal is to ferret out the truth: 'that no force except that of the better argument is exercised; and that, as a result, all motives except that of the cooperative search for truth are excluded'.[50] Consensus arrived at under these ideal conditions is said to express a 'rational will'. Rationality is thus identified as a process of abstraction from all factors that might restrict or constrain discussion. At this point Habermas' theory seems to emanate discernible echoes of Kant's idea of 'enlarged mentality'.[51]

A rational will arrives at what is wanted by all, the common interest, and arrives at this common interest without constraint or deception. Such a discourse is 'rational' because 'the formal properties of discourse and of the deliberative situation sufficiently guarantee that a consensus can arise only through appropriately interpreted, *generalizable* interests' and needs that can be communicatively shared.[52] In other words, each participant in a practical discourse is obliged 'to transfer his subjective desires into generalizable desires'.[53] Habermas here invokes 'the principle of universalization', which he affirms as 'the only principle in which practical reason expresses itself'.[54] However, Habermas does not wish to get involved in the specification of moral principles and 'maxims of universalization'. 'A cognitivist . . . *Sprachethik* has no need of principles. It is based only on fundamental norms of rational speech that we must always presuppose if we discourse at all':

> the expectation of discursive redemption of normative-validity claims is already contained in the structure of intersubjectivity and makes specially introduced maxims of universalization superfluous. In taking up a practical discourse, we unavoidably suppose an ideal speech situation that, on the strength of its formal properties, allows consensus only through *generalizable* interests.[55]

Thus the aim of universal pragmatics, as Habermas construes it, is to reconstruct the 'transcendental character of ordinary language'.[56]

We determine whether judgments are valid, according to Habermas, by asking ourselves what we *would* rationally agree to in a counterfactual situation of undistorted communication and discourse ideally free of power relations. By projecting ourselves into this ideal space of pure rational dialogue, we win the vantage point for securing the validity of our normative judgments. Habermas' concept of the ideal speech situation is in Kantian terminology a regulative idea: it serves to regulate and guide our judgments. At the same time it elucidates

Habermas' central claim that practical questions *can* admit of truth, and that this indeed is the whole point of entering into discussions of practical norms. Thus it is with concentrated irony that Habermas remarks: 'Anyone who still discusses the admissibility of truth in practical questions is [considered to be], at best, old-fashioned.'[57]

So far the affinities with Arendt seem unmistakable: Habermas, like Arendt, looks to Kant for the model of a theory of rational judgment. But, as was the case in examining the relation between Gadamer and Arendt, here too the differences are no less striking than the affinities. Arendt, as we saw in the first section of this chapter, draws a sharp dichotomy between theoretical truth, which relies upon compelling logical inference, and practical judgment, which is merely persuasive and attempts to 'woo the consent' of those to whom it is potentially addressed. Habermas, by contrast, aims at a union of theory and practice: theoretical inquiry into the conditions of valid truth claims is meant to enlighten us about whether practical states of affairs are entitled to claim moral legitimacy. A *theory* of truth can instruct us about the requirements of political *praxis*. Neither Gadamer nor Arendt would presume to make such claims for theory, and for both of them the world of practice is self-sufficient, guided by its own autonomous standards and criteria, rather than by those of theory.

Habermas elaborates the following critique of Arendt in his article 'Hannah Arendt's communications concept of power':

> Arendt sees a yawning abyss between knowledge and opinion that cannot be closed with arguments.
>
> She holds fast to the classical distinction between theory and practice; practice rests on opinions and convictions that cannot be true or false in the strict sense. . . . An antiquated concept of theoretical knowledge that is based on ultimate insights and certainties keeps Arendt from comprehending the process of reaching agreement about practical questions as rational discourse.[58]

The argument here is that Arendt fails to bring practical discourse within the ambit of rational discourse, denying it cognitive status, and thereby severs knowledge from practical judgment. Arendt's rejoinder would be that the specification of a cognitive foundation for political beliefs (which Habermas seeks) would compromise the integrity of opinion. The dilemma is that one theory threatens the autonomy of the realm of opinion, subordinating practical reason to theoretical reason (and therefore privileging the theoretically informed political judgments of critical theorists); whereas the other theory seems to dispense with any relation between judgment and truth, and forces practical reason to relinquish its claim to cognitive validity.

In the last section we looked at the divergence between Gadamer and Arendt in terms of an opposition between Aristotle and Kant. The present argument between Habermas and Arendt can be treated in the same way. In Kant's critical exposition of reflective judgment we are presented with a sharp dichotomy between the non-cognitive judgments of taste and the cognitive judgments of the understanding.[59] For Kant, reflective judgments are strictly non-cognitive (although they may serve a regulative function for cognition); only determinant judgments can be cognitive. Aristotle, on the other hand, offers an account of *phronesis* that is decidedly cognitivist. The exercise of practical wisdom is a fusion of good action and sound moral cognition.[60]

Finally, the case is similar when we consider the contention between Habermas and Gadamer. For Gadamer it is impossible to abstract from the particular situation that elicits practical judgment; in fact, one gains access to practical truth precisely by exploring, from within, the historically articulated prejudices and pre-understandings that particularize one's ethical identity. Habermas, on the other hand, explicates the idea of practical reason by means of a highly formalized inquiry that is concerned specifically to abstract from substantive moral situations in order to identify universal conditions of validity. The contrast here is between Habermas' Kantian method and Gadamer's preoccupation with Aristotelian *ethos*. So, once again, the competing claims of contemporary theories of political judgment may be illuminated by pursuing them at the level of a confrontation between Kant and Aristotle.

T·H·R·E·E

Kant's concept of taste

All three of the theories sketched in the preceding chapter can in some essential way be traced back to Kant or Aristotle. Habermas remarks in a note in *Theory and Practice*[1] that he is indebted to Arendt and Gadamer for teaching him the fundamental importance of the Aristotelian distinction between *praxis* (the realm of the practical) and *techne* (the realm of the technical): the understanding of politics as a moral-practical activity based on *phronesis*, as opposed to the understanding of politics as a technical-productive activity assimilated to *poiesis*. It is certainly true that this distinction is of great significance for Gadamer, although Aristotelian concepts play a much lesser role in Arendt's thought (her concepts of labour, work, and action are influenced less by Aristotle than by Kant's ideas of free agency as an end in itself and of human dignity as grounded in the strict autonomy of spontaneous action).

The debt owed to Kant in the work of these three theorists is even more pronounced. We have seen that Arendt looks to the *Critique of Judgment* for an '*a priori* principle' by which to prove that man is a political being. Gadamer and Habermas also rely upon Kant's transcendental method for their respective theoretical enterprises. In the foreword to the second edition of *Truth and Method* Gadamer defines the task of philosophical hermeneutics in terms of Kant's conception of transcendental inquiry:

> Kant certainly did not wish to lay down for modern science what it must do in order to stand honourably before the judgment-seat of reason. He asked a philosophic question: What are the conditions of our knowledge, by virtue of which modern science is possible, and how far does it extend? Thus the following investigation also asks a philosophic question. But it does not ask it only of the so-called human sciences. . . . It does not ask it only of science and its modes of experience, but of all human experience of the world and human living. It asks (to put it in Kantian terms): How is understanding possible?[2]

And Habermas is similarly explicit in adopting the method of transcendental inquiry, both in his earlier work on the constitutive conditions of human knowledge,[3] and in his later work on the philosophy of language.[4] As we saw in our exposition of his communicative ethics, Habermas conceives of the enterprise of universal pragmatics as a reconstruction of 'the transcendental character of ordinary language'.

Therefore if we wish to pursue the avenues of inquiry suggested in the previous chapter, it is incumbent on us to examine in some detail the relevant texts of Kant and Aristotle.

TRANSCENDENTAL PHILOSOPHY AND THE JUDGING SUBJECT

Transcendental philosophy as inaugurated by Kant treats the objective, empirical world as constituted by an active judging subject. Thus the activity of the judging subject is a theme throughout Kantian philosophy, not just in the account of reflective judgment in the third *Critique*. Although Kant often distinguishes between objective and subjective principles of judgment, object and subject are in fact correlative in his philosophy; the objective is available only as constituted by the subject, and the subject is forever active in relation to an objective sphere which it serves to constitute. However, this Kantian conception of experience is always based on the distinction between the empirical self and the transcendental self, the former subject to empirical laws of causality, the latter doing the constituting that makes it possible for there to *be* empirical laws of causality. Therefore it is always in question what is the nature and function of the subject in any particular domain of Kant's philosophy.

Since the subject may be viewed both from an empirical and a transcendental point of view, the subject may be at the same time both receptive in relation to the objective empirical world and active in constituting the forms of apprehension that make empirical experience possible. This gives rise to a set of systematic tensions and ambiguities in the concepts of objectivity and subjectivity, activity and receptivity, autonomy and heteronomy. For instance, practical reason is supposed to derive all its force from the autonomy of the moral *subject*, yet in the *Foundations of the Metaphysics of Morals* Kant describes the categorical imperative as laying down *objective* laws for the determination of the will.[5] Or, to take a different example, imagination, viewed as a transcendental faculty, plays an essential part in conferring autonomy upon aesthetic judgment, whereas empirical imagination, in common with all other faculties of the empirical subject, is subject to causal determination, and is therefore heteronomous. Again, in the account of aesthetic judgment the whole emphasis is on contemplative spectatorship; however, for Kant, in contrast to Hume, reason is always active, and therefore the aesthetic contemplation of the rational spectator is not merely receptive but rather, in this respect, always a form of activity.

Because the rational subject, for Kant, may be viewed from two perspectives, empirical and transcendental, it is always problematical how the transcendental perspective that guides Kant in the three *Critiques* can be related back to the actual human concerns of knowing, acting, and judging subjects in the phenomenal world. Here we are presented with problems that apply generally within transcendental idealism. If the transcendental subject is a universal subject and if the only way for it to win a rationally compelling basis for its principles of judgment is by ascending to a universal standpoint detached from all contingent empirical conditions, what is it that gives the deliberations of this subject enough determinacy to have any content at all? In the ascent to universality, at what point is one sufficiently distanced from the particular and the contingent to satisfy the transcendental requirement, and what particularities of human experience can be tolerated without this requirement being violated? And if it is through shedding all particularity and contingency that the Kantian subject secures transcendental validity for its judgments, doesn't the standpoint of the transcendental subject turn into no standpoint at all, and isn't the universal self in danger of becoming self-less? How far can the 'enlarged mentality' expand without ceasing to be the possession of an individuated subject retaining its own identity?[6]

This is a highly compressed statement of the kinds of problems and complexities that face all students of Kant's philosophy, and is meant only to indicate a few of the pitfalls that await the reader. The exposition of aesthetic judgment that follows makes only scant reference to the general context of transcendental philosophy; therefore it is necessary to serve warning in advance that the effort to summarize or condense any aspect of the critical philosophy can proceed only by concealing further labyrinths.

TASTE, AESTHETIC AND POLITICAL

What does Kant mean by judgment, and how does he conceive the faculty of judging? In section IV of the introduction to the *Critique of Judgment*, he offers the following definition: 'Judgment in general is the faculty of thinking the particular as contained under the universal' (1: 18).[7] But judgment as thus defined is in turn subdivided into 'determinant' and 'reflective' judgment. Where the universal (the rule, principle, or law) is given, the judgment is determinant – determines the particular. Where the universal is lacking (as in the case of a teleology of nature), judgment must be posited as reflective – 'not determining anything' but posited as an idea 'for the purpose of reflection'. The determinant judgment, because it is already provided with a universal for subsumption of particulars, 'is subsumptive only', 'it has no need to devise a law for its own guidance to enable it to subordinate the particular in nature to the universal' (ibid.). However, in the case of reflective judgment, on the other hand, 'only the particular is given and the universal has to be found for it'.

> The reflective judgment which is compelled to ascend from the particular in nature to the universal stands, therefore, in need of a principle. This principle it cannot borrow from experience. . . . Such a transcendental principle, therefore, the reflective judgment can only give as a law from and to itself. It cannot derive it from

any other quarter (as it would then be a determinant judgment). (1: 18–19)

Instances of determinant judgment are logical judgments, as dealt with in the *Critique of Pure Reason*, and moral judgments, as dealt with in the *Critique of Practical Reason*. Aesthetic judgments and teleological judgments are both cases of reflective judgment, and thus the *Critique of Judgment* is occupied exclusively with reflective judgments.

The introduction to the *Critique of Judgment* is intended to situate the third *Critique* within Kant's philosophy as a whole, and to identify the position of judgment *vis-à-vis* both theoretical reason and practical reason. Judgment is located between theoretical philosophy (metaphysics of nature) and practical philosophy (metaphysics of morals). 'Judgment . . . in the order of our cognitive faculties forms a middle term between understanding and reason' (preface; 1: 4. Cf. introduction, III; 1: 15). Understanding (*Verstand*) relates to constitutive principles of cognition. Reason (*Vernunft*) relates to regulative principles of desire. Judgment, relating to the feeling of pleasure or displeasure, mediates between understanding and reason. To the three faculties of cognition or understanding, judgment, and reason correspond three faculties of the soul: the faculty of knowledge, the feeling of pleasure and displeasure, and the faculty of desire. '[B]etween the faculties of knowledge and desire stands the feeling of pleasure, just as judgment is intermediate between understanding and reason' (introduction, III; 1: 17). Thus just as in the realm of cognitive faculties judgment is 'a middle term between understanding and reason', so in the realm of mental faculties there is also a middle term, the pleasure arising out of the 'harmonious accord' of 'spontaneity in the play of the cognitive faculties' (introduction, IX; 1: 39). Furthermore, this provides 'a suitable mediating link connecting the realm of the concept of nature with that of the concept of freedom' (ibid.). In the same way, judgment, with its concept of a finality of nature, provides a mediating concept between these concepts of nature and freedom. Therefore, just as judgment reconciles understanding and reason, art reconciles nature and freedom (the political implications of this latter reconciliation were left to Schiller to pursue further in his *Aesthetic Letters*). 'Thus judgment makes possible the transition from the realm of the concept of nature to that of the concept of freedom' (introduction, IX; 1: 38).

In section VIII of the introduction, Kant sets out his distinction between aesthetic judgment and teleological judgment. Both are defined in relation to the notion of finality. By finality, Kant means conceiving of an object as if it were constituted according to ends (see introduction, IV; I: 19). That is, in aesthetic judgment we contemplate an object as if it were specifically intended to confer pleasure upon the subject who reflects on its form; in teleological judgment we, for instance, regard objects as if they were specifically intended to serve human purposes. In neither case can we *know* that the objects of nature were given to us to satisfy these ends (therefore finality can never be a matter of cognition, and reflective judgment cannot be a cognitive judgment). But the supposition of finality is required, in the case of aesthetic judgment to make it possible for us to form judgments of taste at all; in the case of teleological judgments to regulate and guide theoretical investigation of nature. Reflective judgment provides the regulative idea of nature as a functional totality: for instance, in order to pursue the science of biology we need the idea of biological organisms as end-governed wholes, as if these objects were shaped by a rational creator in accordance with an idea of their end. This idea can never be drawn from actual cognition, and therefore must be 'posited' by reflective judgment, to make available regulative ideas necessary for the conduct of science that cognitive judgments themselves could never supply.

The difference between the two types of reflective judgment is that aesthetic judgment is 'the faculty of estimating formal finality (otherwise called subjective) by the feeling of pleasure or displeasure' (introduction, VIII; I: 34); whereas teleological judgment is 'the faculty of estimating the real finality (objective) of nature' (ibid.). That is, although neither faculty can establish a real finality in objects of nature, representations of the object in teleological judgment do refer to the object, whereas what is reflected upon in aesthetic judgments is merely the *form* of the representations that elicit pleasure in the apprehending subject. It is important to note here the association between the aesthetic and the formal or subjective: 'the aesthetic judgment contributes nothing to the cognition of its objects. Hence it must *only* be allocated to the Critique of the judging subject' (introduction, VIII; I: 36). An aesthetic judgment 'does not depend upon any present concept of the object, and does not provide one'; it merely reflects upon the form of the object in order to derive a ground of pleasure that can be universalized for all judging subjects (introduction, VII; 1: 31). 'That which is purely subjective in the representation of an object, i.e., what constitutes its reference to the subject, not to the object, is its aesthetic quality' (introduction, VII; 1: 29). Since there are no cognitive concepts available for the aesthetic estimate of the object, the universality of the judgment must rest wholly upon the form of the apprehension, that is to say, upon subjectivity, or the configuration of faculties of the subject.

Teleological judgment, though, also makes essential reference to the subject. That is why its concept of a finality of nature is merely regulative, not constitutive (introduction, IX; 1: 39). The positing of a finality of nature by teleological judgment 'prescribes a law, not to nature (as autonomy) but to itself (as heautonomy), to guide its reflection upon nature' (introduction, V; 1: 25). In fact, there is a tacit bond between aesthetic judgment and teleological judgment, in that both posit the idea of nature as 'intended' for the human subject, as if it were given to man expressly for the benefit of his reflection upon it, whether aesthetic or teleological. Aesthetic judgment, in assigning to nature a formal or subjective finality, prepares the way for a reflective positing of real finality for nature on the part of teleological judgment. In both, nature is conceived as a spectacle offered up to man as a privileged spectator.

On the basis of this preliminary demarcation of the topic, let us now proceed to consider taste. In section 7 of the *Critique of Judgment* Kant situates the reflective judgment of taste between judgments of the agreeable and judgments of the good. In finding Canary wine agreeable, we can claim only that it is agreeable *for ourselves*, and it would be absurd to expect all men to sense things in precisely the same way. However, in forming a judgment of taste we necessarily issue a more ambitious claim. In judging something to be beautiful, it would be ridiculous to assert our claim by affirming that the object is beautiful for ourselves. This would be not a justification of our claim, but an admission that it cannot be justified. In making judgments about the beautiful we solicit the rational assent of everyone else, pledging that the reasonableness of the judgment will become apparent if one strives to abstract from all interests that tend to obfuscate the real beauty of the object. Even judgments of the agreeable may, contingently, win general concurrence, but judgments of taste demand more: when we put a thing on a pedestal and call it beautiful, we demand the same delight from others. Anyone who recommends his taste 'judges not merely for himself, but

for all men, and then speaks of beauty as if it were a property of things';
he blames others if they judge differently, and denies them taste, which
he still requires of them as something they ought to have (§7; 1: 52).
Here the retreat to individual subjectivity is ruled out. However this
poses a real difficulty: judgments of taste, because they are not cognitive
judgments, cannot compel assent, as can judgments of the good, by
strict demonstrations based on concepts. If I seek to convince someone
that something is good, I reason on the basis of a concept of what the
thing is (§4; 1: 46). But this rational procedure is not available in
matters of taste. Because aesthetic judgments do not involve forming a
cognition of the object, they cannot represent the beautiful as an object
of universal delight *by means of a concept*, although neither can they
withdraw their claim to universality, for this would be to concede that
'there is no such thing at all as taste, i.e. no aesthetic judgment capable
of making a rightful claim upon the assent of all men' (§§6–7; 1:
51–3). The problem then is for Kant to show that one who judges with
taste 'can impute the subjective finality, i.e. his delight in the object,
to everyone else, and suppose his feeling *universally communicable*, and
that, too, *without the mediation of concepts*' (§39; 1: 150; italics mine).

   In order to accentuate those features of Kant's theory of judgment
that are especially relevant to the issue of political judgment, we shall
structure the following exposition of the text around a set of theses that
would constitute a Kantian teaching on political judgment, assuming
that one could be extrapolated from the *Critique of Judgment*. To introduce a certain measure of order into our exposition, let us propose these
theses in advance. We hope that this will prove helpful in organizing
what would otherwise be an unmanageable wealth of material.

1 Judgments of taste must be disinterested.
2 Judgments of taste must be contemplative.
3 Judgments of taste must be as free from morality as from sensation,
   must be equally free from the agreeable and from the good.
4 Aesthetic judgments are wholly distinct from moral judgments (the
   latter are practical, not contemplative).
5 Taste is free, independent of natural need, and therefore belongs in
   the realm of leisure.
6 Taste is not bound to the standards of a specific community
   (particularistic), but universal.

7 Judgments of taste are independent of ends, thus refer only to form.

8 Aesthetic judgments, because unrelated to ends, are wholly distinct from teleological judgments.

9 Teleological judgments refer to ends belonging to the object (although there is also a respect in which they too make reference to the subject), whereas aesthetic judgments refer exclusively to the faculties of the subject.

10 Taste is related to imagination.

11 Judgments of taste are related to common sense (public sense, consensus).

12 Judgment must be public (must pertain to outward appearance).

13 Aesthetic judgments are difficult and uncertain.

14 Aesthetic judgments are contentious, but potentially reconcilable.

15 Taste is conducive to the development of moral sense.

16 Judgments of taste are singular.

17 Judgment must be autonomous, not heteronomous (not subject to coercion or social pressure). The individual himself judges, not the community (aesthetic liberalism).

18 Judgments of the sublime are projections of the idea of respect.

1 *Judgments of taste must be disinterested.*

Kant defines taste as 'the faculty of estimating the beautiful' (§ 1; 1: 41n.). The delight which governs this faculty must be a 'pure disinterested delight', in contrast to the delight 'allied to an interest' (§ 2; 1: 43–4). Interest is defined as 'the delight which we connect with the representation of the real existence of an object' (§ 2; 1: 42). '[W]here the question is whether something is beautiful, we do not want to know, whether we, or any one else, are, or even could be, concerned in the real existence of the thing, but rather what estimate we form of it on mere contemplation' (§ 2; 1: 42–3).

> Everyone must allow that a judgment on the beautiful which is tinged with the slightest interest, is very partial and not a pure judgment of taste. One must not be in the least prepossessed in favour of the real existence of the thing, but must preserve complete indifference in this respect, in order to play the part of judge in matters of taste. (§ 2; 1: 43)

The judgment of taste must be pure, by which Kant means that it must be absolutely indifferent to its object. 'Every interest vitiates the judgment of taste and robs it of its impartiality' (§ 13 ; 1 : 64). 'Charm' and 'emotion' are examples of admixtures of interest that violate taste: 'Taste that requires an added element of charm and emotion for its delight . . . has not yet emerged from barbarism' (§ 13 ; 1 : 65). What Kant is asserting is that enjoyment of the object, apart from its aesthetic form as represented in reflection, precludes judgment. Thus a pure judgment of taste is 'a judgment of taste which is uninfluenced by charm or emotion' (ibid.).

Kant allows that empirical or intellectual (or moral) interest can be conjoined to a pure judgment, *subsequent* to the actual rendering of the disinterested judgment itself. Once the aesthetic judgment has been posited (in its purity), an interest can then 'enter into combination with it', although 'indirect' combination (§ 41; 1: 154). As Kant remarks in a footnote, while the judgment may rely on no interest, it may produce one, so that it 'may be wholly *disinterested* but withal very *interesting*' (§ 2; 1: 43n.). Still, Kant insists that the empirical interest, indirectly attached to the beautiful, 'is, however, of no importance for us here' (§ 41; 1: 156).

2 *Judgments of taste must be contemplative.*

This point is very closely connected with the preceding one. Whereas in the case of interest 'it is not merely the object, but also its real existence that pleases', 'the judgment of taste is simply *contemplative*, i.e., it is a judgment which is indifferent as to the existence of an object, and only decides how its character stands with the feeling of pleasure and displeasure' (§ 5; 1: 48). This contemplative aspect to judgments of taste serves to differentiate them from moral judgments: the former 'is merely contemplative and does not bring about an interest in the object; whereas in the moral judgment it is practical' (§ 12; 1: 64). The question that we shall have to explore is whether political judgment is, like aesthetic judgment, contemplative, or, like moral judgment, practical.

3 *Judgments of taste must be independent of morality and
the good.*

Kant argues that in order to make a judgment about the goodness of something, the judgment must be mediated by a concept of the good, which in turn depends upon the concept of an end. Judgments of beauty, by contrast, are immediate, unmediated by concepts of good or of ends. Any good, even moral good, is interested. No good is disinterested, therefore the good can no more be a basis for judgment than can the agreeable. Both involve a reference to the faculty of desire, whereas beauty refers only to the feeling of pleasure or displeasure. The peculiarity of the beautiful is that although it acts as the intermediary between the agreeable and the good, it stands apart from each of the terms that it mediates. The beautiful is free or disinterested, whereas each of the others serves an interest: in the case of the agreeable, the interest of sense; in the case of the good, the interest of reason (§4; 1: 46–8). In this sense at least, sensation and morality have more in common than the middle term (beauty) that stands between them.

This can be seen in Kant's exclusion of 'perfection' as a criterion of beauty. To posit a concept of perfection as a determinant of beauty would be to do away with Kant's sharp dichotomy between the beautiful and the good, for then 'the judgment of taste would be just as much a cognitive judgment as one by which something is described as good' (§15; 1: 70–1). But the point is to safeguard the beautiful from dual intrusion, from the side of the agreeable as well as from the side of the good. Thus, for instance, fine art can be neither merely 'agreeable', nor subjected to a concept. In both cases the art would please 'not as fine art, but rather as mechanical art' (§45; 1: 167). In this connection, it is particularly interesting how Kant sets himself against both the empiricist account of taste (e.g. Hume) which equates taste with sense, and the rationalist account of taste (e.g. Plato) which equates taste with reason (§57, remark 2; 1: 214–15). *Both* pose threats to the autonomy of aesthetic judgment, which requires a transcendental grounding that is equally distinct from the two opposing poles of aesthetic empiricism and aesthetic rationalism (see §58; 1: 215).

4 Aesthetic judgments are wholly distinct from moral judgments.

This proposition merely sums up what can be concluded from the two foregoing theses. We have already noted that moral judgments are practical, while aesthetic judgments are contemplative. Aesthetic contemplation involves

> *preserving a continuance* of the state of the representation itself and the active engagement of the cognitive powers without ulterior aim. We *dwell* on the contemplation of the beautiful because this contemplation strengthens and reproduces itself. The case is analogous . . . to the way we linger on a charm in the representation of an object which keeps arresting the attention, the mind all the while remaining passive. (§ 12; 1: 64)

A further distinction between aesthetic and moral judgment is that aesthetic judgment merely claims assent, whereas moral judgment, as Kant conceives it, commands assent. The absolutely good, according to Kant, involves 'not a mere *claim*, but a *command* upon everyone to assent' (§ 29, general remark; 1: 118). As noted above, moral judgments for Kant figure as determinant, not reflective, judgments.

5 Taste is free, belonging in the realm of leisure.

Kant insists that the interest of inclination disqualifies one from laying a claim to taste, and points out that it is inclination, not taste, that is speaking in the popular maxim, 'Hunger is the best sauce.' In such circumstances the inclination to eat anything that is edible disallows any judgments of taste. Thus: 'Only when men have got all they want can we tell who among the crowd has taste or not' (§ 5; 1: 49–50). Natural need therefore precludes free judgment. The precondition of taste is leisure. For Kant, taste is a realm of freedom, or leisure, beyond the realms of sense and morality.

This question of the freedom of taste ties in with the autonomy of aesthetic judgment in relation to teleology, its freedom from ends. It also relates to the dependence of taste upon imagination, for the latter 'entertains the mind in a free activity', thus allowing for 'an act of *free* judgment' (§ 29, general remark; 1: 122–3). Aesthetic judgment must be free judgment. Thus Kant likens art to 'play, i.e., an occupation which is agreeable on its own account', in opposition to handicraft or industrial art, which is likened to 'labour, i.e., a business, which on its own account is disagreeable (drudgery), and is only attractive by means of what it results in (e.g., the pay), and which is consequently capable of being a compulsory imposition' (§43; 1: 164).

6 Taste is not bound to the particularistic standards of a specific community but, rather, its claims are universal.

Kant defines the judgment of taste as a claim to subjective universality. The man of taste judges *for all men*. Taste is aesthetic judgment 'capable of making a rightful claim upon the assent of all men' (§7; 1: 52). What this signifies is that taste is not bound to the standards of a particular society, as might be true of consensus about the agreeable – what Kant in section 7 of the *Critique of Judgment* calls *general* judgments (1: 53). Rather, they are *universal* – binding upon all men (ibid.).[8] The context of a given community does not enter in here. While general agreement arises out of 'sociability', universal agreement does not. In this sense, judgments of taste are closer to moral judgments, which also demand universality (although in judgments of taste this universality is achieved without the benefit of a concept; the good, by contrast, is communicated by means of a concept, which sets it apart from both the agreeable and the beautiful). 'Sociability' and considerations of that sort, on the other hand, rest on 'empirical rules', which Kant holds to be irrelevant to judgments of taste (ibid.). This means that the 'substantive' concerns and purposes of community have no bearing on judgment. If transposed into a claim about political judgment, this results in the fairly astounding assertion that the universality of the judgment overrides particular sympathies and must abstract from substantive ends. As we shall see, this lies at the crux of the dispute between the Kantian and Aristotelian approaches to judgment.

Kant points out that without the claim to universality, judgments of the beautiful could not be reliably distinguished from judgments of the agreeable, and so the predicate 'beautiful' could never even be applied (§8; 1: 53). As for the ground of such universal claims, Kant contends that this is to be found in 'the universal communicability of the sensation (of delight or aversion) . . . – in the accord, so far as possible, of all ages and nations as to this feeling in the representation of certain objects'. Taste is thus derived 'from grounds deep-seated and shared alike by all men, underlying their agreement in estimating the forms under which objects are given to them' (§ 17; I: 75). Therefore Kant defines 'the judging subject' as 'the subject in a comprehensive sense, as inclusive of all who belong to the human race' (§ 76; II: 55). To summarize, then, it is not enough to claim the agreement of those constituting one's own community; one must aspire to the agreement of *all* men. Thus, because his transcendental grounding of judgment is purely formal, Kant provides no *principle of community* (and refuses, in principle, to provide such) from which to derive aesthetic agreement or consensus.

7 *Judgments of taste are independent of ends, referring only to form.*

For Kant, the judgment of taste is independent of both subjective and objective ends; it is, rather, constituted by form alone:

> We are ... left with the subjective finality in the representation of an object, exclusive of any end (objective or subjective) – consequently the bare form of finality in the representation ... – as that which is alone capable of constituting the delight which, apart from any concept, we estimate as universally communicable, and so of forming the determining ground of the judgment of taste. (§ 11; I: 62–3)

This thesis is essential to our claim, to be developed later, that the Kantian and Aristotelian theories of judgment represent a fundamental polarity between the formal (severed from particular ends and purposes) and the substantive (conjoined to a political teleology).

While beauty pertains to pure form, 'charm' and 'emotion' represent 'matter'. To take charm for beauty is thus to have 'the matter of delight passed off for the form' (§ 13; I: 65). The more securely the judgment is grounded upon form, and the more abstracted from 'matter' (e.g. charm or emotion), the purer will be the judgment. A pure judgment of taste will therefore refer exclusively to finality of form, and not at all to substantive ends. Kant distinguishes between empirical and pure aesthetic judgments: the former, judgments of sense, are material; the latter, judgments of taste proper, are formal (§ 14; 1: 65). Judgments that 'depend merely on the matter of the representations – in other words, simply on sensation, . . . only entitles them to be called agreeable' (§ 14; 1: 66). On the other hand, 'a determination which at once goes to their form . . . is the only one which these representations possess that admits with certainty of being universally communicated' (ibid.).

Kant goes to special pains to disassociate the 'formal finality' of aesthetic judgment from the 'objective finality' of teleological judgment. As we saw above, Kant dismisses 'perfection' as a criterion of beauty, but we can see now that it is because of its implication in the 'representation of an end', and the consequent impossibility of deriving art as perfection from mere form, that Kant refuses its claim to participate in beauty (§ 15; 1: 70). Furthermore, any attention paid to the teleological principle of the organization of things in nature (e.g. snow-figures, flowers, the plumage of birds) infringes upon the judgment of their 'aesthetically final forms, independent of any particular guiding ends' (§ 58; 1: 219). In short, the aesthetic judgment must be kept quite distinct from the teleological judgment.

8 *Aesthetic judgments, because unrelated to ends, are wholly distinct from teleological judgments.*

This point follows directly from the preceding one. Pure aesthetic judgment must exclude all teleological aspects – ends embodied in products of human culture, such as cultural works of art 'where a human end determines the form as well as the magnitude' (of sublimity), or even in nature insofar as it can be conceived teleologically (§ 26; 1: 100). Thus the 'works of art' that Heidegger concerns himself with (e.g. Greek temples) are, as far as Kant is concerned, not aesthetically *pure* ('unmixed with any teleological judgment') (ibid.). We might recall also that the good is excluded from judgments of the beautiful for the very reason that in any notion of the good, 'the concept of an end is implied' (§ 4; 1: 46). In this sense, moral judgments are a species of teleological judgment, and it is for this reason that they are divorced from aesthetic judgments.

Kant's insistence upon a segregation of the aesthetic and the teleological is summed up best in the following passage:

in the transcendental aesthetic of judgment there must be no question of anything but pure aesthetic judgments. Consequently examples are not to be selected from such beautiful or sublime objects as presuppose the concept of an end. For then the finality would be either teleological, or based upon mere sensations of an object (gratification or pain) and so, in the first case, not aesthetic, and, in the second, not merely formal. (§ 29, general remark; 1: 121)

9 Teleological judgments refer to ends belonging to the object; aesthetic judgments refer exclusively to the subject.

This point retraces ground covered previously concerning the subjectivism of aesthetic judgments. Kant writes that aesthetic judgments 'have no bearing upon the object' (§ 8; 1: 55). Therefore the aesthetic universality attributed to a judgment 'does not join the predicate of beauty to the concept of the *object* taken in its entire logical sphere', but rather 'extends this predicate over the whole sphere of *judging subjects*' (ibid.). In this connection Kant distinguishes between logical and aesthetic judgments, whereby the latter, in contrast to the former, 'does not involve any objective quantity of the judgment, but only one that is subjective' (§ 8; 1: 54). Kant writes that in a judgment of taste, the predicate beauty is applied 'just *as if* . . . beauty was to be regarded as a quality of the object forming part of its inherent determination according to concepts; although beauty is for itself, *apart from any reference to the feeling of the subject, nothing*' (§ 9; 1: 59; italics mine). This sentence supplies telling evidence in support of Heidegger's and Gadamer's accusations against romantic aesthetics.

'A pure judgment upon the sublime must . . . have no end belonging to the object as its determining ground, if it is to be aesthetic and not to be tainted with any judgment of understanding or reason' (§ 26; 1: 101). Judgment must not be '*tainted*' by any end belonging to the object. Thus the very term 'aesthetic' (denoting sensory receptivity of the subject) implies subjectivity (in section 90 (II: 133) Kant does in fact at one point employ 'subjective' and 'aesthetic' interchangeably). Again:

the principle of the ideality of the finality in the beauty of nature is the one upon which we . . . invariably take our stand in our aesthetic judgments, forbidding us to have recourse to any realism of a natural end. . . . [I]n our general estimate of beauty, we seek its standing *a priori* in ourselves. . . . For in such an estimate the question does not turn on what nature is, or even on what it is for us in the way of an end, but on *how we receive it.* For nature to have fashioned its forms for our delight would inevitably imply an objective finality on the part of nature, instead of a subjective finality resting on the play of imagination in its freedom, where *it is we who receive nature with favour, and not nature that does us a favour.*   (§ 58; I: 219–20; italics mine)

Here we must probe deeper, to uncover what actually lies at the bottom of this opposition between objective finality and subjective finality. The key terms emerge in this same passage:

That nature affords us an opportunity for perceiving the inner finality in the relation of our mental powers engaged in the estimate of certain of its products . . . is a property of nature which cannot belong to it as its end, or rather, cannot be estimated by us to be such an end. For otherwise the judgment that would be determined by reference to such an end would found upon *heteronomy*, instead of founding upon *autonomy* and being free, as befits a judgment of taste.   (§ 58; I: 220; italics mine)

Here Kant finally discloses his overriding preoccupation: the autonomy of aesthetic judgment versus the heteronomy of teleological judgment (or, freedom versus nature). Heteronomous judgment must not be allowed to infringe upon autonomous judgment; teleology must not violate autonomy. In Kant's philosophy of judgment, as elsewhere in his work, the pivotal issue is freedom as against nature, autonomy as against teleology. So we see that the major concern of his practical philosophy works its way into his aesthetic philosophy. Both are actuated by the same fundamental drive.

Since we have now broached the question of autonomy and teleology, which lies at the heart of the conflict between Kant and Aristotle, let us define the Kantian theory of judgment as concerned with the subjectivity of judgment, and the Aristotelian theory of judgment as concerned with the objectivity of judgment. In the light of this disparity between a subjective theory of judgment and an objective theory of judgment, we can anticipate that the considerations that Aristotle will wish to bring into judgment will be resisted by Kant as being heteronomous. Kant would accuse Aristotle of subjecting the faculty of judgment to empirical, and therefore heteronomous, factors. We see then that for Kant the assertion of the subjectivity of judgment is in effect an affirmation of the autonomy of judgment. This is why the faculty of estimating the beautiful is kept strictly formal, to the exclusion of all substantive (i.e. heteronomous) factors or considerations. The contest between Kant's subjective theory of judgment and Aristotle's objective theory of judgment is thus the presentation in another guise of the modern debate between autonomy and teleology (as evidenced in the contention between naturalism and non-naturalism within contemporary moral philosophy).

10 Taste is related to imagination.

One of the ways in which taste secures its freedom is by virtue of its association with the imagination, for the primary connotation that imagination has for Kant is freedom. Thus we see that the term 'free play' usually occurs alongside the term 'imagination'. This affirmation of the freedom of imagination is bound up with the exclusion of teleology from aesthetics. Thus Kant sets up an opposition between purpose and imagination, the former exhibiting regularity and symmetry, the latter exhibiting non-regularity and freedom. The former applies to instrumentality, the latter to taste. Hence taste is closely associated with the 'free play of imagination' (regarded as a transcendental concept) (§ 22, general remark; 1: 85–9).

This is not to say that imagination is the sole constituent of aesthetic judgment, but only that it is an essential component. It is in the inspired art of genius that imagination has free rein. The judgment of taste 'is the discipline (or corrective) of genius' (§ 50; 1: 183). Accordingly, the power of judgment is the faculty that makes imagination 'consonant with understanding' (ibid.). Kant lists four requisites of fine art – imagination, understanding, soul, and taste, adding that 'the first three faculties are first *brought into union* by means of the fourth' (§ 50; 1: 183n.). Thus taste *subsumes* imagination, thereby reconciling it with understanding.

It can be seen that imagination enters into the very structure of judgment, so much so that it is even apparent in teleological judgment. We recall that judgment means subsumption of particulars under a universal. Thus judgment must rise above particulars as given in sensory perception in order to subsume them under a universal, rather than remaining wholly bound to the given particulars. 'In respect of the particular . . . judgment can recognize no finality.' Unless, therefore, judgment has the capacity to transcend given particulars, it will be incapable of locating that finality which is the aspiration of teleological judgment. In this way imagination is built into the very structure of the faculty of judgment. (Judgment is in this respect a counterpart to the operation of the schematism, as explicated in the *Critique of Pure Reason*.)[9]

11 Judgments of taste are related to common sense.

Kant writes: 'We are suitors for agreement from everyone else, because we are fortified with a ground common to all' (§ 19; 1: 82). Judgments of taste (having conditioned necessity) stand somewhere between cognitive judgments (unconditioned necessity) and taste of sense (no necessity at all) (§ 20; 1: 82). The ground of this conditioned necessity to be found in judgments of taste is a subjective principle of common sense. This notion of common sense he distinguishes from common understanding: the former 'determines what pleases or displeases by means of feeling only and not through concepts, but yet with universal validity'; the latter is not a judgment by feeling, but always one by concepts (§ 20; 1: 82–3).

> The judgment of taste . . . depends on our presupposing the existence of a common sense. (But this is not to be taken to mean some external sense, but the effect arising from the free play of our powers of cognition.) Only under the presupposition, I repeat, of such a common sense, are we able to lay down a judgment of taste. (§ 20; 1: 83)

The existence of this common sense, Kant derives from the fact that cognitions and judgments 'admit of being universally communicated' (§ 21; 1: 83). '[T]he universal communicability of a feeling presupposes a common sense. . . . [W]e assume a common sense as the necessary condition of the universal communicability of our knowledge' (§ 21; 1: 84).

Furthermore, 'we introduce this fundamental feeling not as a private feeling, but as a public sense', a 'consensus of different judging subjects'. With every judgment upon the beautiful, one asserts a *normative* claim: 'I put forward my judgment of taste as an example of the judgment of common sense, and attribute to it on that account *exemplary* validity' (§ 22; 1: 84). The idea of common sense is a transcendental requirement of our presuming to demand universal assent for our judgments: 'This indeterminate norm of a common sense is, as a matter of fact, presupposed by us; as is shown by our presuming to lay down judgments of taste' (§ 22; 1: 85).

In section 40 Kant elaborates upon his distinction between common sense in the sense of taste (*sensus communis aestheticus*) and common human understanding (*sensus communis logicus*) (§ 40; 1: 153n.).

> Common human understanding which, as mere sound (not yet cultivated) understanding, is looked upon as the least we can expect from anyone claiming the name of man, has therefore the doubtful honour of having the name of common sense (*sensus communis*) bestowed upon it; and bestowed, too, in an acceptation of the word *common* . . . which makes it amount to what is vulgar. . . . However, by the name *sensus communis* is to be understood the idea of a *public* sense, i.e. a critical faculty which in its reflective act takes account (*a priori*) of the mode of representation of everyone else, in order, *as it were*, to weigh its judgment with the collective reason of mankind. . . . (§ 40; 1: 151)

'[T]aste can with more justice be called a *sensus communis* than can sound understanding; . . . the aesthetic, rather than the intellectual, judgment can bear the name of a public sense' (§ 40; 1: 153).

Kant quite definitely discerned a political import to this concept of common sense. He notes at one point that a law-governed political community capable of reconciling freedom and equality on the one hand and authority on the other relies upon

> the art of reciprocal communication of ideas between the more cultured and ruder sections of the community, . . . to bridge the difference between the amplitude and refinement of the former and the natural simplicity and originality of the latter – in this way hitting upon that mean between higher culture and the

modest worth of nature, that forms for taste also, as a sense
common to all mankind, that true standard which no universal
rules can supply. (§60; 1: 227)

12 Judgment must be public.

We are now entering upon that area of Kant's philosophy of judgment
most relevant to the formulation of a theory of political judgment. In
the context of his discussion of common sense, Kant distinguishes three
basic maxims of common human understanding: (1) to think for
oneself; (2) to think from the standpoint of everyone else; (3) always to
think consistently. 'The first is the maxim of unprejudiced thought,
the second that of enlarged thought, the third that of consistent
thought' (§40; 1: 152). '[T]he first of these is the maxim of understanding, the second that of judgment, the third that of reason'
(§40; 1: 153). Obviously it is the second of these maxims that is of
concern to us here. Kant observes that 'we have quite got into the way
of calling a man narrow (narrow, as opposed to being of enlarged mind)
whose talents fall short of what is required for employment upon work
of any magnitude. . . . But the question here is not one of the faculty
of cognition, but of the mental habit of making a final use of it'
(§40; 1: 152–3). It is not a question of the range and degree of a man's
natural endowments, but rather of how these are put to use. Someone
is a person of enlarged mind 'if he detaches himself from the subjective
personal conditions of his judgment, which cramp the minds of so
many others, and reflects upon his own judgment from a universal
standpoint (which he can only determine by shifting his ground to the
standpoint of others)' (§40; 1: 153). The point is to

> avoid the illusion arising from subjective and personal conditions
> which could readily be taken for objective, an illusion that would
> exert a prejudicial influence upon its judgment. This is accom-
> plished by weighing the judgment, not so much with actual, as
> rather with the merely possible, judgments of others, and by
> putting ourselves in the position of everyone else, as a result of a
> mere abstraction from the limitations which contingently affect
> our own estimate. This, in turn, is effected by so far as possible
> letting go the element of matter, i.e., sensation, in our general
> state of representative activity, and confining attention to the

formal peculiarities of our representation or general state of representative activity. (§ 40; 1: 151)

Since this depends not upon the scope of one's faculties, but on how these faculties, possessed by *all*, are used, the exercise of judgment or common sense is within the potentiality of *everyone*. The second point to be stressed is that one does not strive to bring one's judgment into accord with a particular community of judging subjects ('actual' judgments), but rather, we put ourselves in the standpoint of others so as, by that means, to attain to a *universal* judgment ('possible' judgments). As pointed out above (under thesis 6), this capacity for enlarged thought does not rely upon any principle of community whatsoever.

In his critique of Burke's 'physiological' account of taste, Kant calls attention to the pluralistic nature of taste (§ 29, general remark; 1: 130-2).[10] 'The import of the judgment of taste, where we appraise it as a judgment entitled to require the concurrence of everyone, cannot be *egoistic*, but must necessarily, from its inner nature, be allowed a *pluralistic* validity' (1: 132). Kant's objection to Burke is that the reduction of taste to *empirical* conditions – love and fear, gratification and pain – privatizes judgment, instead of submitting judgment to public criteria. It is for the same reason that Kant is so concerned to keep the agreeable and the beautiful entirely distinct: 'As regards the agreeable, everyone concedes that his judgment, which he bases on a private feeling, and in which he declares that an object pleases him, is restricted merely to himself personally. . . . The beautiful stands on quite a different footing' (§ 7; 1: 51-2). Judgments upon the agreeable represent merely private judgment. The same point is made in sections 20-2, where Kant classifies common sense 'not as a private feeling, but as a public sense' (1: 84). The distinction between judgment and feeling corresponds to the distinction between public and private. The publicness of aesthetic judgments arises from the fact that judgments of the beautiful relate to public appearances. Thus Kant refers to 'the outward appearance . . . that usually assumes such importance in our judgment' (§ 54; 1: 202).

13   Aesthetic judgments are difficult and uncertain.

This is the point upon which the Kantian and Aristotelian approaches to judgment meet in unqualified agreement. Kant notes that correct subsumption of particulars in reflective judgment 'has to face unavoidable difficulties which do not affect the logical judgment' (§ 38, remark; 1: 147). The rendering of a valid aesthetic judgment is thus much more problematical than the rendering of a logical judgment. None the less, Kant insists that 'the difficulty and uncertainty concerning the correctness of the subsumption' does not affect the transcendental legitimacy of the faculty of aesthetic judgment (§ 38, remark; 1: 148). This point is closely bound up with the fact that 'there is no *science* of the beautiful' (§ 44; 1: 165; cf. § 60; 1: 225). Thus the relationship between reflective judgment, where the subsumption of particulars is unavoidably problematical, and determinant judgment, where the subsumption is much less so, is comparable to the relationship between *phronesis* and *techne*, as conceptualized by Aristotle.

14 Aesthetic judgments are contentious, but potentially reconcilable.

Kant's solution to the antinomy of aesthetic judgment (sections 55–7) resides in a distinction between 'contention' and 'dispute'. Kant defines dispute as 'decision by means of proofs', based therefore upon concepts. '[T]hough contention and dispute have this point in common, that they aim at bringing judgments into accordance out of and by means of their mutual opposition; yet they differ in the latter hoping to effect this from definite concepts, as grounds of proof, and, consequently, adopting objective concepts as grounds of the judgment' (§ 56; 1: 205). In the case of a judgment of taste, 'no *decision* can be reached by proofs, although it is quite open to us to *contend* upon the matter, and to contend with right'. Thus: 'there may be contention about taste (although not a dispute)'. While there cannot be decision by means of proofs, 'there must be a hope of coming to terms. Hence one must be able to reckon grounds of judgment that possess more than private validity and are thus not merely subjective' (ibid.).

The antinomy concerning principles of taste arises from the fact that there must both be, and not be, concepts upon which the judgment of taste is based. If there were concepts, there could be dispute in the sense of decision by means of proofs. If there were no concepts whatsoever upon which to base judgment, 'there could be no room even for contention in the matter' (§ 56; 1: 206). Kant resolves this by allowing that 'the judgment of taste must have reference to some concept or other', but insisting at the same time that 'it need not on that account be provable from a concept' (§ 57; 1: 206). The antinomy dissolves in recognizing that 'the judgment of taste does depend upon a concept ... but one from which nothing can be cognized in respect of the object, and nothing proved' (§ 57; 1: 207–8). With this solution, Kant is able to affirm that 'the judgment of taste contains beyond doubt an enlarged reference ... which lays the foundation of an extension of judgments of this kind to necessity for everyone' (§ 57; 1: 207). Having thereby secured the possibility of contention about matters of taste (and at the same time outlawed conclusive 'proofs'), Kant has justified his supposition that 'we are suitors for agreement from everyone else' (§ 19; 1: 82).

15 Taste is conducive to the development of moral sense.

At the end of the 'Critique of aesthetic judgment', Kant calls the beautiful 'the symbol of the morally good' (§ 59; 1: 223). He specifies the following analogies between the aesthetic and the moral: both please immediately, both please apart from all interest, both exhibit freedom (the freedom of the aesthetic resides in the imagination; the freedom of the moral resides in the will), and both are universal. As we shall soon see, this amounts to saying that both are autonomous. Kant concludes that aesthetic judgments 'excite sensations containing something analogous to the consciousness of the state of mind produced by moral judgments. Taste makes, as it were, the transition from the charm of sense to habitual moral interest possible' (§ 59; 1: 225). In other words, taste mediates between the sensuous and the moral. (It was this aspect of Kantian aesthetics that fascinated and preoccupied Schiller.) This requires a qualification (or perhaps amendment) of our earlier remarks about the radical separation of aesthetic and moral judgment.

Kant writes that 'the propaedeutic to all fine art ... appears to lie, not in precepts, but in the culture of the mental powers produced by a sound preparatory education in ... the *humaniora*' (§ 60; 1: 226). The purpose of the latter is to develop one's *humanity*, which in turn fosters the '*social spirit* of mankind'. This, in turn, leads to 'a concept of the happy union, in one and the same people, of the law-directed constraint belonging to the highest culture, with the force and truth of a free nature sensible of its proper worth', which constitutes a sound *politics*. Thus taste and politics are interwoven with one another, by way of 'humanity', 'social spirit', and 'moral sense'. Accordingly, Kant concludes the 'Critique of aesthetic judgment' in these words:

> taste is, in the ultimate analysis, a critical faculty that judges of the rendering of moral ideas in terms of sense (through the intervention of a certain analogy in reflection on both); and it is this rendering also, and the increased sensibility, founded upon it, for the feeling which these ideas evoke (termed moral sense), that are the origin of that pleasure which taste declares valid for mankind in general and not merely for the private feeling of each individual. This makes clear that the true propaedeutic for laying the foundations of taste is the development of moral ideas and the culture of the moral feeling. For only when sensibility is brought into harmony with moral feeling can genuine taste assume a definite unchangeable form. (§ 60; 1: 227)

This shows quite conclusively that Kant was not insensitive to the possible moral ramifications of taste.

However, it must be understood that this reciprocity between taste and moral sense comes within what Kant calls the 'methodology' of taste, and does not belong to the transcendental critique of aesthetic judgment proper. That is to say, it relates to the way one comes to acquire taste and develop it, not how it receives its transcendental legitimacy. This allows us to clarify our earlier statements about the relationship between the moral and the aesthetic. In so far as its transcendental validity is concerned, the aesthetic judgment must have no admixture of the moral. Apart from this question of how to secure for the judgment its transcendental status, however, Kant displays a thorough awareness of how the acquisition of taste and the establishment of a civilized and moral politics mutually bolster and interpenetrate one another. The reconciliation of sensibility and morality represents both the stabilizing of taste and the humanizing of politics.

16 Judgments of taste are singular.

Kant holds that 'the judgment of taste is invariably laid down as a singular judgment upon the object' (§ 33 ; 1: 140). A universal judgment, e.g. 'All tulips are beautiful', is 'not one of taste, but is a logical judgment. . . . [I]t is only the judgment whereby I regard an individual given tulip as beautiful . . . that is a judgment of taste' (§33; 1: 140–1). Taste judges particulars, not universals. Kant actually makes the distinction between aesthetic and logical judgments hinge upon the fact that the former are singular (but are *potentially universalizable*), the latter are non-singular (i.e. *are* universal). Thus:

> by taking the singular representation of the object of the judgment of taste, and by comparison converting it into a concept according to the conditions determining that judgment, we can arrive at a logically universal judgment. For instance, by a judgment of the taste I describe the rose at which I am looking as beautiful. The judgment, on the other hand, resulting from the comparison of a number of singular representations: 'Roses in general are beautiful', is no longer pronounced as a purely aesthetic judgment, but as a logical judgment, founded on one that is aesthetic. (§8; 1: 55)

This singularity of aesthetic judgment is very closely related to Kant's dictum that 'there neither is, nor can be, a science of the beautiful', that 'the judgment of taste is not determinable by principles' (§§60, 44; 1: 225, 165). It is bound up, too, with Kant's assignment of originality as a 'primary property' of fine art, and his definition of genius as 'a talent for producing that for which no definite rule can be given, and not an aptitude in the way of cleverness for what can be learned according to some rule' (§46; 1: 168). No rule can be sufficient for the aesthetic determination of the particular, and this is true for both the production of beauty by genius and the estimation of beauty by taste. In both cases, natural 'genius' rather than 'scientific' principles accounts for the aesthetic phenomenon.

17 Judgment must be autonomous, not heteronomous. The individual judges for himself.

We now confront the theme that forms the very heart of Kant's theory: namely, the autonomy of judgment. With this we raise the question of the possible continuity between Kant's practical philosophy and his philosophy of judgment.

Kant writes: 'Taste lays claim simply to autonomy. To make the judgment of others the determining ground of one's own would be heteronomy' (§ 32; 1: 137). He states even more sharply: 'every judgment which is to show the taste of the individual, is required to be an independent judgment of the individual himself. *There must be no need of groping about among other people's judgments*' (ibid.; italics mine). The judgment must be *a priori*, not empirical, which means that the 'enlarged mind' discussed above must be purely formal, and in no way substantive. 'Hence it is that a youthful poet refuses to allow himself to be dissuaded from the conviction that his poem is beautiful, either by the judgment of the public or of his friends' (ibid.). The autonomy of judgment requires that it exclude accommodation to the judgment of the public (in the sense of a particular community), or of friends, both of these amounting to heteronomy. In fact, any principle of community, aside from the purely formal universality of the human subject as such, serves to reduce judgment to heteronomy, as we have seen above. What Kant means by heteronomy is indicated in a remark about the sublimity of 'isolation from all society'. Social isolation achieves its quality of the sublime by virtue of its 'superiority to wants' (§ 29, general remark; 1: 129). The sublime is applied here as a moral category. Dependence upon community is classified as a 'natural want', therefore heteronomous in the terms of Kant's moral philosophy.

A posteriori sources of taste, according to Kant, 'contradict the autonomy of taste in each individual' (§ 32; 1: 138). This does not completely rule out the claim of tradition, but it certainly limits it. The case here is the same as in religion, 'where undoubtedly everyone has to derive his rule of conduct from himself, seeing that *he himself remains responsible* for it and, when he goes wrong, cannot shift the blame upon others' (ibid.; italics mine). One *can* appeal to the 'exemplary' models of tradition, which Kant likens to the example of virtue or holiness which 'does not dispense with the autonomy of virtue . . . or convert this into a mechanical process of imitation', but this does not in any way diminish one's own ultimate responsibility for the judgment (ibid.).

In section 40 (as commented upon under thesis 12 above), Kant distinguishes between the maxim of unprejudiced thought ('to think for oneself') and the maxim of enlarged thought ('to think from the standpoint of everyone else'). We see now how these two maxims converge.

Kant describes the former as 'the maxim of a never-*passive* reason. To be given to such passivity, consequently to heteronomy of reason, is called prejudice; and the greatest of all prejudices is . . . *superstition*. Emancipation from superstition is called *enlightenment*' (§40; 1: 152). We can now see that all these attributes of the 'maxim of understanding' apply equally well to the 'maxim of judgment'. The latter, too, represents the ideals of the Enlightenment, which Kant formulates as heteronomy of reason giving way to autonomy.

'The judgment of others, where unfavourable to ours, may, no doubt, rightly make us suspicious in respect of our own, but convince us that it is wrong it never can. Hence there is no empirical ground of proof that can coerce anyone's judgment of taste' (§33; 1: 139–40). Therefore: 'I try the dish with *my own* tongue and palate, and I pass judgment according to their verdict (not according to universal principles)' (§33; 1: 140). This assertion of the autonomy of judgment, with its exclusion of any possible coercion to compel judgment, constitutes a 'liberal' theory of judgment.

We see then that Kant's 'aesthetic liberalism' goes hand in hand with his political liberalism. Kant's affirmation of the inviolable moral autonomy of the individual is just as evident, and just as pronounced, in the *Critique of Judgment* as it is in the moral philosophy of the *Critique of Practical Reason*.[11] This is why Kant writes: 'judgment does not find itself subjected to a heteronomy of laws of experience as it does in the empirical estimate of things – in respect of the objects of such a pure delight it gives the law to itself, *just as reason does* in respect of the faculty of desire' (§59; 1: 224, italics mine). From this we learn that Kant's aesthetic philosophy of judgment cannot easily be extricated from his ethical philosophy of practical reason; closer examination of the seeming disparity between them bars any unproblematical exclusion of one from the other. This calls for further examination of the ways in which the notion of practical reason possibly finds its way into Kant's aesthetic philosophy.

18 *Judgments of the sublime are projections of the idea of respect.*

This final thesis is of sufficient interest to merit being considered on its own. We therefore accord it a separate section.

AESTHETIC JUDGMENT AND MORAL RESPECT

As Nathan Rotenstreich correctly argues in an article on Kant's relation-ship to Burke, for Kant the concept of 'sublimity' is neither aesthetic (even though situated within a philosophy of aesthetics), nor religious (as it was for Burke), but rather, ethical – associated with the moral concept of respect.[12]

Kant defines respect as 'the feeling of our incapacity to attain to an idea that is a law for us' (§ 27; 1: 105). Externalization of this inner moral law constitutes the sublime: 'the feeling of the sublime in nature is respect for our own vocation, which we attribute to an object of nature by a certain subreption (substitution of a respect for the object in place of one for the idea of humanity in our own self – the subject)' (§ 27; 1: 106). In sublimity we project onto objects of nature the infinity of our own inner moral law. Respect for the noumenal subject is projected onto respect for sublime objects. Sublimity, then, is not an acknowledgement of the supremacy of nature, but, on the contrary, an affirmation of our own transcendence of nature: 'nature is . . . called sublime merely because it raises the imagination to a presentation of those cases in which the mind can make itself sensible of the appro-priate sublimity of the sphere of its own being, even above nature' (§ 28; 1: 111–12). Far from exalting nature in his concept of the sub-lime, Kant seems intent on the moral subjugation of nature: he remarks that imagination in its capacity as an instrument of reason and its ideas 'is a might enabling us to assert our independence as against the influences of nature, *to degrade what is great in respect of the latter to the level of what is little*, and thus to locate the absolutely great only in the proper estate of the subject' (§ 29, general remark; 1: 121; italics mine). The supposed sublimity of nature therefore turns out to be no more than a sensuous representation of our own moral autonomy over against nature: 'Sublimity . . . does not reside in any of the things of nature, but only in our own mind, insofar as we may become conscious of our superiority over nature within, and thus also over nature without us' (§ 28; 1: 114). Even our respect for God flows not from awe before the display of His might in nature, but rather 'by the faculty which is planted in us of estimating that might without fear, and of regarding our estate as exalted above it' (ibid.).

Kant offers a moral counterpart to Burke's interpretation of the beautiful and the sublime in terms of a distinction between the feminine and the masculine emotion, or between love and terror. Following Burke, and making ample use of Burke's psychological insights, Kant distinguishes between *strenuous* affection (*animus strenuus*, or spirited emotions such as enthusiasm) and *languid* affection (*animus languidus*, or tender emotions such as sentimentality) (§ 29, general remark; 1: 125). What is distinctive about Kant's account, however, is that he gives the distinction a pronounced moral accent. Intellectual delight in the moral law

> estimated aesthetically, instead of being represented as beautiful, must rather be represented as sublime, with the result that it arouses more a feeling of respect (which disdains charm) than of love or of the heart being drawn towards it – for human nature does not of its own proper motion accord with the good, but only by virtue of the dominion which reason exercises over sensibility. (§ 29, general remark; 1: 123–4)

We do not *love* the moral law, we *respect* it. Love corresponds to the beautiful; respect, to the sublime. (This distinction between love and respect also pervades Kant's early work, *Observations on the Feeling of the Beautiful and Sublime* (1764), especially section 2). This derives from a Burkean distinction between attraction and repulsion, the former an attribute of beauty, the latter an attribute of sublimity. The beautiful corresponds to love by virtue of its quality of attraction; the sublime corresponds to respect by virtue of the demand for distance. Thus a 'tender soul' is opposed to 'stern duty'. The tender soul makes 'the heart enervated, insensitive to the stern precepts of duty, and incapable of respect for the worth of humanity in our own person and the rights of men (which is something quite other than their happiness), and in general incapable of all firm principles' (§ 29, general remark; 1: 125–6). A sense of the sublime, in opposition to the feelings of the beautiful, pertains to respect of humanity, the *rights* of men as opposed to their *happiness*. We might sum this up by saying that the experience of the beautiful lacks the 'moral seriousness' of the experience of the sublime, that it represents the freedom of *play* rather than the freedom of a *law*-ordained function 'which is the genuine characteristic of human morality, where reason has to impose its dominion upon sensibility' (§ 29, general remark; 1: 120). The beautiful evinces the frivolousness of play; the sublime evokes the sternness of law.

In a fascinating passage on the 'moral misanthropy' of old age, Kant distinguishes between two kinds of sadness, one sublime because 'founded on ideas', the other beautiful, 'springing from sympathy' (§ 29, general remark; 1: 129–30). Elaborating further upon this distinction, in reference to a line from Sassure about the 'insipid sadness' of a certain Alpine mountain, Kant remarks that melancholy

> may take its place among the vigorous affections, provided it has its root in moral ideas. If, however, it is grounded upon sympathy, and, as such, is lovable, it belongs only to the *languid* affections. And this serves to call attention to the mental temperament which in the first case alone is sublime.   (§ 29, general remark; 1: 130)

What is fascinating about this differentiation between sympathetic sadness and *moral* sadness is that sympathy (insipid sadness, languid melancholy) is denied a moral status on account of its being lovable, being rooted in love. On the other hand, melancholy which is genuinely sublime (sadness which is 'interesting', melancholy which is vigorous) is so by virtue of its being rooted in *moral ideas*. Once again, love is excluded from the moral. Sympathy, because lovable, falls short of the moral dignity of the sublime, and is therefore consigned to the merely beautiful. Love, like beauty itself, is too 'tender', too 'weak', to meet the severe demands of sublime moral duty.

The duality of beauty and sublimity is resolved by Kant into a duality of love and respect. Thus he writes:

> We may regard it as a favour that nature has extended to us, that besides giving us what is useful it has dispensed beauty and charms in such abundance, and for this we may *love* it, just as we view it with *respect* because of its immensity, and feel ourselves ennobled by such contemplation.   (§ 67; 11: 30; italics mine)

Beauty is merely a 'favour' of nature, while nature's sublimity alone is 'ennobling'. There remains no doubt that the beautiful is ranked as morally indifferent as compared with the sublime. We may remember that Kant distinguishes three kinds of delight, corresponding to the agreeable, the beautiful, and the good. The agreeable gratifies, the beautiful pleases, and the good is esteemed. These refer to the three kinds of delight, that of inclination, of favour, and of respect (§ 5; 1: 49). We see clearly, then, that the beautiful, occupying the intermediate position, is subordinate to the third, which is obviously correlated with the sublime. Beauty is ranked below sublimity because it is totally devoid of moral status, whereas sublimity is wholly constituted by its reference to moral respect. The experience of the sublime permits man to assert his human dignity; the experience of the beautiful does not.

Once again it is a question of autonomy, a matter of 'the spiritual feeling of respect for moral ideas, which is not one of gratification, but a self-esteem (an esteem for humanity within us) that raises us above the need of gratification' (§ 54; 1: 202). Where it is our transcendence of nature that is at stake, mere love, mere beauty, is inadequate to the moral idea.

The principal implication that all of this has for politics is the idea of formal equality. As Kant puts it, amending Hume, 'critics' are not privileged over 'cooks', they 'share the same fate' (§ 34; 1: 141). In rendering aesthetic judgment, 'the mind becomes conscious of a certain ennoblement and elevation above mere sensibility to pleasure from impressions of sense, and also appraises the worth of others on the score of a like maxim of their judgment' (§ 59; 1: 224). The formal autonomy of judgment secures the moral worth of all judging subjects. Thus the principle of independent taste is an important reaffirmation of human equality. Respect, which is the basis of this equality, is confirmed in the experience of the sublime. And respect is, above all, a formal principle, whereas love, the opposing term, is a substantive principle. We respect someone on account of their pure (formal) humanity, whereas we love them on account of their particular (substantive) qualities which endear them to us. Formal equality is rooted in formal respect, and both converge in the exercise of the formal right of autonomous aesthetic judgment. Everyone has a right to their own judgment of taste, assuming that it is based not on some mere sensation but grounded a priori. All are accorded this right as a matter of respect, and in this consists their formal equality.

The problem, however, is that in according respect to the autonomy of each and every judging subject, Kant offers no principle (say, a conception of wisdom) by which one might discriminate, epistemically, amongst various bearers of judgment. A Kantian theory of political judgment would not allow one to speak of political know-ledge or political wisdom. The difficulty with such exclusion of know-ledge from political judgment is that it renders one incapable of speak-ing of 'uninformed' judgment, and of distinguishing differential capacities for knowledge so that some may be recognized as more qualified, and some as less qualified, to judge. The specification of knowledge criteria, to determine degrees of perspicacity or discernment in different judging subjects, would run counter to Kant's idea of universal moral equality. Thus the demand for criteria of rationality to help settle competing claims (in the absence of universal rules) is attenuated by the liberal insistence upon respect for formal equality. To acquire a fuller appreciation of this problem, we must inquire into Kant's political theory.

FROM TASTE TO POLITICS: KANT'S REJECTION OF PRUDENCE

Kant's practical philosophy is based on a thoroughgoing renunciation of ancient practical philosophy. The ancients tended to identify the true and the good, Kant decisively severs them. In so doing, Kant deliber-ately opposes the ancients. To divorce the true and the good is to debar wisdom from informing practical judgment, since morality is made equally accessible to all, even to 'common reason'. In other words, the good is made 'immediately' accessible, rather than being 'mediated' by knowledge of the true. It is hardly conceivable that Kant's philo-sophical reflection upon politics could have remained unaffected by this outright rejection of the classical idea of prudence, or practical wisdom.[13]

Kant distinguishes between technically practical principles, where the concept determining the causality is a concept of nature, and morally practical principles, where it is a concept of freedom. The former, Kant declares to be theoretical (natural), not practical (ethical). He writes:

All technically-practical rules (i.e., those of art and skill generally, or even of prudence, as a skill in exercising an influence over men and their wills) must, so far as their principles rest upon concepts, be reckoned only as corollaries to theoretical philosophy. For they

> only touch the possibility of things according to concepts of
> nature. (introduction, 1; 1: 9–10)

This contains two startling revaluations of Aristotelian concepts: first,
it suggests that prudence (*phronesis*) is not practical; second, it denies the
Aristotelian distinction between *phronesis* and *techne*, assimilating the
former to the latter. Prudence is identified with *techne*. Kant insists that
'political economy, the art of social intercourse, . . . or even general
instruction as to the attainment of happiness,' cannot be denominated
practical philosophy; these 'contain nothing more than rules of skill,
which are thus only technically practical' (introduction, 1; 1: 10). Thus
Kant declares that moral faith, assurance from a purely practical point
of view, 'in no way extends either speculation or the practical rules of
prudence' (§91; II: 144). The genuinely practical, for Kant, is completely detached from any concept of practical wisdom.

   This anti-Aristotelian view of practical reason derives from Kant's
distinction between 'hypothetical imperatives' and 'categorical imperatives'. The former, in Kant's terms, can never be moral.[14] 'The
maxim of self-love (prudence) only *advises*; the law of morality *commands*. Now there is a great difference between that which we are *advised*
to do and that which we are *obliged*.'[15] Prudence, as deliberation upon
the choice of means to happiness, is only hypothetical; it advises rather
than commands.[16] The crucial difference between these two distinct
kinds of imperatives, for Kant, is that the prudential requires careful
deliberation, whereas moral duty is 'immediately' accessible. Thus:

> The commonest intelligence can easily and without hesitation see
> what, on the principle of autonomy of the will, requires to be
> done; but on supposition of heteronomy of the will, it is hard and
> requires knowledge of the world to see what is to be done. That is
> to say, what duty is, is plain of itself to everyone; but what is to
> bring durable advantage, such as will extend to the whole of one's
> existence, is always veiled in impenetrable obscurity; and much
> prudence is required to adapt the practical rule founded on it to
> the ends of life, even tolerably, by making proper exceptions. But
> the moral law commands the most punctual obedience from every-
> one; it must, therefore, not be so difficult to judge what it requires
> to be done, that the commonest unpractised understanding, even
> without worldly prudence, should fail to apply it rightly.[17]

Kant maintains that it 'would ruin morality altogether were not the voice of reason in reference to the will so clear, so irrepressible, so distinctly audible, even to the commonest men. . . . So sharply and clearly marked [is morality] that even the commonest eye cannot fail to distinguish [it].'[18] The principle of happiness, on the other hand, 'refers to experience and is founded on it, and then the variety of judgment must be endless'.[19] Prudential judgments rely on experience; practical judgments, as Kant defines them, do not.

The same assumptions are clearly evident in Kant's political writings. Thus he writes in his essay on 'Theory and practice': 'The concept of duty in its complete purity is incomparably simpler, clearer and more natural and easily comprehensible to everyone than any motive derived from, combined with, or influenced by happiness, for motives involving happiness always require a great deal of resourcefulness and deliberation.'[20] Again:

> a will which follows the maxim of happiness vacillates between various motives in trying to reach a decision. For it considers the possible results of its decision, and these are highly uncertain; and it takes a good head to find a way out of the host of arguments and counter-arguments without miscalculating the total effect. On the other hand, if we ask what duty requires, there is no confusion whatsoever about the answer, and we are at once certain what action to take.[21]

In contrast to the sorts of considerations that customarily govern political life, the basic rights of man command '*immediate* respect'.[22]

For Kant, politics is concerned not with happiness, which is based on experience, but with right, which is *a priori*.[23] 'If we consider the welfare of the people, theory is not in fact valid, for everything depends upon practice derived from experience.' Political right 'has an objective, practical reality, irrespective of the good or ill it may produce (for these can only be known by experience). Thus it is based on *a priori* principles, for experience cannot provide knowledge of what is right.'[24] This allows Kant to approve of statesmen who are in default of prudence: 'The legislator may indeed err in judging whether or not the measures he adopts are *prudent*, but not in deciding whether or not the law harmonises with the principle of right.' Prudence is subject to error, right is not. The idea of an original contract provides the legislator with 'an infallible *a priori* standard . . . and he need not wait for experience to show whether the means are suitable'.[25] Hence, this idea of contract actually *obviates* the need for reflective judgment. Finally, we learn that, according to Kant, the promotion of human progress in history is not merely a desideratum but a duty, so that the entertaining of doubts about whether progress is practicable calls forth the reproach of being merely prudential, or 'expedient': 'I cannot exchange my duty for a rule of expediency which says that I ought not to attempt the impracticable.'[26] Prudence is overruled by duty.

We may assume that Kant's notion of prudence was not simply directed against eighteenth-century utilitarians, but was intended to take in the classical concept of *phronesis*, as articulated by Aristotle and transposed into *prudentia* by Aquinas. In Kant's terms, Aristotle and Aquinas are just as far removed from morality as are the utilitarians, and for his purposes the classical teaching may be assigned the same status as that allotted to utilitarianism.[27]

The chief reason why Kant exalted the immediacy of political right and duty was, purely and simply, because he was such a committed democrat (as was also the case with Rousseau). If political rectitude is 'immediately' accessible, unmediated by knowledge formed and shaped by mutual discourse, then it is accessible to all, the common people no less than the wise. It thereby dispenses with 'reflective' deliberation, in the sense that 'reflectivity' demands a higher insight accessible only to the few. The latter supplies a role for political wisdom, a role circumvented by Kant's insistence upon moral immediacy. Kant's democratic renunciation of prudence is, then, a rebuke to the aristocratic principles of the ancients.

The unfortunate implications that Kant's rejection of prudence has for his theorizing about politics are visible in his major political essay 'Perpetual peace'. Kant's advocacy of republicanism, federalism, and world peace in this essay expresses the consistent universalism of his political concerns, yet this is strangely conjoined to a blatant instrumentalism that seems anything but compatible with the lofty moralism of his conception of right. This is illustrated by the famous 'nation of devils' passage:

nature comes to the aid of the universal and rational human will, so admirable in itself but *so impotent in practice*, and makes use of precisely those self-seeking inclinations in order to do so. It only remains for men to create a good organization for the state, . . . and to arrange it in such a way that their self-seeking energies are opposed to one another, each thereby neutralising . . . the rest. . . . [M]an, *even if he is not morally good in himself*, is nevertheless compelled to be a good citizen. As hard as it may sound, the problem of setting up a state can be solved even by a nation of devils (so long as they possess understanding). . . . [T]he constitution must be so designed that, although the citizens are opposed to one another in their private attitudes, these opposing views may inhibit one another in such a way that the public conduct of the citizens will be the same as if they did not have such evil attitudes. . . . [S]*uch a task does not involve the moral improvement of man.* . . . [W]e cannot expect [men's] moral attitudes to produce a good political constitution.[28]

This discloses the reverse side of Kant's liberalism: political instrumentalism, employing the 'mechanism of nature', and manipulating the selfish inclinations of men regarded as natural (amoral) beings, to achieve right. The same applies to Kant's celebration of universal peace: nature

unites nations which the concept of cosmopolitan right would not have protected from violence and war, and does so by means of their mutual self-interest. . . . [O]f all the powers (or means) at the disposal of the power of the state, financial power can probably be relied on most. Thus states find themselves compelled to promote the noble cause of peace, *though not exactly from motives of morality.* [While] large military alliances can only rarely be formed, and will even more rarely be successful . . . nature guarantees perpetual peace by the actual mechanism of human inclinations.[29]

Rather than incorporating a model of rational persuasion and agreement on the basis of his account of aesthetic judgment, Kant conceives human history as a part of nature, to be interpreted with the aid of regulative ideas on the model of teleological judgment. Kant's political theory does indeed follow from, and interlace with, his practical philosophy, but the latter breaks down when required to operate in the realm of politics (disregarding, for the present, the question of whether it even breaks down in the realm of morality itself; it may, of course, be argued that the problem here is rooted in a more general difficulty concerning the relationship between the noumenal and the phenomenal that pervades the whole of Kant's work). Because Kant excludes prudence and deliberation from his concept of political right, he is forced to fall back upon invisible processes of nature to realize absolute moral ends in the political world. A strict reliance upon morality is simply not sufficient to vindicate Kant's hopes as a liberal. Consequently, Kant must look for support from outside his system of practical reason, and this extraneous guarantee of 'progress' clashes with his pure moral principles.

This gives rise to striking contradictions in Kant's political thought. In the appendix to 'Perpetual peace' Kant criticizes political expediency, for which 'much knowledge of nature is required, so that one can use its mechanism to promote the intended end'.[30] But this is in fact the leading theme of 'Perpetual peace' itself: the use of the mechanisms of nature to promote moral goals such as peace and republican freedom. As noted above, Kant's philosophy of history is really concerned with *nature*, and the ineluctable workings of an invisible providence (as posited by reflective historical judgment). Therefore when Kant, again in the appendix, attacks the conception of 'a state in which everything that happens or can happen simply obeys the mechanical workings of nature where politics would mean the art of utilising nature for the government of men, and where this would constitute the whole of practical wisdom, the concept of right then becoming only an empty ideal',[31] he is actually assailing the entire conception of his own 'Perpetual peace'.

The exact nature of the contradiction needs to be clarified. There is no conflict at all between Kant's concept of right and his moral principles. On the contrary, Kantian politics seeks universal conformity to absolute moral laws. Rather, the conflict arises over how to actualize these laws in nature, how to secure for principles of right a realization in the world. The question is why the means employed are wholly amoral; why supersensible right is at the mercy of empirical causality. Part of the answer is that Kant is compelled to rely upon the workings of nature because he has so radically divorced morality from nature that unless the two happen to converge there is no hope of morality influencing or prevailing upon a being entirely given over to nature. Either one abides by the moral law – which is immediately accessible to the good will – or one does not; Kant has little to provide in terms of rational motives or inducements to win over the expedient politician. Moral deliberation never gets started, since it is assumed that the dictates of duty are already felt at the outset. So, inevitably, Kant resorts to 'natural' stimuli (in Kant's sense of natural), the realm of morality having been elevated, beyond nature, to such an absolute height.

This in turn is inextricable from Kant's deliberate and explicit rejection of ancient moral and political theory. At one point Kant draws a distinction between 'political expediency' and 'political wisdom'. The former concerns itself with grading institutional arrangements – questions that preoccupied the ancients – which Kant says involved complicated and necessarily uncertain calculations; whereas Kant's own solution 'presents itself as it were automatically; *it is obvious to everyone*'.[32] This immediate access to moral intuition precludes, rather than defines, political wisdom as the ancients understood it.

Kant says repeatedly (in the appendix to 'Perpetual peace') that rational politics is congruent with moral duty. But how does this congruency actually come about? By men being brought to see the efficacy of reason through the active agency of moral deliberation, or merely by nature producing it behind the backs of men? In his 'Perpetual peace' the latter alternative prevails, without any admission on Kant's part of how much it strains his anti-naturalist moralism. Kant seems to gloss over the magnitude of his concession to nature. In the appendix to 'Perpetual peace' Kant asserts the conformity that is possible between politics and morality, but in the body of the essay he thoroughly dispenses with moral appeals, and goes so far as to concede that they cannot be made operative. This leaves a vacuum, to be filled only by the covert hand of providence. A more satisfactory account would have supplied a role for reflective deliberation, in the sense of public argument and discussion that involves the adducing of rational inducements, as distinct from bare *voix de conscience*.

I would sum up my critique by saying that Kant lacks a sufficient account of political agency and also lacks a sufficient account of rational deliberation. Kant *might* have attempted to develop for politics a model of rational persuasion and judgment based on his analysis of aesthetic judgment. Instead, he explicates politics within the framework of a philosophy of history that is drawn from his account of *teleological* judgment: history is conceived as a natural process that, viewed from the empirical point of view, appears merely haphazard, but for which we may speculatively posit a moral purpose, on analogy with teleological reflective judgment. We are led to posit the regulative idea of purposiveness in history so that we may reflect on history without despair, and act in history with the hope of realizing moral objectives. Thus the realization of moral ideals in politics is ascribed neither to self-conscious agency nor to political deliberation but only to divine providence. And since we cannot *know* (by determinant judgment) that providence operates in history, we merely posit this idea for purposes of reflection, exactly as we do for nature in teleological judgment. In this way, history is conceived as if it were a *natural* process, empirically conditioned rather than subject to autonomous agency.

It seems to me that the deficiency of Kant's account of politics follows quite naturally from his very decisive rejection of ancient moral philosophy. This rejection finds dramatic expression in the following passage from the *Critique of Judgment*:

> What . . . does it all avail, that this man has so much talent, that he is even so active in its employment and thus exerts a useful influence upon social and public life, and that he possesses, therefore, considerable worth alike in relation to his own state of happiness and in relation to what is good for others, if he has not a good will? (§ 86; 11: 109)

The core of the problem, as we see from this passage, is Kant's depreciation of teleology (in the Aristotelian, not Kantian, sense). Kant asserts that perpetual peace 'is desirable not just as a physical good, but also as a state of affairs which must arise out of recognising one's duty'.[33] Similarly, Kant writes: 'we are . . . concerned not with philanthropy, but with *right*'.[34] As in the formulations of the critical philosophy, Kant makes clear that his concern is not with the needs of man, but with the moral relationship subsisting between man and the rational law. But, *pace* Kant, politics *is* about the needs of man (not just 'natural' needs in the sense of Kant's highly constricted definition, but human needs in the broadest sense), and provides for rational discourse about the provision for those needs.

Kant's stress upon autonomy and formal right induces him to exclude teleology, on principle, from his definition of the political, and this leads to a conception of politics that seems indifferent to the provision for human needs. In the 'Theory and practice' essay, Kant insists that his theory has nothing to say about 'the welfare of the people': 'we are not concerned here with any happiness which the subject might expect to derive from the institutions or administration of the commonwealth, but primarily with the rights which would thereby be secured for everyone. . . . No generally valid principle of legislation can be based on happiness.'[35] Again: 'the principle of happiness . . . has ill effects in political right just as in morality'.[36] And this of course shapes the corresponding definition of what counts as a valid political judgment: 'the result usually affects our judgment of the rightfulness of an action, although the result is uncertain, where the principles of right are constant. . . . [S]uch errors arise . . . from the usual fallacy of allowing the principle of happiness to influence the judgment.'[37] Repudiation of political prudence goes hand in hand with the exclusion of teleology from judgment: a politics of dignity opposes itself to a politics of purpose. This raises serious questions about the adequacy of the Kantian concept of judgment for conceptualizing political judgment.

A non-teleological conceptualization of aesthetic judgment is at least plausible (although by no means incontestable).[38] But how can political judgment be sufficiently comprehended apart from ends, and abstracted from teleological deliberation upon desirable purposes? To get an idea of a radically different, indeed a diametrically opposed, concept of judgment, let us turn to Aristotle.

F·O·U·R
Aristotle's concept
of prudence

JUDGING AND JUDGING-WITH: SYMPATHY
AS AN ESSENTIAL MOMENT OF JUDGMENT

Aristotle's treatment of practical wisdom, *phronesis*, in book VI of the
Nicomachean Ethics, exemplifies a position that would today be called
ethical cognitivism. This means that virtuous action is, according to
Aristotle's interpretation, a mode of true cognition. To be virtuous is
to know what is required in a particular moral situation, and to act
consistently on that knowledge. The *phronimos*, the man of practical
wisdom, typically knows what virtues are called for in a given ethical
situation, and is one who excels at 'getting it right'. *Phronesis* is not one
virtue among others, but is the master virtue that encompasses and
orders the various individual virtues. Virtue is the exercise of ethical
knowledge as elicited by particular situations of action, and to act on
the basis of this knowledge as a matter of course is to possess *phronesis*.
Without *phronesis* one cannot properly be said to possess *any* of the
virtues, and to possess *phronesis* is, conversely, to possess *all* the virtues,
for *phronesis* is knowledge of which virtue is appropriate in particular
circumstances, and the ability to act on that knowledge. *Phronesis* is a
comprehensive moral capacity because it involves seeing particular
situations in their true light in interaction with a general grasp of what

it is to be a complete human being, and to live a proper human life. *Phronesis* moves back and forth, from universal to particular, and from particular to universal. It allows mastery of ethical predicaments without dependence upon a set of rules or codified principles to tell us when the particular is an instantiation of the universal (our conception of what is good in general), when it is an exception to the ethical norms we already live by, and when it calls for revision of our conception of the good. As John McDowell points out in his account of practical wisdom, we approach the experience of virtue not 'from the outside in' (on the basis of codified principles of right conduct), but 'from the inside out' (on the basis of a tacit understanding of what it is to live virtuously).[1]

According to the analysis provided in book VI of the *Nicomachean Ethics*, practical wisdom is not identical to the capacity for judgment, but the latter is certainly an essential component of the former. One cannot be in possession of *phronesis* without mature judgment, *gnome*, and the ability to judge well in the realm of ultimate particulars is one of the prime distinguishing marks of the man of practical wisdom. A more detailed account of the relationship between these two terms, *phronesis* and *gnome*, is offered in book VI, chapter 11 of the *Ethics*, and it is on this chapter that an interpretation of Aristotle's theory of judgment should particularly focus. But first let us begin by locating this chapter within the overall context of book VI.

The bulk of book VI falls into roughly two parts: the first is a catalogue of the various intellectual virtues – *episteme, techne, phronesis, nous,* and *sophia*. In the second half of book VI, one of these intellectual virtues, namely *phronesis*, is singled out for more exact determination. It receives this more precise characterization by means of a series of contrastive pairings through which the distinctive features of *phronesis* are placed into relief. Of course it is significant that it is specifically *phronesis*, of the five intellectual virtues listed, that is selected for this privileged treatment.

The catalogue of the intellectual virtues occupies chapters 3 to 7 of book VI. The pairings used to highlight *phronesis* cover chapters 8 to 11 and 13. Each of the terms with which *phronesis* is paired is something from which *phronesis* has to be distinguished, and yet to which it bears a definite relationship. The pairings are as follows: *phronesis* and political knowledge; *phronesis* and excellence in deliberation; *phronesis* and understanding; *phronesis* and insight or judgment; and *phronesis* and ethical virtue. In each case, there is a difference between the two terms and yet there is something fundamental that they hold in common. Thus: *phronesis* and *politike* are said to be the same characteristic, but their essential aspect is not the same. Deliberating well is a mark of *phronesis*. The sphere of understanding, we are told, is the same as that of *phronesis*, yet understanding and *phronesis* are none the less not the same. It is much the same case with *phronesis* and judgment. Finally, with ethical virtue (*arete*), we find that the two are inextricable, but not identical.

All of these various terms are drawn together in book VI, chapter 11, and it is here that the ground of their unity is specified:

> All these characteristics . . . tend toward the same goal. We attribute good sense, understanding, practical wisdom, and intelligence to the same persons, and in saying that they have good sense, at the same time that they have a mature intelligence and that they are men of practical wisdom and understanding.[2]

What they all share is a common concern with 'ultimate particular facts'. Each of these qualities or virtues grasps ultimate particulars, and in this way each contributes to *phronesis*.

This may suffice for an indication of the overall context; let us now probe some of the more detailed connections. In particular, we need to examine the relationship (which is the decisive one for our own purposes) between *phronesis* and judgment. Why does Aristotle see fit to distinguish between them at all (as he does, implicitly, in book VI, chapters 10 and 11 of the *Ethics*)? *Phronesis* is no doubt *grounded in* good judgment, but that is not to say that they are identical. For Aristotle, lack of *phronesis* is not just a failure of judgment, but really a failure of action or, one might say, a failure of *embodied* judgment. *Phronesis*, then, is judgment that is embodied in action; it is judgment consummated in the efficacy of good *praxis*. If I *see* what the situation requires, but am unable to bring myself to act in a manner befitting my understanding, I possess judgment but not *phronesis*. Eric Voegelin, in part II of his essay on 'What is right by nature?', helps to clarify this problem. *Phronesis* is for Aristotle what Voegelin in his commentary calls an 'existential virtue': knowledge of right action

> merges into concrete action, and action is the truth of knowledge;
> . . . That this is indeed the philosophical intention of Aristotle is

confirmed by his distinction of phronesis from *synesis* and *eusynesis*, the virtue of right understanding and judgments (*NE* VI, 10). *Synesis* has the same scope as *phronesis* but is not identical with it, for *phronesis* issues into command (*epitaktike*) about what is to be done and what not, while *synesis* is the virtue of right judgment and understanding (*kritike*). The *synetos*, the man of good judgment, knows how to assess action correctly, but he does not thereby become a *phronimos*, who acts correctly with effectiveness.[3]

Kritike is a necessary but not sufficient condition of *phronesis*; judgment alone is not enough in order to qualify as a *phronimos*. According to Voegelin, judgment maintains a distance between subject and object which *phronesis* seeks precisely to bridge in *eupraxia*. In short: *phronesis* minus *praxis* equals judgment. *Phronesis* is the union of good judgment and the action which is the fitting embodiment of that judgment.

We have noted that each of the terms from which *phronesis* has been differentiated also represents something to which it bears an essential relationship. But why is *phronesis* explicated in relation to these particular terms? The more we consider them, the more questionable they become. For instance, why should *phronesis*, the ability to 'size up' ultimate particulars, be essentially related to hermeneutic understanding, as Aristotle indicates in book VI, chapter 10? Understanding 'implies the use of one's faculty of opinion in judging statements made by another person about matters which belong to the realm of practical wisdom — and in judging such statements rightly, for *good* understanding means that the judgment is right'.[4] The primary import of the Greek term '*sunesis*' is, however, the comprehension of the utterances of another. Why should this hermeneutic insight bear any fundamental relationship to the tackling of practical problems in a concrete situation? To be sure, sensitivity to the meanings intended to be communicated by another is incidentally helpful in coping with the ultimate particulars that constitute a practical situation. But why should the relationship be an essential one?

The matter becomes even more problematical when we turn to sympathy and forbearance, for in what essential way do these bear upon our efforts to lay hold of the ultimate particulars that are the objects of our practical wisdom? To pose the question more directly: why must one be able to experience fellow-feeling or empathy in order to come to

terms with a matter of concrete practical decision? An easy way to begin
answering is by noting that in the original Greek the terms treated in
book VI, chapter 11, are bound together by an etymological connection,
which means that the relationship would have immediately suggested
itself to Aristotle. He plays upon the interrelation between *gnome* –
which is translated as insight, judgment, or good sense – and its
cognates: *suggnome* – translated as forgiveness, pardon, or sympathetic
understanding; and *eugnomon*, the quality of being considerate.[5] Thus
judgment, sympathy, and forgiveness are conceptually interconnected
in a manner that would not be immediately evident in English translation. The Greek term that we translate as, alternatively, sympathy or
forgiveness means literally 'judgment-with', 'judgment on the side of',
another person. In chapters 10 and 11 of book VI, Aristotle links together *gnome*, the ability to perceive and apprehend rightly the ultimate
particulars with which we are confronted and which demand of us deliberate action, and *suggnome*, our capacity for empathetic understanding
and forbearance. This suggests that to judge is to understand, to understand is to sympathize, and to sympathize is to be able to forgive.

   To get some perspective on this, we may consider the contrasting
conceptual implications of the corresponding English terms. Interestingly, the words we have in English that correspond to *suggnome* are also
derived from the Greek – sympathy and empathy – but they have
pathos, feeling (or suffering) as their root. Sympathy is literally feeling-
with (or suffering-with); empathy, literally feeling-into. What is
especially noteworthy about this distinction between the Greek and
English equivalents here is that the Greek, *suggnome*, is related to a root
that is active, namely judgment, while the English is derived from a
root that is passive, namely feeling – which even more directly connotes
passivity in the Greek than in the English, the Greek *pathos* being conceptually opposed to *praxis*, action.[6] Where *suggnome*, through *gnome*, is
related to *praxis*, sympathy, through *pathos*, is opposed to *praxis*; in
sympathy one merely endures, bears, suffers. *Suggnome* implies judging,
and therefore acting, for to judge-with arises out of a context of acting-
with. The English, in failing to convey this implicit association, con-
veying in fact the very opposite association, likewise fails to capture any
active, *praxis*-oriented dimension to sympathy.[7]

   This opposition between *praxis* and *pathos* (action and passion,
doing and suffering, activity and passivity) is of further relevance to our

topic. In book I, chapter 3 of the *Ethics*, Aristotle relates judgment to *praxis* and *pathos* respectively. On the one hand, the good judge is a man of experience, long schooled in the hard and demanding experiences of life. On the other hand, the young lack judgment: 'a young man is not equipped to be a student of politics; for he has no experience in the actions which life demands of him'.[8] However, an important part of the deficiency of the young in this area has to do with the fact that the youth 'follows his passions', 'pursuing all his interests under the influence of his passions'.[9] In book VIII, chapter 3, Aristotle insists that young people are guided by passion.[10] It would seem then that what qualifies the man of experience for exercising judgment is precisely his experience in the world of *praxis*, and correspondingly, what disqualifies the young from the exercise of political judgment is precisely the fact of their being subject to *pathos*, their dependence on passion. In other words, judgment must be experienced actively, in actual situations of practical choice; judgment will not develop through merely passive exercise, say, in a contemplative or spectator situation. One develops qualities of judgment by being actually thrust into the exigencies of *praxis*.

But, more specifically, what is it about being under the sway of passions that disqualifies youth from wielding political judgment? The answer lies in attending with care to the opposing connotations of *praxis* and *pathos*. The latter signifies 'being acted upon', in contrast to 'acting'. Thus, on this reading, the man of experience is qualified for judgment because he is used to acting, while the young are incapable of commanding good judgment because they are constantly being 'acted upon'. *Praxis* is associated with judgment, and *pathos* with lack of judgment, because judgment accrues from acting, not from being acted upon. All of this serves to underline the importance of sympathy being understood as an active judging-with, and not merely a passive suffering-with.

The relationship between 'judging' and 'judging-with' is well brought out in Gadamer's commentary on this aspect of Aristotle. Gadamer writes:

> Understanding is a modification of the virtue of moral knowledge. It appears in the fact of concern, not about myself, but about the other person. Thus it is a mode of moral judgment. We are obviously speaking of understanding when, using this kind of

judgment, we place ourselves in the concrete situation in which the other person has to act. The question here, then, is not of a general kind of knowledge, but of its specification at a particular moment. This knowledge also is not in any sense technical knowledge or the application of such. The person who is experienced in the world, the man who knows all the tricks and dodges and is experienced in everything there is, does not as such have the right understanding which a person who is acting needs; he has it only if he satisfies one requirement, namely that he too is seeking what is right, i.e., that he is united with the other person in this mutual interest. The concrete example of this is the phenomenon of advice in 'questions of conscience'. Both the person who asks for advice and the person giving it assume that the other is his friend. Only friends can advise each other or, to put it another way, only a piece of advice that is meant in a friendly way has meaning for the person advised. Once again we discover that the person with understanding does not know and judge as one who stands apart and unaffected; but rather, as one united by a specific bond with the other, he thinks with the other and undergoes the situation with him.[11]

Gadamer concerns himself mainly with the relationship between *phronesis* and *sunesis*, prudence and understanding (book VI, chapter 10), because for him it shows that Aristotle's analysis is 'a kind of model of the problems of hermeneutics'[12] and that, conversely, Gadamer's own philosophical hermeneutics is a rightful successor to classical practical philosophy.[13] However, he also makes note of the relationship between *phronesis* on the one hand, *gnome* and *suggnome* on the other hand (in book VI, chapter 11). Thus insight and fellow-feeling are recognized as 'further varieties of moral reflection': 'A person with insight is prepared to accept the particular situation of the other person, and hence he is also most inclined to be forbearing or to forgive. Here again it is clear that it is not a technical knowledge.'[14]

What Gadamer helps us to appreciate is that the *hexis* (habit or settled ability) that is *phronesis*, in one of its most essential aspects, equips the virtuous and prudent man with a capacity to project himself into the genuine situation of another. It is this hermeneutic self-projection into the position occupied by another that lends to judgment its qualitative or 'depth' dimension, so that it cannot be captured in mere technical expertise. Moreover, the cognitive function of judgment implies that knowledge is acquired not only by the route of science and *techne*, but that practical reason, no less than theoretical reason, makes a rightful claim to knowledge.

We started by asking what basic relationship judgment could bear to sympathy and forgiveness, and followed some hints suggested by the etymological link between *gnome* and *suggnome*. We see now that the answer must reside in the capacity of the prudent man, the *phronimos*, not just to judge, but at the same time to judge-*with* (as among citizens) – judgment guided by shared concern, informed by reciprocal involvement in situations held in common. In this sense, sympathetic understanding and capacity for forgiveness are essential moments of any judgment upon human affairs, and all authentic judgment contains within it the potentiality for judgment-with. Aristotle, by pairing *phronesis* with understanding, judgment, and fellow-feeling, thereby contributes to an awareness of the substantive human conditions of practical judgment.

JUDGMENT AND FRIENDSHIP

In our discussion of the Aristotelian concept of judgment, we have referred to the phenomenon of advice in questions of conscience as treated by Gadamer. What we have now to consider is whether such matters of sympathy and fellow-feeling are in some fundamental respect foreign to the proper sphere of political judgment. For instance, it might be supposed that this incorporation of sympathy within the judgment of the citizen imports a wholly inappropriate aspect of intimacy into the realm of the political. To clarify matters it is necessary to call attention to the place of friendship within Aristotle's political thought and, at the same time, to differentiate between *philia*, to which two prominent books of the *Nicomachean Ethics* are devoted, and *eros*, which is accorded no significant treatment.

What I want to suggest is that to take Gadamer's discussion of the phenomenon of friendly advice as an introduction of intimacy into judgment would be to mistake *eros* for *philia*.[15] One possible way of drawing the distinction is to view *eros* as striving continually, even if only in principle, to close the space that separates those who experience it, in contrast to *philia* as involving projection of oneself into the place of the other while leaving intact the space between as that which is held in common. It is precisely this that constitutes friendship as the political relationship par excellence, and accounts for the attention Aristotle devotes to *philia* in the *Ethics*.

Friendship, for Aristotle, is a matter of community, and community, in turn, is a matter of justice. Thus friendship is defined as sharing a common view of what is just:

> friendship and the just deal with the same objects and involve the same persons. . . . Friendship is present to the extent that men share something in common, for that is also the extent to which they share a view of what is just. And the proverb 'friends hold in common what they have' is correct, for friendship consists in community. . . . [F]riendship and what is just exist in the same relationship and are coextensive in range.[16]

What friends hold in common is a common view of what is just, and it is to this extent that friendship is a form of community. It is this that constitutes the continuity between friendship and politics, between political community and the community of friends. Thus Aristotle's discussion of friendship leads naturally into a discussion of political constitutions. '[A]ll associations seem to be parts of the political community, but the kind of friendship prevalent in each will be determined by the kind of association it is.'[17] An analysis of political relationships is coterminous with analysis of the various kinds of friendship.

This intersection between friendship and politics is particularly embodied in the concept of *homonoia* – concord or what we may call political friendship – to which Aristotle devotes chapter 6 of book IX. *Homonoia* means literally 'being of the same mind', 'thinking in harmony'.[18] But Aristotle takes care to point out that it is not identity of opinion, or concurrence of judgment, 'on any subject whatever it may be'. And it is not ascribed to any people whose opinions or judgments so concur. Rather, the identity of judgment must fall within the ambit of political judgment, and the relationship it describes must be one of friendship. Those to whom we apply the term *homonoia* must be friends, and the shared judgments concerned must be about the common interest: 'we attribute *homonoia* to states, when the citizens have the same judgment about their common interest, when they choose the same things, and when they execute what they have decided in common.

In other words, *homonoia* is found in the realm of action.'[19] Needless to say, a concept of political friendship defined in terms of identity of judgment about the common interest is of manifest relevance to an inquiry into political judgment.

'*Homonoia* is friendship among fellow citizens, and that is indeed the common use of the term. For its sphere is what is in the common interest and what is important for life.'[20] What is important about this concept is that it represents an attempt on Aristotle's part to identify citizenship and friendship, basing both on a fundamental harmony of judgments, in particular, judgments about what is just, about what is in the common interest. The opposite of concord is faction, where thoughts and opinions clash, and fundamental judgments are in disharmony. The discord of faction impairs the friendship of citizens.

Homonoia is also intermeshed with virtue, and political friendship is inseparable from ethical qualities.

> [T]his kind of concord exists among good men. They are of the same mind each with himself and all with one another. . . . They wish for what is just and what is in the common interest, and these are their common goals. Bad men, on the other hand, cannot live in concord, except to a small extent, any more than they can be friends.[21]

Friendship and political concord correspond. Hence just as the bad man is disqualified from friendship, so is he disqualified from sharing in concord, or political friendship. The judgments of the citizen are not separable from moral qualities, and the shared judgments that constitute relationships of friendship are likewise bound up with moral character. Friendship and citizenship are jointly constituted by ethical judgment.

But what of the condition of intimacy that we normally associate with friendship, so that the deepest friendships are held to be found always between two people? Aristotle addresses this question in book IX, chapter 10, and while granting that this is so in regard to personal friends, he enters a special clause concerning 'friendship among fellow citizens'. Whereas intimate friendship is restricted to the few, political friendship can be extended to many. '[I]n the kind of friendship that exists among fellow citizens, it is actually possible to be friends with many people without being obsequious and while remaining a truly good man.'[22] Thus political friendship provides the widest possible range of friendship.

From books VIII and IX of Aristotle's *Nicomachean Ethics* the conclusion can be drawn that the quest for a theory of political judgment leads irresistibly to the formulation of a corresponding theory of friendship. To judge is to judge-with, to judge-with is to be a friend. To judge well is a staple of politics. The inference is that friendship is quintessentially political. If we accept Aristotle's premises, it follows that both a theory of politics and a theory of judgment are fully bound up with a theory of friendship, and that the provision of a theory of friendship goes hand in hand with the provision of a theory of judgment. We shall return to this issue in chapter 6 below.

Judgment
and rhetoric

ARISTOTLE: DELIBERATION, RHETORIC, AND JUDGMENT

One who forms a judgment on any point, but cannot explain himself clearly to the people, might as well have never thought at all on the subject. (Thucydides, *History of the Peloponnesian War*, book II, chapter 6)

There is an additional set of considerations that favours the inclusion of sympathy or fellow-feeling within judgment. This concerns the nature of judgment defined as the decision issuing from a process of deliberation. Such a process of deliberation is governed by insight into the effect of one's contribution to the deliberation. In short, he who deliberates well must have insight into rhetoric. But such insight involves understanding of the emotions, character, and moral purpose of one's listeners, as well as anticipation of the emotions, character, and moral purpose that they the listeners will tend to ascribe to you the speaker. It is an account of these factors that occupies Aristotle in his *Rhetoric*. But to appreciate to what extent the study of rhetoric draws upon sympathetic understanding and moral reflection, we must obtain a more detailed account of the nature of political deliberation and of its relationship to the judgment to which it gives rise.

The first thing we might reflect on is the very fact that Aristotle undertakes to provide a philosophical *Rhetoric*. Why indeed does he see the provision of a *Rhetoric* as a worthy pursuit of the philosopher? In short, what significance ought we to attach to the very fact that Aristotle sees fit to write a *Rhetoric*? Gadamer presents Aristotle's theory of rhetoric as a fulfilment of Plato's philosophical programme posed in the *Phaedrus*,[1] namely, the demand for a 'theory of the mutual accommodation of speech and soul': 'the task is to master the faculty of speaking in such an effectively persuasive way that the arguments brought forward are always appropriate to the specific receptivity of the souls to which they are directed'.[2] This calls for 'a profound knowledge of the souls of those one wishes to persuade'.[3] A genuine art of rhetoric, as opposed to the bogus claims of the sophists, must rest upon knowledge of the receptivity of the souls to which one's speech is addressed, and this of course is a hermeneutic knowledge. This rhetorical art is for Gadamer a model of what hermeneutic knowledge as such entails: namely, a mode of truth not accessible to modern epistemological methodologies. Rhetoric, Gadamer writes, 'from oldest tradition has been the only advocate of a claim to truth that defends the probable, the *eikos* (verisimile), and that which is convincing to the ordinary reason, against the claim of science to accept as true only what can be demonstrated and tested! Convincing and persuading, without being able to prove'[4] – this mode of truth is common to rhetoric and to hermeneutics. But it is precisely this form of truth that is invalidated by such thinkers as Descartes, who openly excludes rhetoric from the domain of knowledge. Against Descartes, Gadamer summons Vico, who was himself a teacher of oratory. In his *On the Study Methods of our Time*, Vico seeks to defend rhetoric against the onslaught of Cartesianism. He urges that we devote ourselves to 'topics' as well as geometry, that we 'not spurn reasons that wear a semblance of probability and verisimilitude'. Vico implores:

> Let our efforts not be directed towards achieving superiority over the Ancients merely in the field of science, while they surpass us in wisdom; let us not be merely more exact and more true than the Ancients, while allowing them to be more eloquent than we are; let us equal the Ancients in the fields of wisdom and eloquence as we excel them in the domain of science.[5]

What is noteworthy here is how Vico couples wisdom with eloquence. The latter is a necessary accompaniment of the former, a hermeneutic requirement that Gadamer seeks to restore, against the ravages of the Cartesian quest for certainty based on method. The lesson of philosophical hermeneutics is that one does not reach a judgment in abstraction from the opinions of others, but rather in communion with their feelings and desires, and the judgment is communicated with a view to its proper reception. The judgment is never abstracted from the context of the audience for which it is intended. This is the object of philosophical reflection upon rhetoric, and explains why a philosopher writes a *Rhetoric*.

Aristotle's *Rhetoric* is a study of political judgment; it examines the qualities of judgment that enable a political orator to select the most appropriate modes of persuasion; it conceptualizes the relationship between the judgments of assemblies and the processes of deliberation that culminate in judgment; and it shows the art of rhetoric to be a necessary ingredient in the rendering of judgments, both on the part of the orator and of his audience. Aristotle thus demonstrates for us that to inquire into rhetoric is simultaneously to inquire into political judgment. 'The duty of rhetoric is to deal with such matters as we deliberate upon without arts or systems to guide us' (1357a1–2).[6] This virtually defines the task of judgment.

The main concern of book I of the *Rhetoric* is to distinguish the three types of oratory – political or deliberative, forensic or legal, and epideictic or ceremonial. In section 1, Aristotle expresses a special concern about the extent to which legal oratory has been the dominant focus of attention, especially among the sophists, to the neglect of political oratory. Aristotle finds this insufficient attention paid to political oratory particularly distressing because not only is politics 'a nobler business, and fitter for a citizen, than that which concerns the relations of private individuals', but also because 'in political oratory there is less inducement to talk about non-essentials': 'it treats of wider issues'. Whereas in legal judgments 'it is other people's affairs that are to be decided', and therefore the judges are less liable to be studiously involved in judging impartially, 'in a political debate the man who is forming a judgment is making a decision about his own vital interests'. Therefore the results of the deliberation are of more immediate consequence for those participating in judgment. Aristotle notes that whereas in lawcourts irrelevant speaking has to be forbidden, in the public assembly this is not necessary since 'those who have to form a judgment', because their own interests are at stake, 'are themselves well able to guard against that' (1354b24–1355a3). In sum, political oratory, because it touches issues that are the most comprehensive and that affect most immediately the interests of those sitting in judgment, should be the primary concern of the student of rhetoric.

Aristotle defines rhetoric as 'the faculty of observing in any given case the available means of persuasion' (1355b25–27), and defines the study of rhetoric as concerned with the modes of persuasion. He distinguishes between rhetoric and dialectic on the one hand, and between rhetoric and science on the other. He insists that rhetoric cannot be reduced to a science:

> rhetoric is a combination of the science of logic and of the ethical branch of politics; and it is partly like dialectic, partly like sophistical reasoning. But the more we try to make either dialectic or rhetoric not, what they really are, practical faculties, but sciences, the more we shall inadvertently be destroying their true nature; for we shall be re-fashioning them.   (1359b9–16)

It is this attribute of rhetoric, namely its status not as a science but as a 'practical faculty', that establishes its essential kinship with the capacity of judgment.

What are the objects of rhetoric? Rhetoric comes into operation in the judging of probabilities, and the judging of contingencies. The mode of persuasion it deals with is the enthymeme, that is, a persuasion that does not admit of strict syllogisms. But the assessment of probabilities is not entirely distinct from the rendering of logical judgments: 'The true and the approximately true are apprehended by the same faculty; . . . men have a sufficient natural instinct for what is true, and usually do arrive at the truth. Hence the man who makes a good guess at truth is likely to make a good guess at probabilities' (1355a14–18). But for the very reason that rhetoric enters when probabilities must be weighed, it is at the same time addressed to contingencies: 'The subjects of our deliberation are such as seem to present us with alternative possibilities' (1357a4–5). This is because the probabilities that we are called upon to weigh have to do with human action:

Most of the things about which we make decisions, and into which therefore we inquire, present us with alternative possibilities. For it is about our actions that we deliberate and inquire, and all our actions have a contingent character; hardly any of them are determined by necessity. (1357a23–27)

This is especially so in matters of political oratory: 'counsel can only be given on matters about which people deliberate; matters, namely, that ultimately depend on ourselves, and which we have it in our power to set going. For we turn a thing over in our mind until we have reached the point of seeing whether we can do it or not' (1359a36–40). Thus the persuasion of the political orator enters into the fabric of *phronesis*; selecting among more probable and less probable contingencies on the basis of his persuasive enthymemes is an integral part of the exercise of one's faculty of practical wisdom. The basis of this relationship between rhetoric and *phronesis* is that here too, as in book VI, chapter 11 of the *Ethics*, we find ourselves in the sphere of particulars, and are called upon to judge not universal principles, but particular contingencies.

But *phronesis* is to be found not only on the side of the audience that listens, judges, and decides, but just as much on the side of the orator himself, who must select the most appropriate language, style, and means of persuasion. These judgments of appropriateness (dealt with in book III, chapter 7) demand tact, discrimination, sympathy, sensitivity, and all the other qualities of practical wisdom. Aristotle instructs us to discern the mean: 'Remember what the man said to the baker who asked whether he was to make the cake hard or soft: "What, can't you make it *right?*"' (1416b30–31). Rightness consists 'in the happy mean'.

Three elements enter into the ability to persuade: character (of the speaker); emotion (of the audience); and rationality (of the arguments of the speech itself) (1356a1–25). Persuasion consists in mastering these three, and the whole of the *Rhetoric* is nothing but an elaboration of the details of each. The successful orator must command the following: an understanding of human character and goodness in their various forms (with a view to presenting a convincing appearance of his own personal character); an understanding of the emotions (with a view to putting the audience into a certain frame of mind); and an ability to reason logically (so as to provide acceptable proof in the body of the speech itself). Thus the orator who seeks to lay a claim to genuine *phronesis* in the mode of addressing his audience must be thoroughly familiar with ascriptions of moral character, moral purpose, virtue, goodwill, trustworthiness, and so on, so as to have the best possible motives, character, and purpose ascribed to himself; must be possessed of an awareness of the full range of emotions – anger and calmness, friendship and enmity, fear and confidence, etc. – so that he knows at all times how these emotions are liable to affect a given judgment; and finally, must completely master the various forms of ratiocination, to have the best possible arguments at his disposal. These three sources of persuasion, then, exhaust the art of rhetoric – emotion (of the judges); character (of the speaker); and truth (of the arguments). Thus Aristotle concludes: 'persuasion must in every case be effected either (1) by working on the emotions of the judges themselves, (2) by giving them the right impression of the speakers' character, or (3) by proving the truth of the statements made' (1403b10–14). To show oneself to be a man of moral purpose, to be aware of how emotion interacts with judgment, and to choose the most effective enthymemes, arguments, style, language, delivery, and arrangement of the speech is to achieve in rhetoric the equivalent of what the man in possession of *phronesis* achieves in acting with practical wisdom in a given situation of choice and action. Rhetoric is the counterpart in the realm of speech to what *phronesis* is in the realm of *praxis*.

In book 1, chapter 3, Aristotle differentiates between the three kinds of oratory, namely political, forensic, and ceremonial, as follows: The tripartite division is

> determined by the three classes of listeners to speeches. For of the three elements in speech-making – speaker, subject, and person addressed – it is the last one, the hearer, that determines the speech's end and object. The hearer must be either a judge, with a decision to make about things past or future, or an observer. A member of the assembly decides about future events, a juryman about past events: while those who merely decide on the orator's skill are observers. (1358a36–1358b7)

Here Aristotle specifies the distinguishing feature of political speech, and thereby indicates what he takes to be the distinctive essence of political judgment. The relevant distinctions are made more explicit in the following passage:

These three kinds of rhetoric refer to three different kinds of time. The political orator is concerned with the future: it is about things to be done hereafter that he advises, for or against. The party in a case at law is concerned with the past; one man accuses the other, and the other defends himself, with reference to things already done. The ceremonial orator is, properly speaking, concerned with the present. (1358b12–18)

Thus the typology of rhetoric is based upon time: political oratory is future-oriented, legal oratory is past-oriented, and ceremonial oratory is present-oriented. Of these, the first two types have to do with practical judgment, and it is primarily these that occupy us here. Both political and forensic oratory concern practical judgment because each involves recommending alternative decisions, alternative policies, or alternative courses of action. 'Political speaking urges us either to do or not to do something: one of these two courses is always taken' by counsellors or men who address public assemblies. Similarly, 'forensic speaking either attacks or defends somebody: one or other of these two things must always be done by the parties in a case' (1358b7–12). (The third type of oratory involves praise and blame, so it might be said that it, in turn, issues in 'judgments of character', though these are not practical judgments, strictly speaking.) Both political and legal rhetoric are directed towards judgment because 'rhetoric exists to affect the giving of decisions – the hearers decide between one political speaker and another, and a legal verdict is a decision' (1377b21–23). But what distinguishes these two is that forensic oratory is addressed to judgment upon the past, political oratory is geared to judgment upon the future. In both cases, rhetoric by its very nature leads to judgment.

The same analysis is repeated in book II, chapter 18: 'The use of persuasive speech is to lead to decisions, . . . anyone is your judge whom you have to persuade.' Although the 'onlookers' at a ceremonial speech are treated as judges, 'broadly speaking, the only sort of person who can strictly be called a judge is the man who decides the issue in some matter of public controversy; that is, in law suits and in political debates, in both of which there are issues to be decided' (1391b7–20). General lines of argument concerned with the past are most appropriate to 'forensic speeches, where the required decision is always about the past; that concerned with possibility and the future, to political speeches' (1392a5–8). This distinction obviously affects the kind of argumentation to be employed. Thus for instance:

> 'Examples' are most suitable to deliberative speeches, for we judge of future events by divination from past events. Enthymemes are most suitable to forensic speeches; it is our doubts about past events that most admit of arguments showing why a thing must have happened or proving that it did happen.
>
> (1368a29–33)

Another case in point is offered in book III, chapter 16: 'In political oratory there is little opening for narration; nobody can "narrate" what has not yet happened. If there is narration at all, it will be of past events, the recollection of which is to help the hearers to make better plans for the future' (1417b12–15). One further instance is to be found in book II, chapter 20: 'it is more valuable for the political speaker to supply illustrative parallels by quoting what has actually happened than by inventing fables, since in most respects the future will be like what the past has been' (1394a7–9). Hence whether the judgment is geared to the past or to the future bears a definite relevance to the orator's choice of rhetorical devices.

We have seen that Aristotle differentiates political judgment from legal judgment by reference to time, defining the former as future-oriented. This leads us to the fundamental Aristotelian concept of deliberation, for if political judgment is defined in terms of the future, this at the same time defines deliberation: what is deliberated is a course of action to be undertaken. We find a crucially important account of the relationship between judgment and deliberation in book III, chapter XI of the *Politics*. Aristotle there contrasts the judgment of expertise, of the solitary expert, with the *phronesis* exercised in the common deliberation of the Many. Although each of the deliberators by himself may not be of a good quality,

> when they all come together it is possible that they may surpass – collectively and as a body, although not individually – the quality of the few best. Feasts to which many contribute may excel those provided at one man's expense. In the same way, when there are many, each can bring his share of goodness and moral prudence; and when all meet together the people may thus become some-

thing in the nature of a single person, who – as he has many feet, many hands, and many senses – may also have many qualities of character and intelligence.[7]

Interestingly, Aristotle in this context employs an analogy to aesthetic judgment, arguing that 'the Many are also better judges of music and the writing of poets: some appreciate one part, some another, and all together appreciate all'. This is in direct opposition to Plato's critique of the democratization of aesthetic judgment in the *Laws* (700a5–701c4).

Common deliberation remedies (or at least mitigates) the imperfections of democracy. Each is imperfect in the judgments he forms by himself, yet 'when they all meet together, the people display a good enough gift of perception'. Aristotle proceeds to answer those who object that only experts are qualified to decide political questions, just as medical experts alone are qualified to practise the medical art. For men who have some general knowledge of the art of medicine may also be called doctors 'and we credit them with the power of judging as much as we do the experts'.[8] And it is general knowledge of this sort that characterizes participants in the political assembly. 'Each individual may indeed be a worse judge than the experts; but all, when they meet together, are either better than experts or at any rate no worse.' Moreover, it is not always or necessarily the case that the expert practitioner of an art is the most suitable judge of what issues from his art. There are arts 'whose product can be understood and judged even by those who do not possess any skill in the art. A house, for instance, is something which can be understood by others besides the builder': the user of a house will judge it even better than he does. Similarly: 'the diner – not the cook – will be the best judge of a feast'.[9] The comprehensiveness of political deliberation surpasses the limited perspective of the expert, and the breadth of survey commanded by the Many in deliberation exceeds that of the few possessing expertise.

Deliberation is a crucial term in the equation that relates *phronesis* and judgment, for it is in the course of deliberation that the man of practical wisdom exercises his judgment:

Practical wisdom . . . is concerned with human affairs [in contrast to the supra-human knowledge of the philosophers] and with matters about which deliberation is possible. . . . [T]he most characteristic function of a man of practical wisdom is to deliberate well: no one deliberates about things that cannot be other than they are, nor about things that are not directed to some end, an end that is a good attainable by action. In an unqualified sense, that man is good at deliberating who, by reasoning, can aim at and hit the best thing attainable to man by action.[10]

The function of deliberation is obviously to decide the course of action. Deliberation results in a judgment, and on the basis of that judgment, the man of action, the *phronimos*, proceeds to act: 'Practical wisdom issues commands: its end is to tell us what we ought to do and what we ought not to do. Understanding, on the other hand, only passes judgment.'[11] The distinction here is between 'critical and imperative faculties', or between 'theoretical and practical cognition'[12]: understanding judges, *phronesis* commands. What distinguishes the *phronimos* is that in his case understanding always leads, by way of judgment, to *praxis*.

Once again, the domain of practical deliberation is defined in terms of contingencies and particulars. The latter, especially, is seen as the characteristic mark of deliberative reason. Deliberation is assigned the role of applying universals in the midst of the particular. Practical wisdom must 'be familiar with particulars, since it is concerned with action and action has to do with particulars'. Aristotle claims that this accounts for why men who have no scientific knowledge can be 'more adept in practical matters' than those who do have such technical expertise.[13] The scientific (*sophia* and *techne*) pertains to universals; *phronesis*, on the other hand, judges particulars, and the applicability of universals to particulars. Whereas wisdom seeks to discern universal (and necessary) truths, practical wisdom claims only to have apprehended truth relative to the particular (and contingent) situation of men in contexts of action. Thus: '"wise" [possession of *sophia*] must mean the same for everyone, but "practically wise" [possession of *phronesis*] will be different. For each particular being ascribes practical wisdom in matters relating to itself to that thing which observes its interests well.'[14] The same point, but stated in reference to deliberative oratory, is to be found in the *Rhetoric*:

Since in each type of oratory the object under discussion is some kind of good – whether it is utility, nobleness, or justice – it is clear that every orator must obtain the materials of amplification through these channels. To go further than this, and try to

establish abstract laws of greatness and superiority, is to argue
without an object; in practical life, particular facts count more
than generalizations. (1393a12–18)

Deliberation is not to investigate objects in general, as in science; 'to
deliberate is to investigate a particular kind of object'.[15]

Aristotle's fullest theoretical account of deliberation is his chapter
'Practical wisdom and excellence in deliberation' in the *Ethics* (book VI,
chapter 9). Aristotle seeks to show how deliberation is 'generically
different' from either scientific knowledge or opinion or shrewd
guessing. It is a form of reasoning, but it operates in the realm of the
unknown, in the sense that it deals with objects that remain to be
determined rather than with objects that are already fixed and determined. Furthermore it is a kind of reasoning that proceeds 'deliber-
ately', that is to say, in a measured and prudent fashion: 'deliberation
takes a long time. As the saying goes, the action which follows deliberation should be quick, but deliberation itself should be slow.'[16]
Aristotle proceeds to identify deliberation as 'a kind of correctness', for
'good deliberation is a kind of correctness of deliberation', and 'he who
deliberates well deliberates correctly'. However, since one can reach the
correct outcome without good deliberation (say, by attaining the end by
the wrong means), Aristotle further specifies the correctness of deliberation in terms of its adequacy to the *telos* at which it aims: 'since it
is a mark of men of practical wisdom to have deliberated well, excellence
in deliberation will be correctness in assessing what is conducive to the
end, concerning which practical wisdom gives a true conviction'.[17]

But this chapter of the *Ethics* raises an important problem which
must be confronted: namely, whether deliberation is simply instrumental, or something more. At certain points, Aristotle seems to state
quite clearly that what is deliberated upon is strictly the means to one's
ends. For instance, in the *Rhetoric* he writes: 'the political or deliberative
orator's aim is utility: deliberation seeks to determine not ends but the
means to ends, i.e., what it is most useful to do' (1362a17–20). He
also asserts that the principal consideration in political deliberation is
expedience, and remarks: 'The political orator aims at establishing the
expediency or the harmfulness of a proposed course of action'
(1358b20–30), implying that utility outweighs nobility and justice as
the criterion of deliberative judgment. As Gadamer rightly points out,

though, 'Aristotle's definitions of *phronesis* have a marked uncertainty about them, in that this knowledge is sometimes related more to the end, and sometimes more to the means to the end.'[18] Although 'Aristotle says in general that *phronesis* is concerned with the means (*ta pros to telos*) and not with the *telos* itself', Gadamer believes that 'it is probably the contrast with the Platonic conception of the idea of the good that makes him emphasize that'. In fact, according to Gadamer: 'That *phronesis* is not simply the capacity to make the right choice of means, but is itself a moral *hexis* that also sees the *telos* towards which the person acting is aiming with his moral being, emerges clearly from its place within the system of Aristotle's ethics.'[19] In support of this thesis, book VI, chapter 9 of the *Ethics* may itself be cited:

> it is possible for a person to have deliberated well either in general, in an unqualified sense, or in relation to some particular end. Good deliberation in the unqualified sense of course brings success in relation to what is, in an unqualified sense, the end [namely, the good life]. Excellence in deliberation as directed toward some particular end, however, brings success in the attainment of some particular end.[20]

Whereas deliberation about a specific policy is instrumental, there is excellence in deliberation in a broader sense, namely, deliberating in conformity with the right *telos*, the proper end for man.

> The capacity of deliberating well about what is good and advantageous for oneself is regarded as typical of a man of practical wisdom – not deliberating well about what is good and advantageous in a partial sense, for example, what contributes to health or strength, but what sort of thing contributes to the good life in general.[21]

When they calculate well with respect to some worthwhile end, 'we speak of men as having practical wisdom in a particular respect', not in an unqualified sense (we attribute to them partial, not unqualified, *phronesis*). Thus deliberative *praxis*, unlike production (*poiesis*), does not have 'an end other than itself': 'good action (*eupraxia*) is itself an end. That is why we think that Pericles and men like him have practical wisdom. They have the capacity of seeing what is good for themselves and for mankind, and these are, we believe, the qualities of men capable of managing households and states.'[22]

The themes of deliberation, rhetoric, and judgment assume the importance that they do within Aristotle's political philosophy because practical judgment, unlike contemplative aesthetic judgment, is essentially teleological, geared to determination of the proper ends. Indeed, this thesis is stated in the very first sentence of the *Nicomachean Ethics*: 'every action and choice seem to aim at some good; the good, therefore, has been well defined as that at which all things aim'.[23] Knowledge of the highest end, Aristotle claims, equips us, 'like archers who have a target to aim at, to hit the proper mark'.[24] What Aristotle affirms here is that teleological pursuit of the good is built into the very fabric of politics. This teleologically structured character of political life is exemplified in the deliberative process, as shaped by rhetoric. Deliberative oratory recommends possible ends to be pursued. Rhetorical speech sets the 'target' at which we should 'aim'.

But we must be careful not to misunderstand the place of rhetoric within this teleology. It is not an 'external' teleology, where rhetoric merely serves as means to an independently posited end. The point is not that we *use* rhetoric to obtain our ends, but that our ends are themselves inextricably situated in a rhetorical medium, and are constitutively shaped by this medium. Our ends are not merely pursued rhetorically, they are themselves constituted rhetorically. This is what it means to say that political ends are subject to deliberation (and not simply manipulation).

According to this understanding of rhetoric as not merely an instrument of policy, but as the very medium of choice and decision, rhetoric operates not just where one is pursuing an outcome favourable to oneself by winning the sympathy of others, but is just as active where, for instance, one knows one's words will be greeted with hostility and resistance. The traditional model upon which rhetoric has tended to be construed is that first I discern what I want, what my ends are, and then I choose the most efficacious medium in which to pursue it, the most effective means to the end. It is this model that has, as it were, 'given rhetoric a bad name'. But this latter understanding of rhetoric is both distorted and much too narrow. Pursuit of the end is 'always already' embedded in the medium of its pursuit: discernment of what I want is inseparable from the words and manner of expression in which I express what I want. Furthermore, employment of rhetoric covers a much broader field than merely the instrumental pursuit of pre-established ends. Suppose I judge that a community that I wish to address is far too complacent, and that discourse within the community can only be revitalized by provoking, perhaps even shocking, those whom I address. Here, awareness of the medium in which I speak does not enable me to *use* my hearers to serve particular ends, decided in advance, by evoking their sympathy; on the contrary, I seek rhetorically to regenerate discourse with others by 'assaulting' them with language, the immediate effect of which may be revulsion and anger. So it is not a case of dressing up one's speech in the most attractive paraphernalia, but of understanding the reception one's discourse will evoke through a rhetorical appreciation of the medium in which one communicates with others. Thus conceived, the operation of rhetoric covers a universal domain, not merely restricted to instrumental employment, and it is in this sense that rhetoric and rhetorical insight bear a 'constitutive' relation to political judgment and deliberation.

But whether Aristotle himself had precisely such an understanding of rhetoric is a different – and much more complicated – question. It is clear that Aristotle had a definite appreciation of rhetoric as an essential constitutive feature of political life. What is not so clear is whether he merely understood it as the necessarily imperfect medium within which political life is conducted, or whether he also saw it as a positive expression of the mediated quality of social life. The aspect of prudential judgment, situated within the context of deliberation, choice, and action – this dimension of rhetoric is undeniably communicated by Aristotle with great power. But what remains open to question is whether his *Rhetoric* was merely a handbook for the instrumental employment of this medium or whether it pointed toward an affirmation of the medium itself.[25]

There is one indication at least that Aristotle was appreciative of the constitutive function we have been discussing. This is his awareness of the critical importance of 'finding the right words at the right moment quite apart from the information or communication they may convey'.[26] If sympathy and friendship are cardinal virtues of judgment in situations of *praxis*, then, correspondingly, the cardinal virtue of judgment in rhetoric is appropriateness, the virtue by which one discerns 'aptness of language':

> Your language will be *appropriate* if it expresses emotion and character, and if it corresponds to its subject. 'Correspondence to

subject' means that we must neither speak casually about weighty matters, nor solemnly about trivial ones; . . . To express emotion, you will employ the language of anger in speaking of outrage; the language of disgust and discreet reluctance to utter a word when speaking of impiety or foulness; the language of exultation for a tale of glory, and that of humiliation for a tale of pity; and so in all other cases. (1408a10–19)

The orator who chooses the appropriate manner of speech shows himself to be a man of moral purpose, and a man of judgment. It is in this way that he recommends himself – and thereby recommends the words of counsel he offers – to his judging audience. With this to recommend his speech, he may then say, with assurance:

I have done. You have heard me. The facts are before you. I ask for your judgment. (1420b2–5)

Presentation of the case, mediated by oratory, issues in judgment. It is appropriate, then, that the final word of the *Rhetoric* is *krinate*, the rendering of a decision or judgment.

KANT: JUDGMENT VERSUS RHETORIC

Needless to say, we get from Kant a very different assessment of the relation of rhetoric to judgment than that which we have been observing in Aristotle. The task of the following analysis shall be to prove the underlying basis of this divergence: to uncover why a Kantian understanding of rhetoric is radically opposed to the Aristotelian account; why, indeed, a Kantian outlook on politics would actually exclude rhetoric from judgment.

Kant's renunciation of rhetoric is located in sections 51 and 53 of the *Critique of Judgment*. First of all, rhetoric is defined in relation to poetry, the former conceived as understanding conformed to imagination; the latter, as imagination conformed to understanding:

Rhetoric is the art of transacting a serious business of the understanding as if it were a free play of the imagination; poetry that of conducting a free play of the imagination as if it were a serious business of the understanding.

Thus the orator announces a serious business, and for the

purpose of entertaining his audience conducts it as if it were a mere play with ideas. The poet promises merely an entertaining play with ideas, and yet for the understanding there enures as much as if the promotion of its business had been his one intention. (§51; 1: 184–5)[27]

The rhetorician comes short of his promise to engage the understanding. The poet exceeds his promise to give free play to the imagination. Poetry is as rewarding as rhetoric is deficient. This implied devaluation of rhetoric runs directly counter to Aristotle's teaching.

Crucial here is the accentuated opposition between the serious business of the understanding and the imputed frivolity, the frivolousness, of imagination, between the austere seriousness of ideas and the 'play' of sensibility, between business and play. Kant applies this exacting standard of austerity and *gravitas* because he judges fine arts in terms of their moral seriousness. Thus: 'Where fine arts are not, either proximately or remotely, brought into combination with moral ideas, which alone are attended with a self-sufficing delight, . . . the fate that ultimately awaits them' is as follows: 'the aim is merely enjoyment, which leaves nothing behind it in the idea, and renders the soul dull, the object in the course of time distasteful, and the mind dissatisfied with itself and ill-humoured, owing to a consciousness that in the judgment of reason its disposition is perverse' (§52; 1: 191). Fine arts

then only serve for a diversion, of which one continually feels an increasing need in proportion as one has availed oneself of it as a means of dispelling the discontent of one's mind, with the result that one makes oneself ever more and more unprofitable and dissatisfied with oneself. (ibid.)

Kant differentiates sharply between the manner belonging to merely 'agreeable' art and that appropriate to fine art, 'because the object of the latter must always have an evident intrinsic worth about it, and thus demands a certain seriousness in its presentation, as taste does in estimating it' (§54; 1: 203). From this we may gauge the gravity of the charge that rhetoric falls far short of the genuine seriousness to which it pretends.

Kant escalates his attack in section 53. Whereas 'poetry (which owes its origin almost entirely to genius and is least willing to be led by precepts or example) holds the first rank among all the arts', rhetoric, on the other hand,

> so far as this is taken to mean the art of persuasion, i.e., the art of deluding by means of a fair semblance (as *ars oratoria*), and not merely excellence of speech (eloquence and style), is a dialectic, which borrows from poetry only so much as is necessary to win over men's minds to the side of the speaker before they have weighed the matter, and to rob their verdict of its freedom.
>
> (§ 53; I: 191–2)

Whereas poetry 'couples with the presentation of the concept a wealth of thought to which no verbal expression is completely adequate, . . . thus rising aesthetically to ideas', and 'invigorates the mind by letting it feel its faculty – free, spontaneous, and independent of determination by nature', rhetoric

> can be recommended neither for the bar nor the pulpit. For where civil laws, the right of individual persons, or the permanent instruction and determination of men's minds to a correct know-ledge and a conscientious observance of their duty is at stake, then it is below the dignity of an undertaking of such moment to exhibit even a trace of the exuberance of wit and imagination, and, still more, of the art of talking men round and prejudicing them in favour of anyone. For although such art is capable of being at times directed to ends intrinsically legitimate and praise-worthy, still it becomes reprehensible on account of the subjective injury done in this way to maxims and sentiments, even where objectively the action may be lawful. For it is not enough to do what is right, but we should practice it solely on the ground of its being right. Further, the simple lucid concept of human concerns of this kind, . . . exerts of itself . . . a sufficient influence upon human minds to obviate the necessity of having recourse here to the machinery of persuasion, which, being equally available for the purpose of putting a fine gloss or a cloak upon vice and error, fails to rid one completely of the lurking suspicion that one is being artfully hoodwinked.   (§ 53; I: 191–3)

In contrast to the manipulative semblance of rhetoric, poetry 'plays with semblance, which it produces . . . not as an instrument of deception;

for its avowed pursuit is merely one of play, which, however, under-standing may turn to good account and employ for its own purpose' (§53; I: 192). 'In poetry everything is straight and above board. It shows its hand: it desires to carry on a mere entertaining play with the imagination, and one consonant, in respect of form, with the laws of understanding, and it does not seek to steal upon and ensnare the understanding with a sensuous presentation' (§53; I: 193).

It is very important to note here that all the terms of criticism being applied against rhetoric are, without exception, moral categories. Rhetoric robs men's verdict of its *freedom*; it intrudes itself into the sphere of the *right* of individual persons, and that of conscientious observance of *duty*, and tends to reduce the *dignity* of such moral vocations. By making men act on grounds other than pure duty, rhetoric infringes upon morality, violating the purity of the moral motive. While poetry exhibits freedom and uplifts men to a sense of the moral ideas, rhetoric seeks to determine the will according to the con-straining principles of natural sensibility. In short, poetry is governed by human autonomy; rhetoric, by utter heteronomy.

Kant sums up his indictment in these words:

> I must confess to the pure delight which I have ever been afforded by a beautiful poem; whereas the reading of the best speech of a Roman forensic orator, a modern parliamentary debater, or a preacher, has invariably been mingled with an unpleasant sense of disapproval of an insidious art that knows how, in matters of moment, to move men like machines to a judgment that must lose all its weight with them upon calm reflection. Force and elegance of speech (which together constitute rhetoric) belong to fine art; but oratory (*ars oratoria*), being the art of playing for one's own purpose upon the weaknesses (let this purpose be ever so good in intention or even in fact) merits no *respect* whatever.
>
> (§53; I: 193n.)

Rhetorical persuasion is unworthy of respect. Within the terms of Kant's 'aesthetics of moral respect', no more damning accusation could possibly be levelled against oratory.

The reason that Kant finds rhetoric lacking in moral 'seriousness' is that he discounts its teleological dimension (even *good* purposes cannot win respect for oratory), and considers only its aspect of artifice and dissimulation. But what imbues the orator with serious moral purpose is his adoption and recommendation of a targeted end which will, if embraced, guide us into the future. Kant writes: 'the judgment of taste is simply *contemplative*, i.e., it is a judgment which is indifferent as to the existence of an object' (§ 5; 1: 48). But the political orator is *not* indifferent to the existence of his object. He projects it as an end worthy of adoption and pursuance into the future. He advocates it as the *telos* by which to orient *praxis*, setting it up as the 'target' at which to 'aim'. And the judgments rendered in the situation of *praxis* are not merely 'contemplative'. Rather, such judgments set in motion the teleology of political practice. This motion is a temporal (forward-directed) process: teleological deliberation shaped by rhetoric.

What we are presented with here is an opposition between what may be called the 'representational' and 'constitutive' understandings of rhetoric.[28] Kant concentrates on how rhetorical persuasion deviates from correct correspondence, or adequation, to reality. In this respect, he remains within the Platonic tradition, as opposed to the Aristotelian tradition (to which Gadamer appeals). The latter is much more concerned with how rhetoric is a way of expressing one's sense of community. One affirms one's membership in a given community, confirming one's commitment to it, by adjusting one's speech to the opinions and sensitivities of one's fellows. Rhetoric expresses this sense of community by accommodating itself to the particular, substantive, beliefs and desires of the listeners it addresses, rather than holding to abstract or formal principles of judgment. In taking cognizance of the particular needs and aspirations of his audience, the orator expresses his community with them. This is a purpose embodied in rhetoric that cannot be captured merely by tracing the extent to which persuasive utterances correspond adequately to reality.

The problem of rhetoric focuses in a particularly acute way on the striking contrast between the formal principles of the Kantian theory of judgment and the substantive principles of the Aristotelian theory. Rhetoric along with sympathy and friendship constitute substantive conditions of political life, and of political judgment.

With sympathy and detachment: horizons of a comprehensive perspective

Kant or Aristotle? It should be evident that a comprehensive under-standing of human judgment will be unable to dispense with either. What is required is a wider perspective capable of embracing both autonomy and teleology, both the conception of the autonomous judging subject as a bearer of universal rights and an appreciation of the ends, purposes, and human needs that set for judgment its substantive context.[1] Political judgment must be aesthetic *and* teleological: it must encompass formal-transcendental features of the faculty of judgment, as well as orient itself to rationally desirable human ends. To exclude either is one-sided and partial. From Kant we are to get the transcen-dental perspective by which to provide an account of the formal con-stitutive features of politics as such (reconstructing the 'transcendental character' of political judgment). From Aristotle we get the substantive features of political life by which to fill in the content of this formal delineation (judgment as judging-with issuing out of common de-liberation).

With Aristotle now available to us as a backdrop against which to survey Kant, we may see that the 'aesthetics of respect' of the latter constitutes taste without community and judgment without sympathy. However, on the other hand, we may question whether the Aristotelian principles of judgment make sufficient provision for the sense of universal dignity which receives its fullest articulation in the liberalism of Kant, and in terms of which he defines citizenship under a republican constitution.

FORMAL AND SUBSTANTIVE CONDITIONS OF JUDGMENT

We have stated the need for a 'comprehensive' theory[2] of political judgment; that is, one which 'comprehends' both the Kantian and Aristotelian dimensions of judgment. Such a theory would seek to explore two kinds of condition of political judgment, formal and substantive. The formal kind of condition is that elaborated by Kant. For Kant, any rational agent has a right to autonomy of taste, simply by virtue of being a judging subject, and independent of any shared needs or ends, common purposes or bonds of sympathy, or generally, any relationships of community that might condition the judgment. This is demanded by the pure idea of formal respect, and the subject proves himself worthy of this respect in projecting onto objects of nature his own inner sublimity. This aspiration to moral autonomy cannot be denied, but we are not thereby precluded from noting its deficiency: we can acknowledge its claims upon us without deeming it sufficient.

We have seen one instance of this insufficiency displayed in the discussion of rhetoric in the preceding chapter. It is the formalism of Kant's conception of aesthetic judgment that leads him to exclude rhetoric. A consideration of substantive human needs and ends incorporated within his theory of judgment would have prompted Kant to place a much higher premium upon rhetoric. Aristotle's 'constitutive' conception of rhetoric, in contrast, incorporates the aspect of rhetoric as a mode of community, as an expression of one's participation in an ongoing joint deliberation. To this extent, we endorse Gadamer's conclusion that a Kantian formulation of judgment is in itself unsatisfactory because it formalizes judgment, turns it into a formal operation of the interplay of human faculties, and abstracts from substantive conditions of human interaction.

In postulating the need for a comprehensive theory of political judgment, we suggest that the Kantian and Aristotelian theories of judgment each have their own 'moment of truth'. The moment of truth of the Kantian is the formal right of judgment. The moment of truth of the Aristotelian is the substantive ends of judgment. What must be sought (if possible) is a synthetic approach to judgment, integrating the truth of each of these two moments. We should now try to explore briefly the possibility that Kantian and Aristotelian concepts of judgment are not simply contradictory, but may in some sense complement each other. Let us consider the distinction between the judging of the spectator and the judging of the actor or participant. (In Kant's aesthetics, this dichotomy is reflected in the distinction between taste and genius, where the artistic genius first forges the work of art, and the critic or man of taste then judges it.) We have already called attention to the contemplative, disinterested dimension of Kantian judgment, and contrasted it with the active, *praxis*-oriented dimension of Aristotelian judgment. On the one hand, the judging spectator must be able to 'step back', to extricate himself from pre-occupying interests and purposes, to see the object of judgment 'from a distance'. On the other hand, the judging agent must be schooled in the pursuit of public purposes, must be accustomed to the active exercise of prudential judgment, must be experienced. These different perspectives yield two distinct sets of conditions that govern the operation of human judging.

Pursuing these examples, we may characterize 'distancing' as a formal requirement of judgment: 'If people are to act effectively, they must be able to make rational judgments about their real interests. Such judgments presuppose the capacity of the self to stand back from its immediate feeling and acquire some "distance".'[3] But the paradigm for understanding 'distance' is the case of the aesthetic spectator: 'I can never judge of the same thing exactly in the same way. I cannot judge of my work, while doing it. I must do as the artists, stand at a distance.'[4] Conversely, we may characterize experience as a substantive requirement of judgment. The classic formulation of this requirement is book one, chapter 3 of Aristotle's *Nicomachean Ethics*:

> Each man can judge competently the things he knows, and of these he is a good judge. Accordingly, a good judge in each particular field is one who has been trained in it, and a good judge in general, a man who has received an all-round schooling. For that reason, a young man is not equipped to be a student of politics;

for he has no experience in the actions which life demands of him, and these actions form the basis and subject matter of the discussion. . . . [T]he end of this kind of study is not knowledge but action. Whether he is young in years or immature in character makes no difference; for his deficiency is not a matter of time but of living. . . . Knowledge brings no benefit to this kind of person.[5]

No amount of schooling in a *techne* can supply the experience that is the indispensable requirement of *praxis*.

The disinterested spectator, then, evinces the formal requisite of judgment, namely distance. The active participant in worldly affairs, on the other hand, displays the substantive requisite of judgment, namely experience. This is not to say that the two are not often found in combination; the point, rather, is to begin distinguishing ideal types. These concepts of distance and experience, in turn, suggest other conditions of judging. Good judgment requires space and time. On the one hand, judgment requires space: the space in which to 'step back', to achieve 'distance', to get perspective so as to be able to reflect 'from a distance'. 'We must avoid coming too near just as much as remaining too far away.'[6] On the other hand, judgment requires time: the time in which to weigh one's judgment, time to think things over and to reflect, the pause before the moment of decision. 'The action which follows deliberation should be quick, but deliberation itself should be slow.'[7]

These conditions, space and time as well as detachment and experience, make clear that judgment cannot be a matter of spontaneous, immediate, intuition. Human beings possess no god-like clairvoyance that guides their judgment; they inhabit a world of experience where insight is always a fragile achievement, forever subject to opacity and distortion. Thus judgment calls for a determined effort, a pausing-and-reflecting, and a self-distance. In the words of Vico:

> The actions of men cannot be measured with the straight ruler of the understanding, which is rigid. . . . The imprudent scholars, who go directly from the universally true to the singular, rupture the inter-connections of life. The wise men, however, who attain the eternal truth by the uneven and insecure paths of practice, make a detour, as it is not possible to attain this by a direct road.[8]

Practical wisdom, or prudence, is necessarily mediated, by experience, maturity, and understanding. Theory which tries to dispense with the necessary 'detours' of practice will unavoidably falter.[9] But this is true not only of the judgment of prudence. Kant's account of reflective judgment also depicts the mediated character of judging, as is witnessed in his notions of disinterestedness, detachment, and enlarged mentality. Taste too has its own 'detours'. Both Kantian and Aristotelian perspectives on political judgment portray the activity of judging as essentially mediated – by reflection, by imagination, by spatial and temporal distance, by detachment, by practical and historical experience, by prudential knowledge, by the positing of alternative judgments, by the plurality of judging subjects.

Our inquiry suggests that there are basically two ways to proceed with a theory of political judgment. One way lies through a theory of taste; the other, through a theory of *phronesis* (or a theory of prudence).[10] Posed as a theory of political judgment, the former seems to concern itself primarily with retrospective (or historical) judgment; the latter, with prospective judgment. The former pertains to the political spectator, or critic; the latter, to the agent or political actor. As formulated by Kant, the former limits itself to explicating formal conditions of judgment,[11] whereas the latter – as developed by Aristotle – unfolds substantive conditions of judgment.

But in addition to asking what sets Aristotle apart from Kant, we must also inquire into what they hold in common, in order to locate a common point of departure for a comprehensive theory of human judgment. The first point of agreement between them is that both lay essential emphasis on the judging of particulars. Second, both concur that there are no fixed universals for the subsumption of such particulars. They are agreed on the elusiveness of principles upon which to judge particulars. Third, both insist that a 'community of judgment' comes into play in some way for the subject or agent that judges – the judgments of his fellows are not irrelevant (in some sense) to his own; he cannot remain indifferent to their judgment. Both thus invoke a certain 'principle of community' bearing upon judgment (although, as stressed in earlier chapters, for Kant this 'community' is no more than an abstract and formalized condition of the possibility of judgment).

The two perspectives begin to diverge when we note that for Kant all this applies only to reflective judgment, and furthermore, that practical judgment is not for Kant a mode of reflective judgment, but rather determined by the categorical imperative as a determinant universal. It follows from this that practical judgment in Kant's sense of the term dispenses with any notion of what is signified by *phronesis* within the Aristotelian horizon of moral life. From a classical standpoint, *phronesis* is 'the living nutrient of human existence'.[12] The Kantian emphasis upon rule-governed behaviour, according to Stanley Rosen, militates against an appreciation of this on the part of Kant,[13] and this in turn tells against the possibility of a full theory of judgment being generated within an exclusively Kantian perspective.

We have argued that there are two ways of approaching what Kant calls 'reflective' – as opposed to logical or 'determinant' – judgment. The first way is in terms of formal conditions, such as disinterestedness, detachment, distance. The second is in terms of substantive conditions, such as experience, maturity, and so on. Among the three thinkers that we considered in chapter 2 above, Arendt, in seeking to conceptualize political judgment, adopts the first approach. Gadamer, in seeking to conceptualize hermeneutic judgment, adopts the second. But political deliberation, so we would argue, is a mode of hermeneutic judgment. Therefore it must be asked how any possible conceptualization of political judgment could avoid the substantive dimension of judgment.

If this were all that there was to be said on the matter, it might be suggested that Kant be simply jettisoned, and the theory of taste reconstructed from within an Aristotelian framework. But this conclusion would be ruled out if it could be shown that the two standpoints elaborated here, namely the standpoint of the spectator and the standpoint of the actor, correspond to two irreducible aspects of political life. I would like to claim that the two concepts of judgment that we have been considering are each governed by a separate principle, and that these two principles are indeed basic, and irreducible, constituents of the political: namely, meaning and purpose. The spectator discerns the meaning of a political event, and thereby bestows dignity on those involved. Through the search for meaning, the judging spectator rescues the actors from the flux of time. The critical distance which the spectator establishes between himself and the events judged enables him to perform this dignity-bestowing function. The standpoint of the spectator, then, is governed by the principle of dignity. The standpoint of the agent, by contrast, is governed by the principle of wisdom in the pursuit of substantive purposes. And political life is constituted by both these principles, both purpose and meaning, both wisdom in the realization of human goals and the dignity of distance. Politics may thus be conceived as embracing autonomy and teleology, involving pursuit of natural ends mediated by the distanced plurality of autonomous bearers of dignity.

If we were to personify these two principles of political life, we could say that Pericles represents the prototype of the man of sound practical judgment, and that, correspondingly, it is Thucydides, exiled from Athenian political life and therefore placed in an ideal position from which to judge,[14] who embodies the prototype of the political spectator. Whereas Pericles renders his judgments while immersed in the exigencies and passions of the particular situation, Thucydides is the judging spectator who bestows lasting and universal significance upon the deeds and speeches of the former. Thucydides' exclusion from political activity equips him with a unique measure of detachment, although he maintains a dedicated vigil over the fortunes and destiny of the polis that banished him. He can step back and place the political achievements of Pericles in the appropriate perspective. While he does not have the kind of personal stake that animates Pericles, Thucydides remains dramatically implicated in the events he judges. The judgment of Pericles is mediated by the needs and goals of a particular political community whose very survival is in question; the judgment of Thucydides is mediated by the ever-attentive audience of posterity for whom he delivers his verdict.

Clearly, two distinguishable sets of conditions are at work in these two kinds of judging subjects, actor and spectator. And yet this exemplification discloses the limitations of the theoretical abstraction relied upon in the foregoing analyses. Thucydides is no more lacking in political experience than is Pericles incapable of political disinterestedness. It was Thucydides' wide experience in things political which better equipped him to render disinterested judgment, just as it was Pericles' capacity for detached judgment which informed his profound practical wisdom. But this does not serve to invalidate the theoretical abstractions of the analysis offered above, it merely places them in their proper perspective. The conditions analysed here are not mutually exclusive but, rather, reflect two poles of political life that mutually complement, and indeed interpenetrate and interlace, one another.

A politics of formal dignity alone and a politics of substantive purpose alone are both equally insufficient and 'abstract'. Here we may echo Hegel: 'The maxim: "Ignore the consequences of actions" and the other: "Judge actions by their consequences and make these the criterion of right and good" are both alike maxims of the abstract Understanding.'[15] To forfeit the standpoint of the spectator is to sacrifice dignity, which arises through distancing oneself from the particularity of natural purposes. To forfeit the standpoint of the agent is to sacrifice wisdom, which comes from long and rich experience in the pursuit of human ends. Our conclusion is that political judgment must embrace the standpoints of both the spectator and the actor: it calls for both distance and experience, and its consequence is both dignity and wisdom.

Arendt concerns herself with the judgment of the spectator because she is bent on salvaging a vestige of human dignity, which has suffered such ignominious reverses in the course of modern political history.[16] Therefore she appeals to Kant in formulating political judgment. Gadamer, in contrast, concerns himself with practical judgment because it activates experience, which allows for wisdom in appropriating the gifts of tradition. Therefore he appeals to Aristotle in formulating hermeneutic judgment. Following Arendt, we see the dignity conferred by the spectator as an essential constituent of political judgment. But following Gadamer, we see politics as partaking of the qualities of the hermeneutic, and therefore we must appeal to Aristotle as well as to Kant.

JUDGMENT AND RESPONSIBILITY

Kant defined judgment as subsumption of a particular under a universal. But if the matter rested here, Kant would not have been impelled to provide a critique of judgment (i.e. of 'reflective' judgment).[17] Indeed a critique of judgment, or for that matter any theory of judgment, is necessitated by the fact that such subsumption is inescapably problematical. Unproblematical judgment would render superfluous a theory of judgment. Thus the task of a critique of aesthetic judgment represents an effort to come to terms with problematical (and necessarily problematical) subsumption of particulars under a universal. The attempt to give an account of how it is that while straightforward subsumption is not possible, yet subsumption of some kind can be performed, defines the undertaking of the third *Critique*.

This appreciation of the necessarily problematical character of the relation between universal and particular is by no means universally granted. If one is theoretically committed to the provision of a 'decision procedure', whether in aesthetics, morals, or politics, then one will feel no need for a theory of judgment. On the assumption of facility, in principle, of subsumption under a universal such a theory may be dispensed with altogether. In fact, each of the dominant moral philosophies of today seeks rules for the guidance of moral life – utilitarianism, natural law, the Kantian categorical imperative. Each of these in some way deprives the judging subject of responsibility by providing rules for the mere subsumption of particular cases.

Utilitarianism does not require a theory of reflective judgment because in propounding the universal principle of utility, the greatest happiness of the greatest number, it lays down a rule for the resolution (in principle) of all conflicts in moral and political life.[18] To call for a concept of reflective judgment here would be analogous to requiring a conception of tragedy for a situation in which conflict was perfectly well resolvable. It is true that utilitarianism demands the exercise of 'determinant judgment'. And it is equally true that the exercise of determinant judgment can involve a quite problematical and skilled determination of conditions of application of the given rule (so that determinant judgment tends to shade off into reflective judgment). But this still falls far short of the full dimension of judgment that is being discussed here – namely, the generation from out of particulars of the universal itself. Quite the contrary, utilitarianism precludes such an understanding of judgment because it recommends subsumption of all policy under a universal rule, namely, a quantitative calculus of utility.

Although it was the impossibility of such simple subsumption under a universal rule that prompted Kant to inquire into the nature of reflective judgment in the aesthetic sphere, it must be noted that Kant himself, for that matter, did not have a theory of moral judgment (in the sense of 'reflective' judgment). Morality operates under a determinate (albeit unintuitable) concept of reason, and this is a source of determinant judgment, thereby obviating a theory of reflective judgment for morality. This is why a theory of political or practical judgment cannot be located in the second *Critique*.

Finally, we might observe that 'natural law' doctrines too, in general, allow no room for the free exercise of judgment. (The status of St Thomas' theory of prudence *vis-à-vis* his natural law teaching cannot be taken up here without leading us too far afield, but suffice it to say that the divergence between the Thomist and Aristotelian teachings on practical wisdom is considerable.[19]) Natural law rests upon the supposition that a universal can be discerned for the (in principle) unproblematical subsumption of particulars (leaving aside the residual difficulties of *actually* subsuming particulars under the given universal – which can still be very considerable). This is why Gadamer makes a special effort of disassociating Aristotle from the 'natural law' tradition, so as to appropriate Aristotle's notion of *phronesis* for the development of a hermeneutics governed by historicity. (The ultimate meaning of historicity is that in principle no universal could ever be discerned such as could have subsumed under it all historical particulars. Each new circumstance cast up by history requires a fresh effort of historical understanding.) As far as Gadamer is concerned, historicity of judgment on its own is sufficient to stand in the way of easy subsumption, so that the problematical character of judging is primarily attributable to historicity alone. For Kant, however, simple subsumption could not be allowed for even in the case of (supposedly) ahistorical aesthetic contemplation, and therefore he concluded that there was something in the very structure of such judgment which ruled out easy subsumption, apart from any considerations of historicity.

To reiterate, then: to call the provision of a universal rule a mode of 'judgment' would be the same as calling that which resolved tragic demands into simple commensurables a notion of tragedy. Just as the latter actually obviates tragic conflict, so the former obviates genuine efforts of judgment. It is clear that to analyse tragic claims into re-soluble components is to dissipate tragedy. The dilemma would be not tragic but manageable. The same holds for judgment: to set down an absolute standard of subsumption is to dissipate the burden of judgment.

This is related to a conception of the subject who assumes responsibility for judging. If judgment can be reduced to a formula of subsumption, then it would no longer be meaningful to conceive of judgment as a task or burden, in so far as the universal precept would absolve the judging subject of responsibility. Because the precept itself judges all, the subject comes merely to apply the foregone standard of judgment. Thus to lay down a pre-ordained universal for subsumption of particulars is to lift the responsibility of judgment. (This is not to deny that, say, administering an already decided policy can involve an important measure of responsibility, in some sense of the term – but it is not the sense appealed to here.)

The weighing of given particulars and their careful adjustment to the demands of an elusive universal – a universal under which the particular cannot be neatly subsumed – are, then, matters of the responsibility of the judging subject. Where the universal obviates such responsibility on the part of the subject, personal accountability for judgment is seriously curtailed. It was this undesirable prospect that prompted Kant to stress so emphatically the relation of judgment to transcendental subjectivity, so that an objective set of criteria would not threaten to deprive the judging subject of personal responsibility for a judgment of taste. When Kant speaks of the necessary 'singularity' of judgment and the inescapable 'subjective conditions of taste', he is really saying that the individual judging subject cannot be deprived of his right to personal judgment by some objectively determinable universal rule. In other words, the need for subsumption cannot be allowed to infringe upon the individual subject's own personal autonomy of judgment. (Although, to be sure, this autonomy of the judging subject differs radically from the autonomy of the moral subject, who must adhere to the determinant imperatives of his own reason. Rather, it is analogous to the autonomy of the political subject.) Such responsibility for judgments of taste can only be lifted at the price of the dignity of the judging subject. And this is as true of political judgments as of aesthetic judgments of taste. This, in turn, harks back to the ideal of majority (*Mündigkeit*) as found in the Kantian definition of Enlightenment: to define freedom as release from self-imposed tutelage is to stipulate that adult citizens educate themselves.[20] An exclusion of claims to knowledge in political judgment naturally entails an exclusion of political education.

But all this, as we have seen, goes to make up the formal side of judgment, which we have identified with Kant. We may define formal (subjective) judgment as assumption of responsibility for mediating between universal and particular: 'everyone has to derive his rule of conduct from himself, seeing that he himself remains responsible for it and, when he goes wrong, cannot shift the blame upon others as teachers or leaders'.[21] We may, correspondingly, define substantive (objective) judgment as pertaining to the contingent circumstances that impinge upon and therefore condition this mediation. The former stipulates that all men are formally equal (in respect of their capacity for justifying their judgments). The latter allows of objectively determinable discrimination among varying (differential) grades of political wisdom. In short, the latter depends upon a concern with political knowledge, the former is independent of any concern with political knowledge. In contrast to a theory of judgment derivable from Aristotle, a Kantian theory of political judgment would not allow one to speak of political wisdom, nor would it allow a place for moral or political education.[22] But this reintroduces the problem adverted to in earlier chapters, namely that such exclusion of knowledge from political judgment renders one incapable of speaking of 'uninformed' or cognitively deficient judgment, and of distinguishing differential capacities for knowledge that mark out some as more qualified and some as less qualified to judge.

The problem is rooted, perhaps, in Kant's very definition of reflective judgment. To speak of subsuming particulars without a universal first being given seems to imply that universals (concepts) are not already involved in the justification of the judgment (Kant does allow that concepts *are* involved in the initial representation, but denies that they are relevant to the transcendental *validity* of the judgment).[23] This is bound up with an overly rigid dichotomization of the cognitive and the non-cognitive in Kant's philosophy. For Kant, in any cognitive judgment the universal strictly determines subsumption of particulars. Conversely, any notion of judgment that seeks to allow some freedom or leeway in the subsumption of particulars must be non-cognitive. A rigid dichotomy between the cognitive and the non-cognitive, excluding any cognitive dimension from aesthetic judgment, seems to neglect the 'reflective' element that pertains even to cognitive judgments (the elements of discretion or 'judgment' in a reflective sense required for problematical cognitive judgments). It also seems to neglect the extent to which even, say, aesthetic judgments depend on cognitive discriminations and cognitive insights (for instance, I may not be able to judge whether the thing before me is beautiful without knowing the kind of thing that it is, i.e. knowing the concept under which it is subsumed). It seems quite plausible that these difficulties or oversights stem from the assumption, in the first *Critique*, that all cognitive judgments are a matter of rule-governed mental activity (in the sense that they are amenable to formalization in algorithmic rules),[24] and that, correspondingly, non-rule-governed judgment must be entirely non-cognitive. The conclusion to be reached is not that the distinction between determinant and reflective, as developed by Kant, is not of great importance, and certainly not that this distinction ought to be discarded, but rather that the boundary between the two may be much less sharp and much more complex than is made out in the first and third *Critiques*.[25] *All* human judgments, including aesthetic (and political) judgments, incorporate a necessary cognitive dimension.

As far as Kant is concerned, to discriminate among differential knowledge-capabilities of men violates the integrity of judgment, which *may* be true for the aesthetic sphere (even here, doubt persists), but surely distorts understanding of judgment in the political sphere – which is indeed impinged upon and inescapably conditioned by contingent factors such as needs, or natural wants and desires, which are subject to cognitive claims that are corrigible. To exclude these from judgment is to fail to see what sets the political apart from the aesthetic, and thus not to discern clearly enough the distinctive essence of political judgment. But to say this is in no way to diminish the quality of responsibility ascribed to judgment, it merely renders men's opinions and judgments rationally and discursively responsible, a responsibility mediated by rational discourse.

Kant's distinction between determinant and reflective judgment implies that human subjects must bear a responsibility for correct subsumption of particulars under an appropriate universal in all cases where the universal is not already available for the subsumption. Reflective judgment is necessarily problematical subsumption of particulars under an elusive universal. This always implies a logical gap between what is available for judging and what is required in the way of judgment, and it falls to the human responsibility of the judging subject to bridge this gap. This is inherent to the very concept of reflective judgment. Naturally this capacity for judging reflectively is not confined to the realm of aesthetic judgment or taste, and even extends to spheres of human experience that Kant had explicitly placed within the province of determinant judgment (such as moral or practical judgment). However, while an important human responsibility is engaged in all exercises of reflective judgment (embracing all areas of human life), we would argue that there is an especially heavy burden of judgment involved in judging political affairs, and responsibility of a qualitatively higher intensity. This is because the stakes are altogether different in questions pertaining to the form that collective existence shall take, the direction of common purposes, and the constitution of one's identity as set within the broader context of social life. (These issues will be pursued in the next chapter.) If reflective judgment in general is defined by the assumption of an inalienable responsibility on the part of a judging subject for mediating between given particulars and an elusive universal, then political judgment as such is distinguished by the higher quality of such responsibility. At times, such responsibility rises to the point where it takes on a tragic dimension, so that a theory of political judgment becomes inseparable from the provision of an account of tragic responsibility.

The condition of detached judgment is critical distance; thus it may come about that judgment can only be bought at the price of a severe alienation of the judging spectator from the community which he judges (the community which may be both the object of his judgment and also the subject *with* whom he judges and *to* whom he addresses his ultimate judgment). Consequently a tragic conflict can arise between political membership and political judgment. Perhaps judgment in such situations inevitably opens the judging subject to the charge of betrayal, perhaps even the very act of judging amounts to an act of betrayal. Where judgment implicitly assumes a community of judgment for the sake of which judgment is delivered, the judging subject puts his own identity at risk in his determination to judge. The judging subject places in question his own subjectivity by cutting himself off from the community to whom he would ordinarily appeal for criteria of shared judgment and possible confirmation of the validity of his judgment. How does the judging subject secure his own subjectivity when the community of judgment appealed to is rendered radically problematical? At this point the judging subject becomes the bearer of a tragic responsibility, and human judgment takes on a tragic dimension. To illustrate the claim that a full theory of political judgment ultimately issues in an appreciation of tragic imperatives, let us now attempt to enter into the domain of political judgment by appealing to a couple of works that deliberately concern themselves with the fantastic and irreducible complexities of judging which are brought to bear in real political-historical situations (for purely theoretical considerations alone fail to convey the authentic pathos of judging human affairs).

One such work is Arendt's *Eichmann in Jerusalem*; another is Maurice Merleau-Ponty's *Humanism and Terror*. The latter attempts to depict what Merleau-Ponty calls 'the ambiguity of history', that is, the fact that we live in a history not of our choosing and not fully under our control, a history that sets imperatives evasion of which betrays moral and political irresponsibility. To evade history, by simply turning our backs on its pre-given alternatives, is an abdication of responsibility, as Max Weber demonstrated so compellingly in his distinction between an 'ethics of ultimate ends' and an 'ethics of responsibility'. Merleau-Ponty elaborates this in reference to the Moscow show trials under Stalin, and tries to make intelligible how sincere men of conviction could be led to affirm (and collaborate in) their own degradation. If Merleau-Ponty's analysis of history is true to its subject matter, what is implied is a theory of judgment that coincides with a theory of tragedy or of tragic responsibility.

Arendt's *Eichmann in Jerusalem* seeks to do justice to the holocaust experience not by representing the war criminals as sub-human creatures that are beneath judgment or the victims as innocents without responsibility that surpass judgment, but by making clear that human judgment can only function where those judged are neither beasts nor angels, but men. Many of Arendt's readers objected that if this is how human judgment must operate, it would be better to abstain from judgment. Thus the Eichmann book is especially instructive for our purposes, since it places in question the very status of judgment itself. This issue was confronted most directly in a fascinating exchange in *Encounter* magazine between Gershom Scholem and Arendt. Arendt's final reply is contained in the postscript to the revised edition of her book, where she writes:

> The argument that we cannot judge if we were not present and involved ourselves seems to convince everyone everywhere, although it seems obvious that *if it were true, neither the administration of justice nor the writing of history would ever be possible.* In contrast to these confusions, the reproach of self-righteousness raised against those who do judge is age-old; but that does not make it any the more valid. Even the judge who condemns a murderer can still say when he goes home: 'And there, but for the grace of God, go I.'[26]

What the two works under discussion share is that both place the effort to understand at the centre of their respective inquiries. When understanding is placed at the service of judgment it requires the free exercise of imagination, in particular, the ability to imagine how things look from a position that we do not in fact occupy. Judgment may require us to make the effort to understand those whose point of view we do not share and which we may indeed even find highly distasteful. Disagreement does not release us from the responsibility to understand that which we none the less reject; if anything, it rather heightens this responsibility. Merleau-Ponty writes: 'true liberty takes others as they are, tries to understand even those doctrines which are its negation, *and never allows itself to judge before understanding*. We must fulfill our freedom of thought in the freedom of understanding.'[27]

If, as Merleau-Ponty teaches, freedom and necessity are interwoven with each other, (objective) history and (subjective) responsibility are interwoven with each other, and guilt and innocence are interwoven with each other, then we are left in the tragic situation of not being able to forgo judgment (e.g. condemnation of Stalinism) and yet not able to judge with good conscience.[28] Judgment thus assumes the tragic tasks of understanding and forgiving, these composing the tragic dimensions of judgment. Arendt's efforts to come to terms with the experience of the holocaust convey the same message.[29] To judge a genuinely human situation is to face the risk of tragic responsibility.

These two works are addressed to two of the most extreme (and most distressing) political experiences of our unhappy century, namely Nazism and Stalinism. Still, they merely serve to illuminate in a more striking and perhaps dramatic manner, the irreducibly tragic quality that inheres in *all* political judgment, and which stems from the requirement that judgment encompass more than can possibly be mastered and resolved by human beings. This genuine pathos of political life was probably captured best of all by Max Weber in his famous lecture on 'Politics as a vocation', and the deep appreciation of political judgment that we find in these works can ultimately be traced back to his understanding of politics. Arendt and Merleau-Ponty simply give particularly vivid expression to a dimension of tragic choice and responsibility that had already been recognized by Weber to inhere in all political phenomena. The use of categories like 'tragic' does not lead to a frivolous 'aestheticization' of politics, for it was after all Weber himself who characterized politics as a 'strong and slow boring of hard boards'.[30] Rather, such categories are the only ones we have available to capture the full phenomenal content of political action and discourse. To see the consequence of reducing politics to more 'prosaic' terms, we need only note the current 'banalization' of politics that we are witnessing (as is manifest, for instance, in the massive shift of responsibilities from legislatures to bureaucracies), the dissipation of the tragic dimension through the reduction of judgment to computation, technique, and expertise – these dismaying developments teach us that judgment and politics suffer devaluation simultaneously, and that to depreciate one is to lose one's appreciation for the other.

The finitude of the resources of judgment, confronted by the unlimited demands of judgment, circumscribes the 'hermeneutical' dimension of judgment. The finite capacities of a human subject are hardly ever sufficient to master the full complexities of a human situation, and to this extent, the inescapable gap between determinant judgment and reflective judgment constitutes a tragic burden. To deliver judgment is to bear a tragic burden, for the one who judges can never escape the awareness that no judgment upon human affairs can master all possibilities and thus render a definitive resolution. But the burden can be borne as long as one does not relinquish hope, for hope without optimism and lack of optimism without despair are what ultimately sustain human judgment.

For Hannah Arendt, as we saw in chapter 2, politics is inherently dramatic. Correlatively, the judgment of political appearances is likewise dramatic. For Arendt, the purpose of judgment, as exercised by the storyteller, is to make human affairs 'bearable and meaningful for men' by retrospective reflection. Thus she appeals to Isak Dinesen's dictum: 'All sorrows can be borne if you put them into a story or tell a story about them.' Arendt comments: 'To the extent that the teller of factual truth is also a storyteller, he brings about that "reconciliation with reality" which Hegel . . . understood as the ultimate goal of all philosophical thought, and which, indeed, has been the secret motor of all historiography that transcends mere learnedness.'[31] Hence the affinity between politics and drama:

We may see, with Aristotle, in the poet's political function the operation of a catharsis, a cleansing or purging of all emotions that could prevent men from acting. The political function of the storyteller – historian or novelist – is to teach acceptance of things as they are. Out of this acceptance, which can also be called truthfulness, arises the faculty of judgment.[32]

Human judgment tends to be tragic judgment. It continually confronts a reality that it can never fully master, but to which it must none the less reconcile itself. It is perhaps for this reason above all that Arendt turns to Kant to guide her reflection on the nature of judging:

> Where human pride is still intact, it is tragedy rather than absurdity which is taken to be the hallmark of human existence. Its greatest representative is Kant, to whom the spontaneity of acting, and the concomitant faculties of practical reason, including force of judgment, remain the outstanding qualities of man, even though his action falls into the determinism of natural laws and his judgment cannot penetrate the secret of absolute reality.[33]

FRIENDSHIP VERSUS LOVE: ARENDT AND THE EICHMANN CASE

What we have been seeking in this chapter is a way of thinking about political judgment that does justice to both the Kantian and Aristotelian dimensions. That is to say, what is sought is a concept of judgment that allows for the sense of common purpose which Aristotle locates in the process of deliberating and arriving at practical judgments through rhetoric; but that also makes provision for the sense of dignity of the judging subject which we have come to associate with the Kantian ideal of autonomy. Arendt, in a noteworthy passage of *The Human Condition*, articulates a notion of friendship that comprehends both the Kantian and Aristotelian requirements of our theory:

> what love is in its own, narrowly circumscribed sphere, respect is in the larger domain of human affairs. Respect, not unlike the Aristotelian *philia politike*, is a kind of 'friendship' without intimacy and without closeness; it is a regard for the person from the distance which the space of the world puts between us.[34]

In chapter 4 above, the concept of friendship was placed under the rubric of Aristotelian judgment. In this passage, however, the Aristotelian notion of *philia* is correlated with a Kantian notion of respect. (We may recall Kant's opposition between love and respect, elaborated in his analytic of the sublime, in sections 27–9 of the *Critique of Judgment*.35) If this correlation can be upheld, the concept of friendship will provide us with the comprehensive concept for which we seek.

At the end of the chapter on Aristotle we suggested that provision of a theory of friendship goes hand in hand with provision of a theory of political judgment. Such a theory of friendship is actually supplied by Hannah Arendt, and is to be found in her essay on Lessing, 'On humanity in dark times'. The Lessing essay constitutes one of the two brilliant analyses of the role of intimacy in public life to be found in Arendt's work, the other being the analysis of compassion in the chapter of *On Revolution* entitled 'The social question'. Both analyses are directed against the spirit of 'fraternity' and the dominating hold of the emotions of pity and compassion that were most powerfully evidenced in the politics of the French Revolution.

In the Lessing essay she addresses the strong urge experienced during 'dark times' to substitute the intimacy of 'brotherhood' for genuine politics, especially among persecuted peoples such as the Jews, and counterposes to this tendency the principle of friendship which she sees most fully evinced in Lessing's *Nathan the Wise*, which she labels 'the classical drama of friendship'.36 Arendt delineates two conceptions of friendship, one modern, the other ancient; one dominated by *eros*, the other properly signified by *philia*; one epitomized by Rousseau, the other epitomized by Lessing:

> The ancients thought friends indispensable to human life, indeed that a human life without friends was not really worth living. . . . We are wont to see friendship solely as a phenomenon of intimacy, in which the friends open their hearts to each other un-molested by the world and its demands. Rousseau, not Lessing, is the best advocate of this view, which conforms so well to the basic attitude of the modern individual, who in his alienation from the world can truly reveal himself only in privacy and in the intimacy of face-to-face encounters. Thus it is hard for us to understand the political relevance of friendship. When, for example, we read in Aristotle that *philia*, friendship among citizens, is one of the fundamental requirements for the well-being of the City, we tend to think that he was speaking of no more than the absence of

factions and civil war within it. But for the Greeks the essence of friendship consisted in discourse. They held that only the constant interchange of talk united citizens in a polis. In discourse the political importance of friendship, and the humanness peculiar to it, were made manifest. This converse (in contrast to the intimate talk in which individuals speak about themselves), permeated though it may be by pleasure in the friend's presence, is concerned with the common world, which remains 'inhuman' in a very literal sense unless it is constantly talked about by human beings.[37]

This space of discourse which Arendt calls the world, a space that 'relates and separates',[38] is preserved by *philia*, but collapsed by *eros*. *Eros*, whether in the form of the compassion, fraternity, and humanitarianism of the Rousseauian French revolutionaries, or in the form of the intimacy, warmth, and brotherhood of the persecuted Jews, collapses the space of friendship, the space which, by enforcing the distinct identity of each, sustains the mutual integrity of the friends.

That humaneness should be sober and cool rather than sentimental; that humanity is exemplified not in fraternity but in friendship; that friendship is not intimately personal but makes political demands and preserves reference to the world . . .[39]

– these are the characteristics of friendship that Arendt seeks to impress upon us. It is these 'classical' aspects of friendship that, Arendt claims, Lessing teaches.

We have seen what a powerful need men have, in 'dark times', to move closer to one another, to seek in the warmth of intimacy the substitute for that light and illumination which only the public realm can cast. But this means that they avoid disputes and try as far as possible to deal only with people with whom they cannot come into conflict. For a man of Lessing's disposition there was little room in such an age and in such a confined world; where people moved together in order to warm one another, they moved away from him. And yet he, who was polemical to the point of contentiousness, could no more endure loneliness than the excessive closeness of a brotherliness that obliterated all distinctions. He was never eager really to fall out with someone with whom he had entered into a dispute; he was concerned solely with humanizing the world by incessant and continual discourse about its affairs and the things in it. *He wanted to be the friend of many men, but no man's brother.*[40]

Friendship therefore means neither loneliness nor fraternity. Arendt implores that we should be friends, but not brothers.

A similar appeal against the aspiration to fraternity is entered by Philip Roth:

> They are presently holding beatnik parties in the suburbs – which does not convince me, however, that all men are brothers. On the contrary, they are strangers; that fact is made clear to me every day when I read the newspapers. They are strangers, and often they are enemies, and it is because *that* is our condition, that it is incumbent on us not to love one another – which is to deny the truth about ourselves – but to practice no violence and no treachery upon one another, which is to struggle with the darkest forces within us.[41]

Men *need* not be strangers; but from this it does not follow that they *can* be brothers. The concept of a friend is an intermediary between the two.

Let us now begin trying to draw some lessons for political judgment. The principal lesson to be obtained here is that love belongs outside politics because it impairs judgment. This tension between love and judgment is illustrated by Arendt's own involvement in 'the Eichmann affair'. In the exchange of letters between Arendt and Gershom Scholem, referred to in the preceding section, Scholem charges Arendt with a lack of '*Ahabeth Israel*', with a failure 'to love the Jewish people'. Arendt responds: 'I have never in my life "loved" any people or collective. . . . I indeed love "only" my friends and the only kind of love I know of and believe in is the love of persons.'[42] Furthermore, Arendt is accused by Scholem of lacking *Herzenstakt*, that is, lack of soul, lack of heart. To this she replies: 'the role of "heart" in politics seems to me altogether questionable'. She then refers to her analysis of revolutionary compassion in *On Revolution* as an exemplification of 'the disastrous results' that accrue 'when emotions are displayed in public and become a factor in political affairs'[43]: 'Compassion, in this respect not unlike love, abolishes the distance, the in-between which always exists in human intercourse.'[44] What is really at issue between Arendt and Scholem in this exchange is whether love should enter into judgment.

In fact, the entire 'Eichmann controversy' is extremely instructive in regard to this question of the relationship between love and judgment. Daniel Bell, in his contribution to the debate,[45] offers a very interesting discussion of 'the tension between the parochial and the universal':

> Miss Arendt writes from the standpoint of a universal principle which denies any parochial identity. It is this which gives her exposition a cold force and an abstract quality.

Bell relates a Talmudic parable to help make his point: 'If [the Hebrew letter] Daled had stood only for Dabar, the Divine Word, it would have been used [by God to begin the world, instead of the letter "B"], but it stands also for Din, justice, and under a law of justice, without love, the world would fall to ruin.'[46] Dwight Macdonald, in an equally noteworthy rejoinder to this argument,[47] writes:

> It is an interesting, and depressing, historical exercise to imagine what the reactions would have been to a book like this in the thirties, when all of us, from Miss McCarthy to Mr. Abel, despised national and racial feelings and were hot for truth, justice and other *universals*. The suggestion that *certain* people and institutions should be exempt from criticism would have embarassed everybody (except the Stalinists). But the death camps have cast their shadow.

In the contest between particularistic love and universalistic justice (the former is a substantive principle; the latter, a formal principle), Arendt holds that judgment stands wholly and uncompromisingly on the side of the latter.[48]

Macdonald undertakes to answer both Bell and Scholem, whom he considers to be the only two critics of Arendt from whom one can learn, because both are motivated by a genuine desire to understand. Bell had written:

> Many of Miss Arendt's strictures are correct, if one can live by a universalistic standard. In this situation, one's identity as a Jew, as well as a *philosophe*, is relevant. The agony of Miss Arendt's book

is precisely that she takes her stand so unyieldingly on the side of disinterested justice, and that she judges both Nazi and Jew. But abstract justice, as the Talmudic wisdom knew, is sometimes too 'strong' a yardstick to judge the world.

Macdonald notes that this is basically the same complaint as Scholem had made in his *Encounter* letter where he wrote: 'In the Jewish tradition, there is a concept . . . we know as *Ahabeth Israel*: "Love of the Jewish people." In you dear Hannah, . . . I find little trace of this.' Macdonald replies on Arendt's behalf:

I think Mr. Bell and Mr. Scholem have made explicit . . . the concealed . . . assumptions that explains the violence of the Jewish attacks on Miss Arendt's book. Both reproach her because she lacks a special feeling in favour of her fellow Jews. But such a prejudice would have made it impossible for her to speculate on how the catastrophe might have been less complete . . . , or to attempt to a realistic interpretation of the Nazi horror as the work of men (who can be understood) and not of 'monsters' and demons (who cannot). That is, she tried to learn from history, an enterprise in which I don't think either the Talmud or *Ahabeth Israel* would have been useful. I am not Jewish, but if I were, I hope I would not agree with Mr. Bell that 'in this situation, one's identity as a Jew . . . is relevant', if it means applying a different ('weaker') yardstick to Jews. A yardstick is not a yardstick if it is more or less than three feet long, and justice is not justice unless it is 'universalistic'. I am old-fashioned enough (as of the thirties) to still find these favored, special, exceptional categories of race or nation morally suspect and intellectually confusing. And so I take heart in a book like *Eichmann in Jerusalem*.[49]

We have dwelt on the Eichmann case because it illustrates Arendt's argument in *The Human Condition* that 'love, by reason of its passion, destroys the in-between which relates us to and separates us from others'.[50] Love threatens to violate standards of judgment because it strives to collapse the space in between, the 'distance' which is an indispensable condition of judgment. Herein consists the difference between love and friendship.[51]

Judgment must be 'cool and sober', although at the same time informed by sympathy that arises out of common involvement. It is this requirement of judgment that excludes love from politics, and likewise excludes the passions associated with intimacy (e.g. pity, compassion). That is why 'love of the Jewish people' plays no part in a political judgment, although a sense of membership in a common political entity *does* play a part. The two must be carefully disassociated from one another, for the latter is a necessary prerequisite of judgment, the former actually impairs responsible judgment.

Love is excluded from political judgment because politics cannot withstand the immediacy of love – the latter violates the mediated quality of judgment. The point is not that love and friendship never converge; nor do we deny that there are forms of friendship that are heavily constituted by what we call love. The point here is rather that friendship can bring into play a form of relating-together *through* things held in common – namely, what Arendt calls 'a world', a common focus of concern and of action in concert, a *mediated* relating-together not to be encountered in more direct, and intimate, forms of human relationship. This tension between love and judgment is exemplified in the following case: Aldo Moro, the kidnapped (and eventually murdered) leader of the Italian Christian Democratic Party, in a letter to the Italian authorities pleading for compliance with the kidnappers' demands, ordains that no state or party official shall attend his funeral: 'I want to be followed only by those who really loved me.' But for the representatives of the Italian government to 'love' him in this sense would entail that they relinquish responsibility for maintenance of a shared form of life, namely, a particular kind of constitutional order.

We shall conclude with one final illustration of the relationship between judgment and friendship. In the exchange between E. P. Thompson and Leszek Kolakowski in the *Socialist Register*, 1973–4, Thompson ends his letter 'Yours fraternally', whereas Kolakowski ends his 'Yours in friendship'. The point of this change in greetings I take to be this: that in matters of political judgment one can address another, at best, only as a friend, never as a brother.

STORYTELLING AND NARRATIVE TRUTH

As Alasdair MacIntyre notes in his recent book *After Virtue*, much contemporary work in political philosophy restricts itself to the formulation of rules that are supposed to operate in moral and political life.[52] As a consequence, such theories move within a highly contracted horizon of theory. This is no less true even of the work that is taken to have heralded a 'rebirth' of political philosophy: John Rawls' *A Theory of Justice*. Rawls forgoes substantive judgments about the good life and the good for man – the classical questions of western political philosophy – leaving rational individuals to decide for themselves their own 'rational plan of life'. Rather than theorizing about the proper ends of human life, Rawls thinks that the way forward is by means of a theory of political *right* formulated in conjunction with 'a thin theory of the good'. (More precisely: right is to *take priority* over the good. A fuller theory of the good can be elaborated, subsequent to, and on the basis of, a fully developed conception of right.)[53] The implicit assumption is that there is no reliable way of arbitrating between 'thick' theories of the good. We can devise rules that tell us what is *right*, namely the rules of a just society, without being able to specify what the substantive good for man consists in. How then might we return to questions of the good society and the conditions of a good life? How can we adjudicate between 'thick' theories of the good? The three thinkers with whom this inquiry was launched can, I think, suggest possibilities.

The simplest way to begin answering these questions is to say that in attempting to define a conception of the human good, *we tell a story*. Despite the endless plurality of the stories that we tell, the point of the telling is to disclose some truth about the condition of man, and certainly not all stories can serve this purpose with equal felicity or success. If we did not have some capacity for weighing the truth of a narrative, we could not discriminate between stories that are rich and penetrating, and those that are colourless and superficial. It is this same faculty that operates in weighing the stories offered by political theorists and philosophers. And if the theoretical narratives fail to satisfy us, what is sought in the way of truth-content is not so much absolutely compelling deductive inference, but rather a deeper and richer filling out of the story told.

For instance, if we wish to expound the necessary place of political freedom in a meaningfully human life, we may wish to tell a story about how the union organizers of Solidarity in Poland, against all odds, forced a remote party machine to listen to the voice of the Polish people, at least for a certain period of time. Or we may wish to tell the story of how, on the night of the attempted Spanish coup, King Juan Carlos of Spain spent until dawn on the telephone convincing key commanders and governors throughout the country to remain loyal to the democratic constitution. Those who possess ideas of freedom radically different from those implied in these particular stories will be obliged to tell their own stories. It cannot be assumed in advance that our stories will be mutually unintelligible: we must go through the effort of *making* our stories intelligible to others, of rendering them, if not compelling, at least persuasive. Again, the point of telling and sharing such stories is to disclose some truth about our common situation, and the more compelling and convincing we make our narratives, even to those who come from very different backgrounds and start from altogether different assumptions, the more validity we can claim in our storytelling.

As Gadamer shows in his philosophical hermeneutics, we do not inhabit fixed horizons but, rather, our horizons of understanding expand and contract, depending on the *ethos* within which we are raised. Through dialogue with our past and the effort to understand and come to terms with our moral identity, we can come to see more sharply, more perspicuously, or obtain a more comprehensive insight into our situation. The most important means of enlarging our own understanding is by opening ourselves to other horizons, temporal and spatial. This is designated by Gadamer as the process of 'fusing horizons'. The greater the effort to fuse horizons and to enlarge our own horizons by making contact with the horizons of other people and understanding other cultures, the stronger will be our own claim to true cognition.

It cannot be assumed that theorists who forbear from offering teleologies or substantive accounts of the good for man are in any privileged position in respect of the more modest claims that they make for theory. For they too, no less, shall have to tell their own stories, to persuade us of how we can or should refrain from teleological theories – for instance, deontological stories about the primacy of the right over the good.[54] And there is no reason for presuming that in their case the burden of narrative shall be any the less imposing. Our respective stories address a common truth, and therefore bear an equal responsibility to all possible interlocutors. Our most telling illustrations of this narrative character of political thought and political philosophy are of course the dialogues of Plato.

The ultimate measure of the truth of a given story is the depth of experience upon which it draws, and which it in turn communicates to us. We acquire the gift of storytelling by living in the truth of experience. Walter Benjamin has described how the art of storytelling has atrophied, owing to a general contraction in the dimensions of human experience:

> Familiar though his name may be to us, the storyteller in his living immediacy is by no means a present force. He has already become something remote from us and something that is getting even more distant. . . . [T]he art of storytelling is coming to an end. Less and less frequently do we encounter people with the ability to tell a tale properly. More and more often there is embarassment all around when the wish to hear a story is expressed. It is as if something that seemed inalienable to us, the securest among our possessions, were taken from us: the ability to exchange experiences.
>
> One reason for this phenomenon is obvious: experience has fallen in value. And it looks as if it is continuing to fall into bottomlessness. Every glance at a newspaper demonstrates that it has reached a new low, that our picture, not only of the external world but of the moral world as well, overnight has undergone changes which were never thought possible. With the [First] World War a process began to become apparent which has not halted since then. Was it not noticeable at the end of the war that men returned from the battlefield grown silent – not richer, but poorer in communicable experience? What ten years later was poured out in the flood of war books was anything but experience that goes from mouth to mouth. And there was nothing remarkable about that. For never has experience been contradicted more thoroughly than strategic experience by tactical warfare, economic experience by inflation, bodily experience by mechanical warfare, moral experience by those in power.[55]

We shall recommence our task as adjudicators of the human good only when we can begin to recover this lived depth of truth-revealing narrative.

S·E·V·E·N
Towards a theory of political judgment

Reflection on the nature of politics, and on what it means to be a political being, discloses a faculty of human judgment that is intrinsic to political life as such, and intrinsic to man as a political being. This gives rise to a set of philosophical questions: what is it about human beings that endows them with the ability to make reasonable judgments about human affairs and to judge the common world they share with others? What are the underlying conditions of this human capacity, and what implications does it have for the understanding of politics?

How may we go about elaborating such a theory of political judgment? A possible point of departure is provided for us by the distinction between reflective and determinant judgment defined in Kant's *Critique of Judgment*. Judging, according to Kant, is the activity of subsuming particulars under the relevant universal, or finding the correct concept with which to apprehend a given instance. Here is a particular rose; is it beautiful or unattractive? Should we subsume it under this concept or that? Judgment is 'determinant' where the universal (the rule, principle, or law) is given in advance for the subsumption; and it is 'reflective' where the universal is lacking and must somehow be produced from out of the particular. If we are judging something to be a flower we normally have enough in the way of definite criteria to determine the subsumption, and thus the judgment is 'relatively' determinant (although, as we discussed in chapter 6 above, the distinction is less rigid than Kant implies); but if we are judging the flower to be beautiful the appropriate universal is much less accessible, and therefore the judgment is clearly reflective.[1] Political judgment, in common with aesthetic and many other kinds of judgment, belongs to the latter class; hence our interest here is solely with reflective judgment. But this comprises such a large class of different kinds of human judgment that we are faced with the problem of identifying political judgment within this wider category.

The activity of judging is ubiquitous; it pervades every aspect of our daily existence, and comprehends the entire scope of human experience. How, then, can political judgment be isolated, and characterized as distinct from other modes of judgment? A theory of political judgment must supply some means of individuating political judgment relative to other varieties of human judgment (such as aesthetic judgment, moral judgment, historical judgment, legal judgment, and hermeneutic judgment). We cannot hope to fulfil this requirement here, but perhaps we can take a first, tentative, step, and thus contribute in a preliminary way to the eventual provision of a full theory of political judgment. We may find it helpful to sample a few of the more simple types of reflective judgment, beginning with ordinary practical judgments, before ascending to the more elaborate cases encountered in political life.

PRACTICES

Practical judgment means, in the first instance, judgment in the context of practices; that is, ordinary human practices, not necessarily moral practices. These include, for instance: playing a game or preparing a meal, writing an essay or composing a letter, participating in a debate or trying to persuade an interlocutor, decorating a room or designing a work of art. All of these activities are engaged in on the basis of reflective judgment.[2] To take a relatively primitive case, let us consider the pondering of a chess move. The need to imagine fresh possibilities introduces an element of freedom into the game, to such an extent that the full diversity of appropriate moves is unlikely to be absolutely exhausted by programmes fed into a digital computer. In making one's move, one confronts a particular combination of possibilities, the particular configuration of which must be contended with without having been fully computed in advance or foreseen by any number of rules, of whatever degree of complexity. This is because in assessing the situation concretely, we actually draw upon a 'subsidiary' awareness of our position that cannot be formalized, and 'zero in' on what strike us as promising possibilities on the basis of such tacit (and non-rule-governed) awareness. Such a human capacity for non-algorithmic action and judgment has been explored in these terms by philosophers like Michael Polanyi[3] and Hubert L. Dreyfus. Second, whatever rules are available must be applied to the particular situation in hand, and this application cannot itself be dictated by a rule, for then one would fall into an infinite regress of rule governing rule governing rule and so on. Human agents are not subject to such a regress because rule-application for them itself presupposes knowing what it is to apply a rule, which is not in turn dictated by a rule.[4] When we speak of having an available rule, we mean an exact rule in the sense of an algorithm, not rule-following in the sense in which this has been extensively explored in Wittgenstein's *Philosophical Investigations*. In fact, Wittgenstein's investigations point to the ubiquity of what we are calling reflective judgment, since he has shown that rule-following for human agents starts from an implicit underlying grasp of 'what it is to follow a rule', including the very rich practical context within which the rule is situated. The relevance of such insights in the later work of Wittgenstein to the present inquiry is apparent.[5]

The point that even where exact rules or algorithms *are* available, meta-rules are *not* available for application of the first-order rules – so that first-order judgment is determinant, second-order judgment, reflective – can be put in another way by saying that what is determinant at one level can be reflective at another level; or that what is determinant under one form of description may be reflective under another form of description. This second-order level of judgment involved in the application of rules brings into play that whole range of qualities of practised experience and skill that are the mark of a seasoned player – in short, all that would in the political domain go by the name of prudence.

As we have stated, in order for reflective judgment to operate, imagination is necessary. That is, we must make present to our minds possible configurations that are not obvious simply by observing the given situation. They must be 'conjured up', and this may require considerable mental effort. In part, this involves imagining how the game appears from the other side of the board, that is, how things look from the standpoint of one's opponent. I must project myself, imaginatively, into a position I do not actually occupy, in order to enlarge my perspective and thereby open up an awareness of new possibilities, to broaden the range of alternatives from which my judgment then makes its selection. In chess, then, as in politics, I am faced with particulars; that is to say, I do not deliberate about rules, which are general or universal, but about application of rules. This in turn requires, first of all, practical experience in playing chess, and second, a freely operating faculty of imagination which generates new and unforeseeable possibilities, thereby opening up avenues of judgment. Another point, relevant also to higher orders of reflective judgment, is that although there is often no single 'right' answer to the question of the best move, we *can* argue that our choice was the appropriate one in the circumstances, adducing various grounds, and often winning people over to our judgment even if their judgment would have been different had they been in our place. (Of course, sometimes the question of the right move can be settled conclusively, but here we are assuming a situation where various possibilities can be argued for compellingly, depending on the kind of criteria appealed to.) In chess, standards of rationality are operative, even though it is not a kind of rationality that dictates unitary answers – just as in matters of taste or aesthetic judgment. Thus we are not judging strictly for ourselves, but positing the judgment of potential spectators who could question our move, and demand justification for it. In addressing ourselves to those hypothetical interlocutors and critics, we exercise reflective judgment.

One cannot 'prove' that one's judgment was the right one; if one could furnish a proof, one would have a patent case of determinant judgment. But while one does not possess such a proof, one can point to various features of the particular situation that justify one's choice. (In Kant's terms, we engage in 'contention' rather than 'dispute'.) And since the range of possible features that can be appealed to is virtually boundless – or generally so – the meaning of the situation is not univocal, but rather, multivocal. It is not clear in advance which features are relevant. If there were a means of demonstrable proof, there would hardly be a point to the game. Once one had exhausted the set of conclusive rules, it would simply be a matter of demonstrating one's superiority in the mastery of these rules. But clearly this is not generally what the game of chess is about (although obviously mastery of rules will figure to a much greater extent in certain aspects of the game, such as openings and endgames).

In playing chess, only in certain cases is there a single demonstrably 'correct' move. In general, there is rather a plurality of 'good' moves (although this plurality is limited or determinate, not endless and indeterminate), and each of these potentially 'good' moves is arguable, that is, can be argued for on grounds publicly presented for comparison and assessment. (Thus one of the most enjoyable aspects of the game is the possibility of subsequent analysis by the players of whether a particular line of play realized its full promise, or whether it could have been pushed to a fuller realization.) But ultimately, a choice has to be made, with the sustained awareness that other alternatives were open, and arguably as plausible, and that one's own decision can only be rationally affirmed, not 'proven'. It is because the human ability to play chess relies upon judgment that it has proven so notoriously difficult to devise programmes that make it possible for digital computers to equal the reflective judgments of the best human chess-players on the basis of mere algorithms.[6]

At this point we should clarify our use of the term reflective judgment, defining it relative to Kant's (more narrow) usage. Kant opposes reflective judgment to subsumption under an objective concept, the latter providing cognition, as do the concepts of the understanding (whereas in teleological judgment, for instance, rather than knowing, we merely posit our judgments 'for the purpose of reflection'). Aesthetic judgments, according to Kant's account, lack a concept for the subsumption of particulars, for the simple reason that such judgments do not involve reasoning or deliberation about concepts, but rather involve ascriptions of beauty on the basis of given configurations of the faculties of understanding and imagination which elicit (or ought to elicit) pleasure in the subject. This would seem to place a severe restriction on the role of discursive rationality in aesthetic judgment (granting that this rationality operates in a somewhat more problematical way in aesthetic than in other forms of discourse). Kant poses the problem in a manner that is too limited for our purposes, for we need a concept of reflective judgment where it is not only our 'pleasures and displeasures', but also our cognitive efforts, that are at stake.7

According to Kant, aesthetic judgments rest (from the point of view of their claims to validity) upon *no* cognitive content, and it is for this reason that one could derive no '*a priori* proofs' – 'rules of beauty', for instance. In what we are by extension calling reflective judgments, there is clearly *some* cognitive content, but not such as would be sufficient to determine the judgment. Thus the concept of a good chess move does not determine the identification of such a move in the way that, for instance, the concept of an even number determines the identification of such a number. The latter provides clear cognitive criteria, the former does not.

But even descriptive judgments (e.g. 'this is a table') are much closer to reflective judgment than we might be tempted to assume. Julius Kovesi, in his book *Moral Notions*, demonstrates that the identification of a table is never exhausted by what he calls its material elements, but depends upon a grasp of its formal element, namely the purposes, needs, concerns, etc., which demand that we be able to identify tables – the latter never being reducible to an enumeration (however lengthy) of material properties. Kovesi's argument is drawn from Wittgenstein's concept of rule-following: what enables us to recognize something as a table is not exhausted by an explicit formulation of material elements, but presupposes initiation into a form of life within which we have and need a word by which to describe certain things as tables, and to decide conceptual disputes by reference to the needs and purposes of that form of life. For instance, to settle hard cases we have to be able to grasp the *point* of calling something a table. Reflective judgment operates in the *gap* between what we are presented with and what we are called upon to judge.8 Thus our ability to identify and class particulars under the correct description is not exhausted by what we are able to specify by explicit formulation, but presupposes a grasp of the point of classing something under one description rather than another. The fact that our judgment can and must operate within this gap explains why Kant at one point calls reflective judgment 'this strange faculty'.9

The chessplaying example is illuminating because we can see from the achievements of recent computer technology what a massive complexity of rules is needed to simulate activities that human beings engage in to a large extent *without* rules, on the basis of a tacit grasp of a concrete situation. To this the following challenge may be put: if rule-governed operations are substitutable, in principle, for non-rule-governed judgments, is not the exercise of practical judgment then rendered dispensable? Moreover, if *this* barrier could be crossed, what would there be, in principle, to stop one from reducing reflective judgment in *every* domain (not just chess) to sets of determining rules (or decision procedures). To these objections we may reply: first, there are, no doubt, many human activities that can, in principle, be simulated without reliance upon interpretation or a human grasp of the point of engaging in the activity. But this must not confuse us into thinking that the way we actually engage in these activities is rule-bound and independent of interpretation. For the fact is that we can and do play chess in large part without rules of determinant judgment, and it tells us something essential about ourselves that we can 'make do' without them. This fact of our chessplaying ability in the absence of comprehensive rules shows indisputably that we are in the possession of a faculty of reflective judgment. Second, even if it is conceded that certain activities (such as chessplaying) in principle admit of a full set of determining rules that would allow us to dispense with reflective judgment, this in no way commits us to the further admission that the conquest of reflective judgment in all other spheres is an equally conceivable possibility. For there are other exercises of reflective judgment that can never, *in principle*, be substituted for by determinant judgment. Here we must be reminded that thus far we have still been dealing with a very primitive case of reflective judgment. In morals and politics, for instance, not only is it the case that we actually *do* exercise reflective judgment, it is also the case that we *must* (in principle) exercise such judgment. If a near-infinite complexity of rules is required to master a relatively determinate set of possibilities where the end is fixed and only the means must be settled upon, what then can be said of those requirements of judgment where the end itself, and indeed the nature of the subject for whom the end is posited, are left indeterminate and subject to judgment?

PERSONS

Let us now consider another order of reflective judgment, which we will illustrate with judgments of character. Such judgments can never be 'self-validating' or validated absolutely. Rather, they rest upon, and are validated by, one's *own* qualities of character. In venturing an assessment of someone else's integrity, or honesty, or trustworthiness, and so on, one at the same time registers an implicit claim about one's own personal qualities, such as reliability and trustworthiness. In judging, we enter an implicit claim about the character that lies behind such judgments, namely our own (although perhaps there is nothing here distinctive of moral discourse as such; claims of this sort may well be implicit in *all* discourse involving truth-claims). Of course, such claims are never final or incontestable, but neither are they arbitrary. They must point to the qualities of insight, maturity, experience, objectivity, and so on, which ground and give weight to the judgment, winning people's confidence and earning their trust.

I can never 'prove' that X is a dislikable or irritating person, by a chain of argument from premises to conclusion; rather I build up a store of confidence in my judgment so that if I judge a person to be unsavoury, you are likely to be inclined to judge likewise, given sufficient familiarity with the character under scrutiny. I say, in effect, 'trust me, for my judgments have proven accurate in the past, and if my judgment fails me here I risk the diminution of whatever credibility I now enjoy'. We 'put ourselves on the line', for our own character will be impugned if we prove consistently incapable of forming a just estimate of the character and personal qualities of others. In publicly judging others, we subject ourselves to judgment, and are thus 'put to the test'. If I venture the opinion that X is a scoundrel and Y is a man of scrupulous integrity, whereas it turns out upon further experience that the very reverse is the case, it is likely that serious doubt will be cast upon my own claim to practical judgment and moral insight.

Here, as in aesthetic and other forms of reflective judgment, a great deal more enters into the judgment than can be expressed and articulated verbally or even consciously. The criteria or grounds of the judgment remain unformulated and (to an extent) unformulable. Such judgments, to be sure, involve a great deal of 'tacit knowing', which, in Polanyi's words, is characterized by the fact that 'we know more than we can tell'.[10] But this tacit dimension to judging in no way implies a diminishment or curtailment of responsibility for the judgment. Quite the contrary, as Polanyi himself states: the acts of the knower 'are personal judgments exercised responsibly with a view to a reality with which he is seeking to establish contact'. This responsibility cannot be attenuated by reducing the claims asserted.

> The affirmation of a probable statement includes a judgment no less personal than an affirmation of its certainty would do. Any conclusion, be it given as a surmise or claimed as a certainty, represents a commitment of the person who arrives at it. No one can utter more than a responsible commitment of his own, and this completely fulfills the finding of the truth and the telling of it.[11]

Polanyi tells us that his account of tacit knowing is intended to show

> how man can exercise responsible judgment when faced with a problem. His decision in casting around for a solution of an unsolved problem is indeterminate; but his decisions are also responsible in being subject to the obligation to seek the pre-determined solution of his problem. . . . This is a commitment to the anticipation of a hidden reality. . . . Responsibility and truth are in fact but two aspects of such a commitment: the act of judgment is its personal pole and the independent reality on which it bears is its external pole.[12]

Thus the tacit dimension of judging is a personal dimension, and this personal dimension entails that the act of judgment is integrally bound up with responsibility and commitment. In other words, a theory of judgment implies a concept of the person.

Returning now to the case of judgments of character, which is our present illustration: what, we may ask, is the difference between this variety of reflective judgment, and the previous one considered? One principal point of distinction, it seems, is that the type of judgment just delineated brings into play a stronger concept of responsibility than was operative in the other. The kind of reflective judgment that we first considered applies to any sort of practical activity – taking part in a sport or recreational activity, fulfilling the demands of a job or pro-fession, choosing a turn of phrase, executing a plan, building or con-structing something, and so on. And while it is true that we take responsibility for all these activities that we carry on, for instance, take responsibility for the chess move that we have decided upon, the responsibility extends only to the limit of the activity in question (or at least, this is the case in most of our practical activities) – when the chess game ends, so does the exercise of responsibility involved in playing the game. But this is not so for judgments of a more serious kind, for they mark us as reliable or incompetent in a deeper sense than occurs when we appear incompetent chessplayers (although, undoubtedly, it speaks for our character that we take whatever we do seriously, even chess-playing). In other words, in judging the character of X we often carry the responsibility for rendering judgment beyond this particular exercise of judgment. We must 'live with' our having judged X as we did, for it will characterize *us* as being penetrating or shallow, insightful or banal; it is this enduring property of responsibility contained in our judgments that we must 'live with'.

Still, this is but an intermediate form of judgment, for even this falls short of the full dimension of responsibility that – I want to argue – can be located only in the sphere of political judgments.

COMMUNITIES

Let us, then, ascend finally to the realm of the political itself, where yet another dimension of reflective judgment is added. This added dimension of responsibility follows from the very nature of political community, for political judgment entails an implied responsibility for the assumption of what may be termed a shared way of life. All political judgments are – implicitly at least – judgments about the form of collective life that it is desirable for us to pursue within a given context of possibilities. The commonality of judging subjects is internal to, or constitutive of, the judgment, not merely contingent or external to it. (In the latter case, judgment is deliberated upon 'monologically', and therefore submitted to one's fellows for confirmation or negation only subsequent to one's having arrived at the judgment independently of them; in the former, the deliberation is 'dialogical', that is, proceeding from a form of deliberation that does not abstract from one's discourse with one's fellows.) This follows from the nature of the *object* of deliberation, which is directed to the very form of our relating together. For the moment, I can express this no better than by saying that what is at issue here is not 'what should I do?' or 'how should I conduct myself?' but: 'how are we to "be" together, and what is to be the institutional setting for that being-together?'. Where what is at stake are arrangements of mutual accommodation defining how we are to associate with one another, the urgency of coming to an agreement is not merely greater, but indeed of a higher order. Hence the complexities of this form of deliberation are qualitatively, not by degree, enhanced. (It is not *self*-deliberation about my life, but mutual deliberation conducted *between* agents implicated in a common life.) While this higher level of responsibility can be present in private relationships (e.g. in family life), only the public sphere admits of general deliberation about the form of being-together which governs or regulates our interaction on a truly comprehensive scale. It was this comprehensiveness which, according to the argument of book I of Aristotle's *Politics*, distinguished the polis from lesser forms of association, including the family. (Aristotle referred to it as the 'self-sufficiency' of political life.)

If this position can be shown to be compelling, it would follow that in judgments about political relationships, that is, judgments relating to the form of association between men, a quality of intensified responsibility is at work that is not present in delivering a judgment about a chess move, or about the character of a person with whom we are acquainted, or for that matter, about the aesthetic quality of a work of art (all of which are instances of reflective judgment). At most, the form of intersubjective deliberation operative in politics is foreshadowed or anticipated in the less fully developed types of reflective judgment that we have been considering previously. This implies that only political judgment is as a matter of course characterized by the need to come to an agreement about the common form of our relating-together – and it is this quest that animates the presentation of a judgment for common deliberation, consent, or conflict, and ultimately, the movement of coming-to-an-agreement through rational or not-so-rational consensus (and therefore, what is required of a theory of political judgment is to provide some theoretical account of this process of rational deliberation, consensus, and the hope of coming to an agreement). We must now elaborate in further detail what we mean when we say that all political judgments – as distinct from other varieties of reflective judgment – are characterized by implicit judgments about the form of collective life that it is appropriate for a community to pursue; and that it is in this that the added dimension of responsibility specific to politics is situated. This further elaboration can only be accomplished by illustration.

Let us consider the choice of competing political commitments: 'I support Zionism' or 'I oppose Zionism'. Each side of this pro-and-contra encapsulates a whole complex of judgments and understandings, which issue in a compound judgment, namely, that a people should or should not be organized into a nation-state, in contrast to its foregoing history of lacking statehood. A nation-state connotes authoritative control over a given territory for the purpose of national self-expression on the part of a given people. This is not the only way to organize a state, but it has been the dominant mode of political organization since the nineteenth century.[13] This gives rise to related questions, for instance: is the nation-state to be given a (nominally) religious basis, or is it to be an officially secular state? And how are those excluded from the nation to be treated within the nation-state? What political and legal rights will they retain? All these judgments about political institutions require attention, yet we have not even begun to pose vital questions of social, economic, and constitutional organization (democracy or a one-party state, socialism or capitalism, agrarian society or western-style modernization).

How to proceed with the judgment? To begin with, are the basic needs of the people to be served in this way or that? This consideration includes (but not exclusively) needs such as elementary survival as a people, collective self-expression, preservation of collective identity. It is first of all by reference to needs of this sort that the claim to statehood is postulated. But this judgment is accompanied by considerations of dignity and respect. Here it is a question not just of whether the people's own dignity is properly secured by statehood, but whether it infringes the dignity of other peoples, and therefore whether the principle of respect in general is observed or violated. This in turn brings into play historical judgments: was there a pre-existing nation inhabiting the territory beforehand? When was this people constituted into a nation, distinct from surrounding peoples, and did such nationhood (if it was such) entitle it to territory from which it was dispossessed by the founding of the Jewish state? Were rights violated; if so, then who bears the primary responsibility for this violation; and were such rights overridden by conflicting, and pre-eminent, rights? What is the historical timespan over which a people retains its claim to an ancestral homeland, and is such a claim sufficient to override competing claims? These are of course questions of moral legitimacy, and require moral judgments about the rights asserted and rights denied in founding a state. In rendering such judgments about moral legitimacy or right, it is difficult to disentangle political judgments from historical judgments. Indeed, here we see how profoundly intertwined are moral, political, and historical judgments.[14]

The reason why public judgments are possible at all is that the objects of those judgments are shared by those who judge, or are the focus of their *common* concern. For instance, I judge as a member of a community because of a common tradition and shared history, public laws and obligations to which all are subject, common ideals and shared meanings. These 'public objects' or public things (*res publica*) allow for judgment of a public character, for these things concern all of us who participate in these traditions, laws, and institutions, and who therefore share in common meanings. Such judgments concern not merely what *I* want or the way of life *I* desire, but rather, entail intersubjective deliberation about a common life (how *we* should be together).

Let us examine another aspect of our example, where it is not at all clear where the common relationship is situated. Two parties are in disagreement about a right, in this case the right to possession of territory. The disputants must at least share a concept, namely the concept of a right to possess land, in order to dispute the right. But the sharing of a concept implies some agreement about the kinds of criteria that will potentially decide disputes about how to apply the concept. (In Wittgenstein's phrase, communication in language presupposes 'agreement in judgments',[15] no matter how attenuated or oblique the community of judgment concerned.) This certainly does not mean that the *actual* achievement of agreement is assured; rather, one cannot speak of a shared concept where there is no *possibility* of agreement on how to apply the concept. This is not to say that fundamental disagreements cannot arise over such concepts, only that there must be *some* conceptual contact between those in fundamental conflict. (And let us bear in mind that the application of general concepts to particulars is what we have already defined as 'judgment'.) Thus there must be at least this minimal (or formal) shared judgment if conflicts of judgment are to occur. Even divergent judgments of the most deep-seated and fundamental kind are rooted in some relation of community, otherwise one would lack the concepts with which to disagree.[16] It is this always limited but always possible (and always extendable) commensurability which Gadamer implies when he speaks of the universal horizon of language, and the 'fusing of horizons' by means of language. It is forever *possible* to expand the horizon until one achieves a settlement of the competing claims that was hitherto out of reach.[17]

This (limited) commensurability might seem to preclude the assertion of a tragic dimension to judgment; for if the claims upon us are commensurable, in what way can they be in tragic conflict? (One readily thinks of Weber's 'polytheism': for the gods to make tragic claims upon us, there must be no way to adjudicate between them.) But this is mistaken, assuming that by 'commensurable' one does not simply mean 'decidable'. The claims upon us can conflict tragically only if they make conceptual contact with one another, and the only way in which they can come into contact with one another is if there is *some* commensurability between them. Otherwise they would simply pass each other by, without any trace of mutual disturbance. Commensurability in this sense is in fact the *condition* of the possibility of tragic conflict, and theories that postulate moral or intellectual incommensurability are incapable of giving an account of such conflict. (In saying this, I am well aware that 'commensurability' is not really the appropriate term, for it seems to imply a common measure or standard, like utility, which surely *would* dissipate the tragic dimension of judgment.)

How are such questions of right resolved? Necessarily, they must be submitted to criteria of judgment to which (ideally) all those judging can assent. That is, there must be underlying grounds of judgment which human beings, *qua* members of a judging community, share, and which serve to unite in communication even those who disagree (*and who may disagree radically*). The very act of communication implies some basis of common judgment. There must be *some* agreement of judgment on what would count as valid historical evidence, or valid moral considerations, such as would tend to confirm or contradict one political judgment or the other (although it may well be that none of these considerations is strictly conclusive). For judgment at all to be possible, there must be standards of judgment, and this implies a community of judgment, that is, agreement in judgments at a deeper level that grounds those at the level of ordinary political argument. In this sense, discourse rests upon an underlying substratum of agreement in judgments. The very possibility of communication means that disagreement and conflict are grounded in a deeper unity. This is what may be termed, borrowing Kantian language, a 'transcendental' requirement of our discourse.

We have maintained that judgment implies agreement of judgment at the level of the community appealed to for criteria or grounds of judgment. But this in turn raises the question of which community is appealed to for the intersubjective criteria or grounds of judgment, since the latter will vary as one varies the community appealed to. Consider the following questions submitted to judgment: 'Should "we" found a state in 1948 even at the price of waging war with all our neighbouring states?' 'Should "we" cede territory in order to exchange peace for bitter antagonism, even if it means severely risking our national security?' These are questions addressed to a particular community, and the judgment called for is – when posed in this way – largely a prudential one. Judgment here can limit itself to prudential considerations because the 'we' that judges in this case is already (relatively) given ('relatively' because the collective subject is always in a state of continuing self-constitution, and the judgments it makes will have a reflexive effect upon its own identity as a community). But suppose the same questions are submitted for judgment, but addressed to a different 'we': ought one to found a state under such circumstances? Ought one to make these sacrifices? Here one appeals to a world community, and strives for a universal judgment (and not merely as a matter of 'winning over world public opinion', in the sense of 'public relations'). The grounds of judgment vary because the community appealed to for intersubjective criteria of judgment has varied. The question is no longer one of prudential judgment. Thus we require a definition of community in order to know how the judgment shall proceed. What shall take precedence, national solidarity or universal solidarity (solidarity with mankind as a whole)? How am I to judge – as a Zionist (or anti-Zionist), as a Jew (or Gentile), as a member of western civilization, or as a human being, a member of the whole human race? Judgment implies a community that supplies common grounds or criteria by which one attempts to decide. But where allegiances conflict, it is not decided in advance which community will supply the basis of judgment. Does my commitment to a particular people outweigh, or is it outweighed by, my commitment to universal mankind? This too demands judgment (and judgment of a higher order, a sort of higher-order prudence). Thus the claim – judgment implies judging community – gives rise to the question: which community?

But this question, as with all questions of judgment, can only be resolved in the concrete, when confronted with particulars. Theoretical inquiry can only clarify what is at stake, and disclose the conditions that render efforts towards a satisfactory resolution possible; theory cannot itself displace judgment. If theory alone could answer the question, judgment would be rendered superfluous, and political man deprived of that quality of responsibility which we have argued is inalienable. The study of ethics, according to the classical conception, does not tell one what to do or furnish maxims for conduct; rather, it forms the kind of person that one is – making one, for instance, more reflective, more discriminating, more attentive – and it is only in this indirect way that it has an influence upon practice.[18]

MEANS, ENDS, AND IDENTITY

Judgment can be defined, following Kant, as the activity of subsuming particulars under universals. We, as judging subjects, assume responsibility for this subsumption. (However, this is always a *partial*, or qualified, responsibility since to a certain extent particulars come to us already subsumed in virtue of our speaking the language that we do. There is no such thing as a 'pure' particular: particulars are always given to us as instantiations of some universal or other; or expressed differently, the very recognition of particulars is necessarily mediated by linguistic concepts.) The judging subject mediates between a particular object and a universal concept, and this act of mediation involves the assumption of an ultimate responsibility for one's judgment. It follows that responsibility is inherent to the very concept of judgment. If we seek to differentiate political judgment as a distinct form of judgment, one means of doing so may be to classify different levels of responsibility corresponding to the various kinds of judgment. Human responsibility comes into play wherever judgment is, to employ Kant's terms, not 'determinant' but 'reflective'; that is to say, where the particular is not merely subsumed under an already given universal, but rather where the universal must somehow be found for the subsumption. Such responsibility is exercised in all practical activities, including those as common and obvious as hanging a painting, writing a letter, or deciding on the best move in a game of chess. Even where the end is fixed in advance, and therefore the judgment is of an instrumental kind, the selection of the best means is a matter of human responsibility, and therefore belongs to the class of reflective judgments. We must seek then for a principle of individuation that will allow us to single out political judgment as something distinctive within the entire class of reflective judgments.

Obviously, not all judgments involve the same degree, or rather the same quality, of responsibility, and the more that is at stake in a given exercise of judgment, the greater will be the burden that is placed upon the judging subject. In order to begin to situate political judgments among the diverse forms of human judgment, consider the following three questions:

1 Who am I?
2 What do I want?
3 How do I get what I want?

In judging, we as judging subjects attempt to determine, as best we may, who we are, what we want, and how we realize our ends.

It may be observed, upon closer reflection, that what is sought after in these three questions corresponds roughly to the three varieties of reflective judgment dealt with in our survey. Questions of the third sort are purely instrumental, and presuppose fixed answers to the first and second questions. Our first example was of this sort: I know I want to win the chess game, but how do I go about doing so? The second question, in contrast, involves a kind of teleology that is not merely instrumental, but rather, entails deliberation about ends. It activates what is sometimes called ends-rationality, as opposed to means-rationality. This corresponds to some extent to our second example, that of character judgments. When I evaluate someone as a person, I am thereby (by implication) judging what is valuable in human life, what are the standards by which we measure human beings, what virtues comprise the right ends of man, and so on. In judging a person to be worthy of friendship, it is inescapable that I will simultaneously be judging what are the qualities that define worthiness-of-friendship, and these are undoubtedly teleological, not instrumental, judgments. Our third level of reflective judgment, which we illustrated with the case of judgments for or against Zionism, is like the second level in that it exhibits a non-instrumental teleology. However, the teleological deliberation in this third case is not addressed to personal ends, but rather, to shared ends deliberated upon in common. The added dimension of responsibility corresponds to the first of the questions above, namely, 'who am I?' – that is, 'who is the subject who judges here?'. Political judgments tacitly posit a judging subject, and answer the question 'who am I?', or rather, 'who are we?' (although judgments of private morality may also have to define the relevant subject). When one renders judgments addressed to a community or a form of life held in common, it is not transparent or immediately accessible who exactly is judging: the single political agent, or his collocutors, with whom he is deliberating, as well; neither is it immediately apparent to whom the judgment is addressed: a community of the past or one projected into the future; a particular national community or a community of nations; a tiny circle of associates or universal mankind? In positing the subject of the judgment, and defining thereby the community from which grounds are drawn, one affirms a political identity. The indeterminacy that such judgments carry with them constitutes a further order of complexity.

Reviewing our three questions – who am I (or who are we)? what do I (we) want? how do I (we) get what I (we) want? – we find that instrumental judgments address only the third question, and assume the first and second to be fixed. Individual moral judgments address both the second and third (although they may sometimes address also the first). Finally, political and moral-political judgments address all three. If each of these questions represents a different level of responsibility, serving to render the judging subject responsible for the determination of his own identity and purposes, the burden of judgment will increase in proportion to the range of such questions engaged by a given form of judgment.

Needless to say, the rough survey offered here does not presume to be either definitive or exhaustive. Other examples could be explored, and those sketched here could be elaborated in other ways. But the idea of a hierarchy of ascending forms of reflective judgment, with political judgment at its apex, does seem to me a promising avenue of theory, and worthy of further consideration.

When, for example, I pronounce that 'I support Zionism' or 'I oppose Zionism', I not only appeal to relations of community which make available the common concepts, as well as public objects and shared meanings, which ground the judgment; I also posit the community to whom I address the judgment.[19] When I state 'We, as Jews, should do this, and not do that', I appeal to a national community – and submit my claims to prudence, or practical wisdom. When I state 'The Jewish State is morally justified (or not) in what it has undertaken in 1948 and in the present day', I address a universal community, appealing to world opinion and international judgment – and enter a claim to disinterestedness and justice.

Where the claims to prudence and disinterestedness, in this case addressed to particular and universal communities respectively, make contact and perhaps conflict with one another, there the complexities of judgment reach their greatest density, and the task of judgment is most severe. Conor Cruise O'Brien, in a recent column ('In Hebrew it's all a bit earthier', *Observer*, London, 5 December 1982), relates the following remarks quoted from a discussion within Israel: 'Every Israeli is partly Peace Now, partly Gush Emunim. Both sound a chord in all of us. That is what happens here. Eretz Yisrael, and also peace and justice.' The intention here of course is not to privilege one form of political experience over another, but to insist that political experience *as such* is highly mediated in a whole variety of ways; and that where it becomes *most* uncertain how one is to determine the appropriate mode of judgment, there the task of judgment reaches its peak.

When we participate in political life we deploy concepts of a particular kind, such as right, justice, and responsibility. (For instance, in making a judgment for or against Zionism, one must pose the questions: who holds the right to the land? Who bears responsibility for the plight of dispossessed refugees? What does justice demand?) And the deployment or application of these general concepts rests upon a range of conditions which ground the subject's assumption of responsibility for his judgments. These conditions do not direct the application of political concepts, in the sense of determinant judgment; rather, they provide a 'reservoir of appeal', or a pool of criteria from which we draw justification for our judgments, although the ultimate responsibility for application to a given set of particulars rests with the subject who judges. Because of this employment of concepts, political life is constituted by discourse. And political discourse, in turn, is constituted by appeals to shared criteria and grounds of judgment embedded in common forms of life. The exercise of reflective judgment in applying general concepts like right, justice, and responsibility to particular situations is constitutive of political life in general. Judgment is thus the constitutive medium of political life and political discourse, the medium of politics.

However, we should take care not to overemphasize the discursive dimension of politics. Habermas, in particular, sometimes falls into this kind of error. This was the fallacy of the Enlightenment: to assume that the world could be remade by rational inquiry and discourse purged of prejudice. Against this, we have the insight of Gadamer, that the hermeneutical function of language is precisely to explore and render intelligible to ourselves our historically grounded prejudices, for a situation without pre-judgments and pre-understandings would not be a human situation.[20] These givens are not dissolved by talk, for without them there would be nothing to talk *about*; we would lack the stable reference points that serve as the *objects* of our discourse.

In attempting to depict politics as the medium wherein men make sense of their common situation in discourse with one another, we have no desire to endow political judgment with an unwarranted degree of freedom, or to abstract from the non-discursive aspect of political life, in particular, the institutionally given context of factors that constrain and circumscribe the possibilities open to men. Judgment always operates within an institutionally defined structure of opportunities and possibilities. Men never judge in a vacuum; to overlook the objective constraints upon their judgment is to fail to do full justice to the situation that elicits political judgment in the first place. This introduces another essential dimension within which political judgment moves, and that helps to characterize it as distinctively political. This further dimension might be expressed by saying that political judgment must take account of 'givens', both institutional and ideational (which is *not* to say that it can – ever – take its bearings exclusively from these). The state of Israel exists, the PLO exists – these are givens. The Israelis occupy East Jerusalem, the PLO commands appreciable military and guerrilla forces; the Israeli people by and large are reluctant to abandon settlements on the West Bank, the Palestinian people by and large accept the authority of PLO representatives; the Israelis see the PLO as a threat to their very existence, the Palestinians see Israel as pursuing colonialist designs. All these are givens that must be reckoned with by political judgment. Conor Cruise O'Brien, in another recent column in the London *Observer* ('Peace need not pass understanding', 21 March 1982), very incisively notes that many proposed resolutions of political conflict in Northern Ireland and the Middle East contribute nothing whatever to the search for peace because they are founded upon the condition that Ulster Protestant Unionists will cease to be Unionists, and that Israeli Zionists will cease to be Zionists. In judging, we must address ourselves to what is already given, to what the judging subject confronts as given.

On the other hand, the dimension of 'open discourse' invoked in our argument is never wholly absent, and political judgment thus retains a quality of moral complexity that can never be dispensed with. This is so because we can never tell in advance when it is legitimate to remain within the framework of institutional givens, and when a concept of right must be brought to bear against the given. There is no way of deciding in advance what is properly a matter of experience, or of prudence in a much narrower sense than that appealed to in this study, and what, a matter of critical judgment. (Even mere administrative responsibility for carrying out as efficiently as possible an already decided government policy does not eliminate responsibility for judging between right and wrong as to the policy administered – as the limit case of Eichmann shows all too clearly.) It is always an open question: does one rest content within the established structure of possibilities, or does one demand that the agents concerned break out of structural constraints (despite the hazards involved)? Thus the possibility of such moral challenge is ever present, and may at any point be levelled against the agent who claims moral immunity by reference to established standards of action and judgment.

Obviously, one cannot deny that there is more than cliché in all the common maxims about politics as the 'art of the possible', as concerned with present circumstance and actually given contingencies, as pertaining to the 'Is' (exigency) as opposed to the 'Ought-to-be' (right). But it is not the whole truth, and never can be. To say this is certainly not to impugn the importance of Max Weber's concept of an 'ethic of responsibility' (which in 'Politics as a vocation' is distinguished from an 'ethic of ultimate ends'). Indeed, it was Weber who affirmed that 'man would not have attained the possible unless time and again he had reached out for the impossible'.[21] In this respect, perhaps it is Weber's famous lecture on the political vocation that furnishes us with a genuine articulation of the two-sided demand of political judgment – neither abstracting from the existing realities with which political man must contend, nor failing to distance oneself from merely contingent institutional and existential givens. As Weber says, political life demands *both* distance and passion, both detachment and involvement. To judge a political world responsibly is both to accept and to reject, to say 'Yea' and say 'Nay', to face realities that confront one and to 'reach out for the impossible'. In this way Weber does justice to both moments of judgment: judgment as the detached reflection of the spectator, and judgment as the responsible commitment of the man of prudence. Here we have the intimation of a perspective capable of reconciling the truths contained in Aristotle and Kant respectively; confronting an established structure of actualities and possibilities, but bringing to bear a concept of right that critically judges, and therefore distances itself from, the established reality. The concrete achievement of political judgment is a living synthesis of detachment and involvement, of passionate commitment and critical distance.

We have argued that, for example, deciding on a friendship differs in kind from deciding on a chess move, in the following way: non-instrumental judgment implies an activity of judging that is not self-contained, but potentially involves stepping outside one's immediate situation in order to question one's life as a whole. And we have also characterized the difference between deciding whether to befriend someone (individual moral judgment) and deciding in favour of or against Zionism (moral-political judgment) in the following terms: what is at stake in the latter is collective identity, and therefore the institutional embodiment of a being-with others, not just a concern with my own integrity and that of other individuals. The added complexity here arises out of the need to relate to others for the purpose of constituting, in common, a political way of life. Consider the following three cases: a stockbroker who lacks judgment, a friend or relative who lacks judgment, and a political leader who lacks judgment. In the first case, the incompetent stockbroker is no doubt held responsible for his judgments, but (assuming that culpable negligence is not involved, and that his practical incompetence is not compounded by moral incompetence), he is held responsible as a stockbroker, not as a person (in this context, 'I wouldn't trust him' means: 'I wouldn't trust him to handle my stocks'). Contrast this with the third case, that of the political leader who has been disgraced because of incompetence or corruption. Here we hold him responsible not just in the sense of castigating him for ruining his career, or even for making a ruin of his own life and the lives of those immediately around him. Rather, we charge him with violating a public trust, with abusing his position, with failing to live up to the responsibility with which he was charged. Admittedly, personal-moral responsibilities can involve this too, but there remains a considerable difference between cases where an entire political way of life is threatened (e.g. American political life under the Nixon admin-istration) and those where personal (private) relations are disturbed. In any case, practical judgments in the *narrow* sense (non-moral and non-political) rarely express the kind of person I am in the sense in which moral and political judgments regularly do. Of course, there still remains the possibility that these distinctions between forms of judg-ment are merely a matter of degree, and not qualitative at all. Thus it can be objected that collective identity is at stake in personal-moral questions, that moral identity is involved in instrumental judgments, and so on. (Certainly, many of our practices *do* go to the heart of moral existence, and many of our private relationships *do* engage larger questions of identity.) But on the other hand, there is no reason why this should suffice to rule out the very attempt at distinguishing these various levels analytically, and even placing them in a hierarchy (as suggested by Aristotle, in book 1, chapter 2 of the *Nicomachean Ethics*).

Political judgment stands at the apex not only because of the superior comprehensiveness of its object, but because it combines moral and instrumental considerations in a form of deliberation that is neither strictly instrumental nor strictly moral. Moreover, it is not simply a case of a chance combination of instrumental skills and moral qualities in a given individual (as if that were, in itself, an assurance of political wisdom, which it surely is not), but rather, of participation in a distinct kind of judgment which is itself a higher synthesis of practical ability and moral insight. In politics, moral claims are mediated by assumption of responsibility for institutionally embodied forms of life, and, at the same time, deliberation about the most effective policy is mediated by claims to moral legitimacy. As even a cursory reading of Thucydides would bear out, political deliberation would not be political deliberation without both debate about the most effective means of securing the interests of the polity, and at least ostensible claims to legitimacy and justice. (Absence of the former would be mere naivety; absence of the latter, mere coercion.) Political judgment combines and surpasses the complexities of moral and instrumental judgment.

Human subjects have no privileged access to their own identity and purposes. It is through rational dialogue, and especially through political dialogue, that we clarify, even to ourselves, who we are and what we want. It is mistaken to assume that we necessarily enter into dialogue with an already consolidated view of where we stand and what we are after, conceiving of speech merely as a means to be used for winning over others, rather than as an end to be pursued for its own sake. On the contrary, communication between subjects joined in a community of rational dialogue may entail a process of moral self-discovery that will lead us to a better insight into our own ends and a firmer grasp upon our own subjectivity. Here politics functions as a normative concept, describing what collective agency should be like, rather than abiding by its present devalued meaning. The political expression of this ideal is the republican tradition. Thus inquiry into the intersubjective basis of moral and political rationality may contribute to a fuller understanding of what Arendt and Habermas call a public realm or public space, what Charles Taylor has called a deliberative culture, and what in the traditional vocabulary goes by the name of a republic. Our hope is that such reflection will ultimately conduct us back to Aristotle's insight that it is through speech and deliberation that man finds the location of his proper humanity, between beast and god, in the life of the citizen.

E·I·G·H·T
Closing reflections

In the political world of today we are faced with a host of urgently pressing political issues: mass unemployment, poverty, environmental pollution on a global scale, nuclear proliferation, steadily encroaching bureaucratization at all levels of political decision-making, ever-growing complexity of social life that makes it seem beyond the understanding or control of the average citizen, decay of urban life, the breakdown of the family and its consequent implications for social life generally, potentially explosive relations between the developed and the underdeveloped world, new dimensions of war and revolution, nationalism, the challenge to liberal democracies posed by totalitarian regimes, and so on. A theory of political judgment cannot tell us how to judge these various pressing issues or what particular judgments to make in respect of them; rather, a theory of political judgment tells us that we cannot help but judge them, or, if we think they can be judged *for* us, alerts us to the fact that we must be suffering major dislocations in our political life. In the latter case, the theory of political judgment points to the need for a reformulation of the notion of citizenship that will allow us to reclaim our capacity of judgment from those who presume to exercise it on our behalf.

In the case of Adolf Eichmann, as encountered in Hannah

Arendt's striking portrait in her book *Eichmann in Jerusalem*, we confront the paradigmatic figure of the unthinking and unjudging non-citizen of our times. Indeed, it may be easier to give an account of what judgment *is* by reflecting on what it means to *lack* the faculty of judgment. What does it mean when we say, as Arendt does implicitly in the postscript to her book, that Eichmann lacks the faculty of judgment? It seems as if we mean to say not merely that he is incapable of making *sound* political judgments, that he does not possess the capacity for *correctly* attending to relevant particulars, but rather something much stronger. Consider the analogous case of aesthetic taste. Suppose we presented an exquisite rose to someone for him to admire, and said 'Isn't this beautiful?' Under what circumstances would we say that the person *lacked* the faculty of judgment (as opposed to simply judging poorly or wrongly or incompetently)? Suppose he said, 'That isn't a rose, it's an orange.' Would that be a case of *poor* judgment, or would we rather want to say that he wasn't judging *at all*, that we couldn't recognize or had difficulty recognizing his response as a proper case of judgment? But if he merely said, 'I don't see anything beautiful about it, I find it ugly', at what point then would we feel obliged to credit it as a judgment, at what point could we feel entitled to dismiss it altogether as a real judgment? We are not always sure what answer to give in such cases. And how does this compare with the political case? If he replies: 'This isn't murder, it's good management, efficient organization', is this faulty judgment, poor judgment, or does it fail to qualify as judgment at all? What about the inability to experience disgust at the slaughter of countless innocent men, women, and children? Is this perverted judgment, malfunctioning judgment, or is it no judgment at all? Can we be faulted for wanting to say that such a person simply has not begun to exercise a faculty of independent judgment?

This should help us to understand better the equivocal logic of the concept of judging. Political judgment is the estimation of particulars with which we are confronted, like the aesthetic judgment of particular objects to be appreciated: a rose, a painting, a piece of music. Not being able to exercise political judgment is like not being able to judge the beauty of a rose. However, as we see, there are problems in distinguishing the logical contour of the concept of judging. We seem to lack unambiguous dividing lines to determine whether, and at what point, we are entitled to refuse to ascribe judgment at all, even though the

subject seems, *prima facie*, to be making some identification of a particular. This is a logical problem that involves clarification of the various
senses in which we can be said to judge, or to ascribe judgment to
others. It is evident that ascriptions of judgment may be both made and
not made, depending on the sense appealed to, such as: he judged, but
his judgments attested to his utter lack of a sense of political judgment.
This means that several dimensions of judgment may be considered
simultaneously, certain of which may be operative, others not. Something may be identified as a particular, but not identified under a
special form of description: X saw that it was an object, but did not
see that it was a beautiful rose. X saw that he was a man, but did not
see that he was a political actor, engaged in revolutionary activity. In
the first case X is judging, but not judging aesthetically; in the second
case X again judges, but this time does not judge politically. The full
dimensions of the particular escape the judging subject, who therefore,
in a certain relevant aspect, fails to judge. 'Did he judge?' is not a
yes or no question. It must be further defined and specified by the
attendant questions: did he identify a particular at all? Did he identify
it aesthetically? Did he identify it politically? and so on.

But judgment is not only a matter of identification. For in classing
any particular under a universal, we are at the same time distinguishing
it from other particulars. To identify is at the same time to discriminate.
Our world of experience (including political experience) is a world of
identity and difference. To identity and difference correspond the dual
faculties of identification and discrimination. Judgment encompasses
these two correlative capacities. To judge the world is to identify and
discriminate, to determine what is the same and what is different. Thus
the faculty of taste (which Kant identified with aesthetic judgment) has
so often been elucidated in terms of the capacities of discrimination,
discernment, and the ability to attend to relevant differences. Hobbes,
for instance, distinguishes between wit and judgment as follows:

> whereas in [the] succession of men's thought there is nothing to
> observe in the things they think on, but either in what they be
> like one another, or in what they be unlike, or what they serve for,
> or how they serve to such purpose; those that observe their
> similitudes, in case they be such as are but rarely observed by
> others, are said to have a good wit; by which, in this occasion, is

meant a good fancy. But they that observe their differences, and dissimilitudes, which is called distinguishing, and discerning, and judging between thing and thing, in case such discerning be not easy, are said to have a good judgment.[1]

Actually, Hobbes' distinction is misleading, for judgment in fact comprises the apprehension both of similitudes and of dissimilitudes.

Aesthetic judgment and political judgment are species of the genus we call judgment (perhaps even closely related species, perhaps distant relations); we may be judging, and yet lack either aesthetic judgment or political judgment, or both. These faculties do not exhaust judgment. Even if we were never confronted with aesthetic or political objects of judgment, we would still be judging – judging constantly, throughout the whole fabric of our conscious and semi-conscious experience, that is, identifying particulars, for without judgment there *would be* no experience as we know it. Judging is ever present in human experience, for it constitutes it *as* human experience. This is not the case with aesthetic judging or political judging, although aesthetic experience and political experience *are* of course constituted by these respective faculties of judgment.

To say that Eichmann lacks the ability to judge is to charge Eichmann with a much broader failing than the incapacity to make politically astute observations. In this very narrow sense of political judgment, it is *not* being affirmed that Eichmann lacks the gift of judging politically with felicity. What is attended to here is something much deeper, and much more revelatory of the faculty by which men ready themselves for political concerns and for involvement in politics. It is what we may call 'humane judgment', which may be distinguished from the bare capacity for identifying logical particulars that is common to *all* human subjects, and may therefore be designated the human faculty of judging. When we say 'Eichmann lacks judgment' we want to say: 'He does not lack the power to judge in any sense whatever, but he does lack the power of *humane* judgment, he fails to identify correctly particulars that would be evident to any normal, civilized, morally sighted judging subject. To go wrong *here* is to suffer from a kind of blindness, a blindness to the human dimension of things.' Here we confront a faculty that is both broader than the faculty of political judgment, narrowly conceived, and yet narrower than the universal faculty of human judgment, in the bare sense of identifying particulars.

The thesis that Eichmann lacked the faculty of judgment seems therefore to refer to an idea of 'humane judgment' interposed between the narrower conception of political judgment *per se* and the broader human faculty of judgment as such. It wasn't that Eichmann was incapable of judging that these were men, women, and children – he could see that as well as any other human being – and it wasn't just that he failed to perceive the political significance of what was going on around him – such as the fact that he could be liable to prosecution for war crimes by an international tribunal in the event of German defeat – but rather, we want to say, he seems to be missing the *human* significance of these events, his very faculty of moral *perception* (not just political evaluation and foresight) seems to be essentially deficient. Therefore when we say 'Eichmann lacked the capacity of judgment' we want to say something much stronger than 'Eichmann tended to make unfortunate political judgments', but not nearly so strong as 'Eichmann lacked the universal human ability to identify particulars'. We want to say something like this: Eichmann missed the human significance of things, he failed to perceive them in their true light, he was blind to the human dimension.

The universal human faculty of judgment is a necessary (but not sufficient) condition of humane judgment, and humane judgment in turn is the necessary (but not sufficient) condition of political judgment. Without the humane capacity of perceiving the human significance of things we would be incapable of confronting phenomena in the political world (as Eichmann was), but without the bare ability to identify particulars we would be incapable of even beginning to appraise their human significance, that is, to perceive the humane dimension of our world.

To judge is to identify a particular, to class it under one description or another. In Kant's terminology, it is the subsumption of particulars under a universal (concept). Political judgment is the comprehensive faculty by which we come to terms with particulars in the political world. Obviously, the meaning of this definition will vary as one varies what one takes 'political' to mean, and will stretch as broadly or contract as narrowly as one's conception of politics. Consequently, it will not suffice to define *political* judgment as the identification and classing of *political* particulars, for this still leaves the domain of the political quite unspecified. What qualifies as 'political' is yet to be determined. In the discussion of humane judgment we spoke of political judgment 'narrowly conceived', as if this could be neatly circumscribed. But can it? Is the 'humane' dimension ever absent from political judgments in the proper sense? Or is it rather the case that judgments are 'political' only in the most truncated sense if abstracted from this humane dimension? In a sense we are shifting our ground somewhat, now bringing political judgment much closer to what we have up to this point been calling 'humane judgment'. For, we want to argue, political judgment that does not incorporate the kinds of moral discrimination involved in 'being open to the human dimension of things' cannot be considered political judgment in the full sense. In other words, political judgment 'narrowly conceived' does not embrace all that we mean to attach to the concept of political judgment. Political judgment that does not encompass the full dimensions of a situation considered as a human situation is, so we would argue, political judgment only in a very attenuated sense. Political judgment, which at first sight seemed to be narrower than 'humane judgment', is now seen to be as broad as, or even broader than, humane judgment, in that a genuinely political judgment incorporates the humane judgment, in the sense of being open to the full human dimensions of the situation or the particulars being judged. Political judgment in the fullest sense confronts particulars in the light of the whole, namely, the whole of what is meaningful and important to human beings.

We are taken a step further in our reflections by considering the claim that to recognize particulars for what they are and classing them under the appropriate universal is to be a spectator of political particulars, to have a spectator's appreciation of them. This idea of political spectatorship is suggested in a newspaper column by George F. Will during the US presidential campaign of 1976 referring to a statement by presidential candidate Eugene McCarthy that his opportunity lay among the 45 per cent abstaining voters:

> But such voters are persons who, for various reasons, pay little attention to politics. McCarthy's candidacy is for those connoisseurs who pay attention. . . . Obviously McCarthy's appeal will be to persons with sensitive ears, persons to whom politics, like

ballet, has only one 'use', the pleasure it gives the watcher. His candidacy will render an almost aesthetic judgment on the competition, and will appeal to persons who savor the manner that maketh this man.

According to this conception, possessing the faculty of judgment means being a genuine spectator of the particulars that present themselves to one's purview, having a true spectator's appreciation of them.

The concept of spectator seems to imply a distinction between spectatorship and participant involvement, or between spectator judgment and agency. What we are after here is not an objectified classification of political beings into the categories of agent and spectator (as if one could be one to the exclusion of the other). Rather, what we are after is a clarification of what it means to be a political being, *überhaupt*. And here, I think, the concept of the spectator is of help to us.

Needless to say there are radically different senses in which one can be said to be a spectator. One mode of spectator judgment is that of poetics, or the reflective understanding of drama. A radically different mode of spectator judgment is the supposedly 'neutral' judgment of the detached political scientist in search of empirical trends and causal generalizations. Here we may introduce a distinction between understanding spectatorship and objectifying spectatorship. The former is a mode of hermeneutic judgment: it seeks to understand rather than simply to explain; it seeks to encompass the full human dimensions of that which it judges. Understanding judgment tends to be historical, retrospective, concerned to reflect on the meaning of what has occurred historically. Historical judgment is (or should be) a form of understanding spectatorship, as opposed to objectifying spectatorship, which tends to have as its overriding aim, control, and therefore prediction. The former asks: 'What are the human implications of this historical occurrence?'; the latter asks: 'How is the present state of affairs to be brought under human control?' One 'opens itself' to the given, the other seeks to impose its will upon the given. Do both of these two modes of judgment have equal claim to the title of 'spectator'?

When we consider that the explicit purpose of the analysis is 'disclosure of what it means to be a political being', a radical asymmetry between these two modes of spectator judgment comes into view. Objectifying judgment distances itself from the lived experience of political agents, for purposes of 'scientific' control, whereas understanding judgment seeks to penetrate into the actual experiential horizons of those involved in a situation, to gain hermeneutic appreciation of the agents' own understanding of their situation. Understanding judgment seeks to penetrate into what it means to be a political being; objectifying judgment abstracts from this lived experience of the political being in order to extrapolate invisible laws governing his situation. If our aim is to acquire access to the meaning of being a political being, which involves an internal rather than external relationship to political experience, then clearly one of these modes of spectatorship must be privileged over the other. The objectifying social scientist aspires to a form of spectatorship that is entirely removed from the common concerns and shared perspectives in which one will seek to partake as a genuine observer and student of politics.

To isolate the concept of the spectator implies a disjunction of political judgment into prudential judgment (the judgment of the involved participant) and spectator judgment (the judgment of one who stands back and reflects). However, within spectator judgment itself we have uncovered a further disjunction, between the reflective understanding of the historian and the objectifying prediction of the social scientist. Both the reflective understanding of the historian and the prudential judgment of the political actor are modes of reflective judgment; they see political happenings 'from the inside', applying the kind of concrete understanding that is only possible 'from the inside'. In other words, understanding spectatorship is closer to prudential judgment (the participant judgment of the actor) than it is to the objectifying spectatorship of the social scientist seeking causal, nomological, explanation and prediction. The latter mode of spectatorship is judgment seeking to overcome itself, to transcend the limits of finite, historical, reflective understanding of ourselves. Conversely, genuine spectatorship, in common with prudential judgment, is inescapably hermeneutic; it strives for an 'insider's' view of human affairs. But such spectatorship is also inescapably historical; it reflects on what has been. (This distinguishes it from the actor's prudential deliberation on what shall be.) And in this respect, political judgment in the mode of the spectator is akin to poetics, the understanding of drama. The political spectator, like the dramatic spectator, asks: 'What is the meaning of what I have seen?'

The function of the spectator is to interpret, to understand, and to judge. If we are not mistaken, these activities of understanding and judging the 'drama' of human affairs are at the very heart of political experience, of what it means to be politically. This renders an 'ontology of politics' that looks to language, understanding, and judgment as jointly constituting the ontological medium of political life.

We have argued that there are two modes of reflective judgment, the prudential judgment of the actor and the historical judgment of the spectator. But to do no more than offer this distinction is in itself misleading, for of course the concepts of spectator and actor are far more intricate and logically complex than the distinction alone suggests; there is a dialectical relationship here that we have not even begun to capture in theory. Even the most passionately involved agent remains in a significant sense a spectator so long as he continues to possess the faculty of independent reason. And even the most disinterested spectator remains in a significant sense a participant so long as he shares the concepts that enable him to make sense of the thing witnessed as the very thing that it is. Participation and spectatorship compose the strands of a common fabric, and this fabric constitutes the medium of human being-in-the-world. Each moment of such dwelling in a human world is, *simultaneously*, an act of shared involvement and critical distance. To regard exclusively either the agent-dimension or the spectator-dimension is a presumption of theoretical abstraction. And yet this reflexive awareness must not inhibit us from distinguishing these concepts and focusing our attention on one or the other. At the same time, we must strive for a dialectical grasp of their interconnection.

To be in possession of the faculty of judgment is to be (among other things) a spectator of human affairs. Here again the question offers itself: but if we judge poorly, carelessly, or indeed atrociously, are we still spectators in this sense, or pseudo-spectators (attenuated spectators), or do we cease to be genuine spectators at all? We appear to have some basis (or at least, some temptation) for saying all three. We find ourselves saying: 'He seems to be judging in *some* fashion or other, and yet he doesn't *really* seem to be judging. Anyone who *really* sought to attend to these particulars (as one ought when one seeks to judge) would not be *capable* of missing the point the way *he* is missing the point.' Real judgment, we might say, is the expression of agency and autonomy, rather than being the product of passivity and mere convention.

In appealing to the notion of spectatorship, we have no intention at all of acquiescing in the progressive transformation of politics in the contemporary age of mass media into a kind of 'video pageant' (where political events are specifically enacted for the benefit of a television-viewing audience). Every polity is classifiable according to the principle by which it is inspired. Our polity is distinguished, according to its motivating principle, by *boredom*. Politics is turned into mass spectacle, in the hope of jolting us out of our collective inertia and numbness. But the spectacle offered us is commended not by the quality elicited in judgment, but by the force with which it seeks to impress itself upon our sensations. 'Spectacular' politics is turned into a sensorium of affects rather than being reserved to active judgment. The spectacle of modern politics is governed by *pathos* rather than *praxis*, and the subjects of this spectacle are 'patients' absorbing stimuli rather than 'agents' exercising active discrimination and intelligent reflection.

The effort to define or provide theoretical analysis of political judgment does not actually supply a means of recognizing a particular instance of judgment or yield a criterion for determining who possesses judgment. (Indeed, it would be self-contradictory and a betrayal of our definition of judgment to claim otherwise.) Rather, we know what political judgment is, in this sense, only when we encounter *exemplars* (or examples) of judgment, that is, men and women who judge with impeccable consistency and skill, who have mastered the issues from every possible angle, and who embody the full ensemble of qualities needed to render the appropriate verdict. We shall grasp the nature of political judgment only when we are presented with exemplary judges of political affairs[2] (just as we were able to clarify the notion of a lack of judgment only by considering an exemplary figure, namely Eichmann). Political judgment discloses itself only in an exemplary performance, just as aesthetic judgment only discloses itself when we witness someone actually rendering the appropriate verdict upon some particular aesthetic object. Judgment cannot be fully rendered by abstract definition or analysis: we know it when we see it, and when we see it, we see it embodied in some exemplary judging subject.

Example or exemplification is so important for judgment because judgment is bound so closely to particulars, both the particular object that is judged and the particular subject that does the judging. Judgment never occurs in the abstract; it attaches to a particular object and a particular subject. Obviously, it would be impossible to say in advance what *would* be an exemplary act of judgment, for judgment itself involves the capacity for distinguishing what is relevant from what is irrelevant in a given case, and this almost by definition cannot be specified in advance. Judgment is therefore irreducible to algorithm, in the sense of formulation of fully explicit criteria of judgment. What is required is not a 'decision procedure', but an education in hermeneutic insight, taste, and understanding. Consequently the designation of a particular judging subject as exemplary is always a polemical choice, that is, subject to debate and contention (therefore *itself* a matter of judgment). Still, certain men and women do seem to command widely acknowledged (if not universal) authority in certain matters; people place justifiable confidence in their judgments.

Who are these exemplary persons of judgment? They may be journalists, diplomats, or statesmen, historians or ordinary citizens, and they *may* even be political theorists and philosophers, although theoretical insight is by no means a guarantee of political judgment, for the mastery of universals is quite distinct from the capacity for recognizing particulars. (The case of the journalists is a particularly fascinating topic for consideration, since journalists must make their judgments in extreme haste, sizing up political situations and political personalities on a day-to-day basis under the pressure of public scrutiny. Despite a general decline in the standards and status of journalism, there remain some exemplary practitioners of this eminently political art: examples that come to mind include Conor Cruise O'Brien's columns on Ireland and the Middle East in the London *Observer*, Colin Legum's reports on southern Africa, also (formerly) in the *Observer*, and Leopold Unger's articles on eastern Europe, specifically Poland, in the *International Herald Tribune*.) The person of exemplary judgment possesses a certain detachment from the issues being judged, and thus is not swept up into the immediacy of passion and prejudice that often attends pressing political issues. And yet he or she must also possess long and rich experience in the circumstances and context, temporal and spatial, that give to the affairs being judged their particular shape or contour. We can judge only on the basis of a great deal of antecedent knowledge, but we can only put this knowledge to work in freedom from the immediacy of passion and interest. We may be passionately concerned, but must not be driven by passion; we may be intensely interested in the complexities of the case, yet we must exercise our freedom of reflection disinterestedly. Exemplars of judgment do this, and they do it with marvellous adeptness.

Political judgment is not something specified in advance by the formulation of criteria; rather it is something 'exemplified'. We know it when we apprehend it in its concrete exemplification, and not before. Without examples or exemplars to reflect on we could not even begin to imagine what it would be to exercise such a faculty. We ourselves are schooled in the exercise of this faculty by observing the exemplary performances of others. We learn by example.3

At an earlier stage of these reflections we defined political judgment as 'the comprehensive faculty' by which we come to terms with political phenomena. What was meant here in calling this faculty 'comprehensive'? I think the only way of answering this is by showing how the genuine exemplar of judgment embodies this comprehensiveness, exercising his faculty of judgment comprehensively. The concrete exercise of political judgment is always comprehensive, and we know this as soon as we are confronted with a true exemplar. This recalls what we were saying earlier about the fact that political judgment in the proper sense can never abstract from the humane dimension of judgment, in the widest sense (or at least, it so abstracts only at heavy cost to its own integrity as political judgment). If judgment is to be properly political (and not some feeble approximation to the political), it must be open to the domain of moral judgment, aesthetic judgment, and so on; for in order to make sense of human ends, as we must do constantly in our political judgments, we must make sense of them in their full human dimensions (comprehending the moral, the aesthetic, etc.). Nothing known to man is foreign to political judgment. It must comprehend the full range of human experience. Let me cite one instance. We may perhaps think of judgments of character, judgments of persons and of personal qualities, as a facet of private life, as possessing an intimacy far removed from the abstract impersonality of public life. (The assumption may be that politics concerns the workings of institutions rather than the disclosure of persons.) But in fact judgments of persons and of personal character form a large and essential aspect of political judgment, and anyone who is a poor judge of character or whose judgment of persons is deficient will be likewise deficient in matters of political judgment.

The judging of persons is a mode of moral judgment or, one might say, hermeneutic judgment. It rests upon qualities of moral insight, imagination, keen sensitivity, and capacity for fine discriminations. Political judgment is comprehensive insofar as it 'comprehends' this mode of moral-hermeneutic judgment. An indispensable condition of political understanding is the capacity to judge persons, to 'size up' their qualities of integrity, competence, moral intelligence, or the lack of these qualities – to extract the essence of their character. We would not credit the political judgments of someone whom we found to be morally obtuse with respect to the judgment of persons, for his judgments would be missing an essential dimension. In this respect (as in every other) political judgment appears as a comprehensive faculty, for it 'comprehends' a multitude of moral-aesthetic capacities. In judging the political world we exercise taste, but it is a faculty of taste as all-encompassing as human experience itself. To possess the ability to render political judgments with exemplary skill is to comprehend the entirety of human experience, for only someone with a thorough acquaintance with the full range of needs, desires, potentialities of human beings can possibly succeed in delivering a conclusive verdict on any given aspect of political life. One might say that political judgment requires a knowledge of the human soul.

But a serious problem remains. For if, as we have claimed, political judgment is a truly comprehensive faculty of human beings, how are we to individuate it in relation to other modes of judgment such as aesthetic judgment, moral judgment, historical judgment, and so on? In asserting its claim to comprehensiveness, do we not thereby deprive the political of all distinctness as an identifiable field of judgment? Indeed, how can we answer opposing claims to the effect that only philosophical, or perhaps religious, experience can realize the comprehensiveness with which we credit political experience? Must we not return to the narrow conception of political judgment with which we started, according to which it consists in pragmatic, or instrumental, or (in the narrow sense) prudential consideration of what is advisable under the circumstances, given an assessment of the possibilities and an anticipation of expected or likely consequences? With this we find ourselves back within a highly contracted horizon of judgment. We cannot pretend to have a satisfactory answer to such objections; even to attempt to deal with the host of issues opened up by these difficult questions would involve defining the precise scope of the political itself – which it would be impossible to undertake here. Clearly, political judgment as a distinct mode of judgment stands in need of some principle of individuation. But rather than presuming to fulfil this demand, we shall merely affirm that no delimitation of the political on the basis of prevalent assumptions about the nature of politics can possibly do justice to that which has guided the present inquiry, namely, the question of what it means to be a political being *überhaupt*.

We do not claim to have exhausted the topic with these somewhat random concluding reflections; our treatment has been far from systematic. But the topic is not easily exhausted, for – as we have argued – it is a *comprehensive* faculty of human beings, one that comprehends the full dimensions of what it is to be human. But even more or less random observations on this faculty lead us to reflection on the actual capacities of human beings, and therewith, on what it means to be human.

Why this preoccupation with the concept of judging? Why does one make the effort to clarify our understanding of the concept? To be sure, there is a merit in conceptual clarification that is in need of no further justification, whatever the concept singled out for attention. But is analysis of *this* concept privileged in some special way? I am convinced that it is, for judging is in important respects the mark of our humanity; it contributes to the humanizing of our world as no other human faculty does. To attempt to reflect on this human capacity is thus to meditate on what is distinctive of our humanity, on what it is to be human or to constitute a human world.

There is another, perhaps more historically specific, reason for exploring the concept of judging. Judgment, we have argued, is a quintessential faculty of political beings. The contemporary political world, however, allows very little outlet for genuinely political activity, and offers ever diminishing scope for the political dimension of our existence. But judgment, because it is an act of mental reflection, can operate more or less independently of the actual political conditions within which men happen to find themselves situated. It has the inherent capacity to *free* itself from whatever contingent circumstances encumber and constrain human possibilities. This is implied in the twofold character of human judgment: the judging actor deliberates from *within* his actual situation; the judging spectator reflects *on* the actual situation, but his very reflection upon it liberates him from the constraints of the moment. Therefore, attending to the faculty of judgment may be a way of recouping one's status as a citizen, in a world that systematically frustrates any real sense of citizenship. (Judging then becomes a kind of vicarious political action!) Judgment, as well as being the condition of actual political engagement, when that is possible, also provides some compensation for the eclipse of the political. When deprived of the possibility of meaningfully affecting, and therefore meaningfully deliberating about, the basic conditions governing the shape of the world we share with others (and those conditions are increasingly being placed out of our control, so that they confront us as merely external givens), we can at least continue to judge – and in this, hope finds a refuge.

What is political judgment? What does it mean to be in possession of such a faculty, and to exercise it as men do? This question seems so simple, yet, because it is a philosophical question, the answer tends constantly to elude our grasp. If we could succeed in answering the question, we could perhaps secure insights into why a sense of political citizenship is indispensable to human agency. It would be wrong, however, to imagine that an analysis of political judgment could provide a direct guide to actual political conduct. There is no reason to accord to the theorist any special prerogative in pronouncing upon questions of political judgment (the tasks of theory are less proximate). It would be unreasonable to expect everyone to become theorists in order to occupy themselves with politics. It is, on the other hand, entirely reasonable to expect everyone to be concerned with, and involve themselves in, political affairs.

Adolf Eichmann lacks the faculty of judging; you and I do not lack it, we possess and exercise it regularly (or at the very least, our failings, where they arise, are nowhere near as glaringly obvious as his). This seems both the commonest of truisms and among the more far-reaching of philosophical insights into the condition of being a political being. Yet is it not the case that philosophical problems of utmost interest very often have this character, and, by attending to what is most familiar, carry us furthest in illuminating the situation of man?

Notes

CHAPTER 1 WHAT IS POLITICAL JUDGMENT?

1 Hans-Georg Gadamer, 'Hermeneutics and social science', *Cultural Hermeneutics*, 2 (4), 316.

2 Norman Jacobson, *Pride and Solace*, Berkeley, University of California Press, 1978, 18–19.

3 St Thomas Aquinas, 'Treatise on prudence and justice', in *Summa Theologicæ*, second part of second part, questions 47–79 (esp. questions 47–56, 60).

4 Bhikhu Parekh, 'The nature of political philosophy', in Preston King and B. C. Parekh (eds), *Politics and Experience*, Cambridge, Cambridge University Press, 1968, 197.

5 Further clarification is required here. One can distinguish three principal meanings of judgment: (1) judgment as a *logical* operation, by which we assert or negate propositions; (2) judgment as a *cognitive* faculty, or a distinct sphere of mental activity; and (3) judgment as a *practical* faculty, or what might otherwise be called prudence. (Cf. *The Great Ideas: A Syntopicon*, vol. 2, chapter 41 ('Judgment'), Chicago, University of Chicago, 1952, 835–42.) Parekh, in speaking of the idealists' concern with judgment, refers to the concept of judgment in a way that embraces senses (1) and (2). On the other hand, our concern in this work is addressed to the concept of judgment in a way that embraces senses (2) and (3). The concept of judgment has traditionally figured very prominently in treatises in logic, and in

this the idealists were following a much older tradition. But the term has been much less prominent in treatises of political philosophy. What is sought are investigations into what, following Parekh, may be called the epistemology of politics.

6 It may be objected that the philosophical tradition does offer theories of moral judgment that are readily applicable to politics: for instance, natural law, utilitarianism, and the Kantian Categorical Imperative. However, these are theories concerning the *basis* or grounds of valid judgment, rather than theories about the judging faculty itself. They specify what are the correct criteria for forming judgments, rather than inquire into what judgment actually is or explore the conditions that govern the very process of judging. Moreover, in so far as they claim to supply universal rules or principles for determining all judgment, such theories situate politics within the sphere of determinant judgment, and fail to capture the dimension of reflective judgment that characterizes the world of human affairs as something not calculable but essentially dramatic.

7 Ludwig Wittgenstein, *Philosophical Investigations*, 3rd edn, New York, Macmillan, 1968, para. 129, 50.

8 See Hannah Arendt, *Lectures on Kant's Political Philosophy*, ed. Ronald Beiner, Chicago, University of Chicago Press, 1982.

9 In this paragraph I have borrowed from the helpful discussion of these three meanings of judgment in *The Great Ideas: A Syntopicon*, chapter 41 ('Judgment').

10 Aquinas, *Summa Theologicæ*, 2a2æ, question 60, article 1.

11 For a good summary of the relevant issues, see Thomas McCarthy, 'A theory of communicative competence', in Paul Connerton (ed.), *Critical Sociology*, Harmondsworth, Penguin, 1976, 470–97.

CHAPTER 2 POSSIBLE AVENUES OF INQUIRY

1 For a more comprehensive account of Hannah Arendt's theory of judging, see my interpretive essay accompanying her *Lectures on Kant's Political Philosophy*, Chicago, University of Chicago Press, 1982. For present purposes, I confine myself to her earlier writings on the theme of judgment.

2 Hannah Arendt, *The Human Condition*, Chicago, University of Chicago Press, 1958, 199.

3 Arendt, 'What is freedom?', in *Between Past and Future: Eight Exercises in Political Thought*, enlarged edn, New York, Viking Press, 1968, 153–4.

4 ibid., 154–5.

5 Sophocles, *Oedipus at Colonus*, lines 1224 ff.

6 Arendt, *On Revolution*, New York, Viking Press, 1965, 285.

7 Arendt, 'Thinking and moral considerations: a lecture', *Social Research*, 38 (3), 446.

8 Arendt, 'Freedom and politics', in A. Hunold (ed.), *Freedom and Serfdom: An Anthology of Western Thought*, Dordrecht, D. Reidel, 1961, 207.

9 Arendt, unpublished lecture from a course at the University of Chicago on 'Kant's political philosophy', Fall 1964, Hannah Arendt Papers, Library of Congress, Container 41, 032272.

10 ibid., 032259.

11 Arendt, 'The crisis in culture: its social and its political significance', in *Between Past and Future*, 218.

12 ibid., 219.

13 ibid., 220.

14 ibid., 221.

15 Arendt, 'The concept of history', in *Between Past and Future*, 53.

16 Arendt, 'The crisis in culture', 222.

17 ibid., 223.

18 Arendt, 'Truth and politics', in *Between Past and Future*, 241.

19 ibid.

20 ibid., 241-2.

21 ibid., 242.

22 Arendt, 'The crisis in culture', 225.

23 ibid., 226.

24 ibid., 223.

25 ibid.

26 ibid., 224 (italics mine).

27 Arendt, 'The concept of history', 52.

28 Arendt, 'The crisis in culture', 210.

29 Cf. Arendt, 'The concept of history', 64: the function of the historian is 'to say what is'; and 81: meanings cannot be 'made', but, 'like truth, will only disclose or reveal themselves'.

30 With the burgeoning of interest in Gadamer's work, a large literature on hermeneutics has developed. For an influential attempt to apply hermeneutics to the social sciences, see Charles Taylor, 'Interpretation and the sciences of man', *Review of Metaphysics*, 25 (3), 3-51; and for a more recent defence of hermeneutics in the context of the philosophy of science, see Richard Rorty, *Philosophy and the Mirror of Nature*, Princeton, Princeton University Press, 1979, chapters 7-8.

31 Hans-Georg Gadamer, *Truth and Method*, New York, Seabury Press, 1975, 38-9.

32 Arendt, 'The crisis in culture', 224, 297, n. 17.

33 Gadamer, *Truth and Method*, 10.

34 ibid., 19–29 ('*Sensus communis*'). Gadamer refers to Vico's *On the Study Methods of Our Time*, and to Shaftesbury's *Characteristics*, treatise II ('*Sensus Communis: an essay on the freedom of wit and humour*'), esp. part III, § 1.

35 See Gadamer, *Truth and Method*, 22, 26, 29.

36 ibid., 31.

37 Kant, *Critique of Judgment*, §60; and *Anthropology from a Pragmatic Point of View*, §§42–4, 67–71. Cf. Gadamer, *Truth and Method*, 41. Kant himself remarks, in the preface to the *Critique of Judgment*: 'The present investigation of taste, as a faculty of aesthetic judgment, not being undertaken with a view to the formation or culture of taste, (which will pursue its course in the future, as in the past, independently of such inquiries,) but being merely directed to its transcendental aspects, I feel assured of its indulgent criticism in respect of any shortcomings on that score.'

38 Relevant here is Arendt's appeal to Lessing's aesthetics: Lessing was not at all concerned with 'the perfection of the work of art in itself', but 'rather . . . in agreement with Aristotle . . . concerned with the effect upon the spectator, who as it were represents the world, or rather, that worldly space which has come into being between the artist or writer and his fellow men as a world common to them' (Arendt, 'On humanity in dark times', in *Men in Dark Times*, Harmondsworth, Penguin, 1973, 14).

39 Gadamer, *Truth and Method*, 80 ff., 278 ff., 472, 489–90. See also Gadamer, 'Practical philosophy as a model of the human sciences', *Research in Phenomenology*, vol. 9, 74–85.

40 Arendt, 'Truth and politics', 241.

41 Jürgen Habermas, 'On the German-Jewish heritage', *Telos*, vol. 44, 128.

42 ibid., 130–1.

43 Habermas, *Legitimation Crisis*, London, Heinemann, 1976, 95.

44 ibid., 115.

45 ibid., 100.

46 ibid., 120.

47 ibid., 105.

48 ibid.

49 ibid., 107.

50 ibid., 108.

51 To the extent that Habermas' theory is a Kantian one, it falls subject to the same kinds of difficulties that are common to all Kantian moral theories (that is, all theories, from Hare to Rawls, seeking a rational procedure for universalizing moral judgments): namely, how far can one distance oneself from the particular and the contingent without taking leave of the human moral situation altogether? In Habermas' case the problem is whether the subjects in the ideal speech situation retain their

real identities, or whether the conditions of undistorted communication can only be met by positing the equivalent of a transcendental subject stripped of all the parochial attachments and commitments that constitute the identity of actual subjects. For a discussion of problems in defining Habermas' idea of universalization, with reference to Rawls and J. L. Mackie, see Steven Lukes, 'Of gods and demons: Habermas and practical reason', in John B. Thompson and David Held (eds), *Habermas: Critical Debates*, London, Macmillan, 1982, 134–48.

52 *Legitimation Crisis*, 108.
53 ibid., 109.
54 ibid., 108.
55 ibid., 110.
56 ibid.
57 ibid., 123.
58 Habermas, 'Hannah Arendt's communications concept of power', *Social Research*, 44 (1), 22–3.
59 See, for instance, *Critique of Judgment*, §§ 1, 38 (remark): 'the judgment of taste is not a cognitive judgment'.
60 For an Aristotelian account of cognitivist moral psychology, see John McDowell, 'Virtue and reason', *The Monist*, 62 (3), 331–50.

CHAPTER 3   KANT'S CONCEPT OF TASTE

1 Jürgen Habermas, 'The classical doctrine of politics in relation to social philosophy', in *Theory and Practice*, trans. John Viertel, London, Heinemann, 1974, 286, n. 4.
2 Hans-Georg Gadamer, *Truth and Method*, New York, Seabury Press, 1975, xvii–xviii. See Kant, *Critique of Pure Reason*, trans. N. K. Smith, New York, St Martin's Press, 1963, 59, 96. On the concept of transcendental inquiry, see Charles Taylor, 'The opening arguments of the *Phenomenology*', in Alasdair MacIntyre (ed.), *Hegel*, New York, Anchor, 1972, 151–87; and Stanley Cavell, *Must We Mean What We Say?*, Cambridge, Cambridge University Press, 1976, 64–5.
3 See Habermas, *Knowledge and Human Interests*, trans. J. J. Shapiro, Boston, Beacon Press, 1971.
4 See Habermas, 'On systematically distorted communication', *Inquiry*, 1970, vol. 13, 205–18; 'Towards a theory of communicative competence', *Inquiry*, 1970, vol. 13, 360–75; 'Some distinctions in universal pragmatics', *Theory and Society*, 1976, vol. 3, 155–67; and 'What is universal pragmatics?', in *Communication and the Evolution of Society*, Boston, Beacon Press, 1979, 1–68.

5 See Kant, *Foundations of the Metaphysics of Morals*, trans. L. W. Beck, Indianapolis, Bobbs-Merrill, 1959, 29 ff.

6 For an important discussion of some of these problems, in the context of Rawls' Kantianism, see Michael Sandel, *Liberalism and the Limits of Justice*, Cambridge, Cambridge University Press, 1982.

7 This and all the following references to Kant's *Critique of Judgment* are to the translation by James Creed Meredith, Oxford, Clarendon Press, 1952. In the brackets, the section reference corresponds to the original numbering of the *Critique of Judgment*; this is followed by a page citation referring to the Meredith translation. In the Meredith edition, separate page numbering is given for the 'Critique of aesthetic judgment' and the 'Critique of teleological judgment', so 'I' or 'II' serves to indicate whether the page reference is to part I or part II. (Certain words in the quotations have been de-italicized or changed from upper case to lower case so as not overly to distract the reader.)

8 The original German text reads: 'Aber hier wird die Allgemeinheit nur comparativ genommen; und da giebt es nur generale (wie die empirischen alle sind), nicht universale Regeln', referring to judgments of the agreeable *as opposed to* judgments of taste. Of course, the German term *allgemein* comprehends both the 'general' and the 'universal'. Consequently, when Kant speaks of a validity that is *allgemein*, it is always ambiguous whether he is claiming for judgments of taste a universality analogous to that of moral judgments, or mere generality related to empirical human communities. This passage is therefore of crucial importance in clarifying the scope of Kant's *Allgemeinheit*. Kant's point is that judgments of taste, like representations of the good (and unlike judgments based on mere sociability), elicit 'universal delight', but that this universality rests upon a different *basis*: universal judgments of the good are arrived at *by means of a concept*, whereas judgments of the beautiful, like judgments of the agreeable, are not.

9 See §9; I: 59 and §59; I: 221–2. Heidegger (in *Kant and the Problem of Metaphysics*) goes so far as to locate in the schematism the key to the entire *Critique of Pure Reason*, inasmuch as the schematism (at least as presented in the first edition of the *Critique*) serves to establish the utter centrality of Transcendental Imagination. Cf. Arendt, 'Imagination', in *Lectures on Kant's Political Philosophy*, ed. R. Beiner, Chicago, University of Chicago Press, 1982, 79–85.

10 Nathan Rotenstreich argues that Burke was quite as well aware of the transcendental, and pluralistic, aspects of taste as Kant was. According to Rotenstreich, Burke speaks about taste as a form of judgment. Burke assumes that taste is not an egoistic quality but is related to the agreement

of mankind, therefore pluralistic. 'For Burke what is called taste is not a simple idea; it is made up of a perception of the primary pleasures of sense, of the secondary pleasures of the imagination, and of the conclusions of the reasoning faculty, as well as the various relations of these and their relations to human fashions, manners, and actions' (Rotenstreich, 'Sublimity and terror', *Idealistic Studies*, 3 (3), 238–9).

11 It must be emphasized, however, that the moral individual, for Kant, is always conceived as an instantiation of the universal, namely, universal human dignity. Therefore it would be more accurate to speak of the 'autonomy of the universal as instantiated in the individual' rather than of 'the autonomy of the individual'. But this emphasis on the universal actually grounds rather than contradicts his moral individualism.

12 Rotenstreich, 'Sublimity and terror'.

13 See Habermas, 'The classical doctrine of politics in relation to social philosophy', 42.

14 Kant, *Foundations of the Metaphysics of Morals*, 31 ff.

15 Kant, *Critique of Practical Reason*, §VIII, remark II, in *Kant's Critique of Practical Reason and Other Works on the Theory of Ethics*, trans. Thomas Kingsmill Abbott, 6th edn, London, Longmans, 1909, 126.

16 Kant, *Foundations of the Metaphysics of Morals*, 33–4, 36.

17 Kant, *Critique of Practical Reason*, 126.

18 ibid., 124–5.

19 ibid., 125.

20 'On the common saying: "This may be true in theory, but it does not apply in practice"', in *Kant's Political Writings*, ed. Hans Reiss, trans. H. B. Nisbet, Cambridge, Cambridge University Press, 1971, 70.

21 ibid., 71.

22 ibid., 86 (italics mine).

23 ibid., 80.

24 ibid., 86.

25 ibid., 80.

26 ibid., 89.

27 Cf. *The Great Ideas: A Syntopicon*, vol. 3, chapter 73 ('Prudence'), Chicago, University of Chicago, 1952, 475: 'In Kant's view, Aristotle and Aquinas, no less than Mill, are pragmatists rather than moralists. They are all utilitarians in the sense that they regard happiness as the first principle of human conduct and concern themselves with the ordering of means to this end. Since the consideration of means necessarily involves the weighing of alternatives as more or less expedient, prudence becomes indispensable to the pursuit of happiness. The choice of the best means is second in importance only to the election of the right end. Kant admits that those

who live for happiness require a great deal of prudence, in order to adapt practical rules to variable circumstances and to make the proper exceptions in applying them. None is required by those who live according to the moral law.' Also, see Pierre Aubenque, 'La prudence chez Kant' (*Revue de métaphysique et morale*, vol. 80, 1975, 156–82), for a thorough examination of 'Kant's polemic against the traditional doctrine of prudence'.

28 'Perpetual peace', in *Kant's Political Writings*, 112–13 (italics mine).
29 ibid., 114 (italics mine).
30 ibid., 122.
31 ibid., 117.
32 ibid., 122 (italics mine).
33 ibid.
34 ibid., 105.
35 'Theory and practice', in *Kant's Political Writings*, 86, 80.
36 ibid., 83. Happiness does play an important role in Kant's practical philosophy, not as a motive for practice but as an ultimate reward for virtue that we are compelled to posit as a necessary postulate of practical reason. See the discussion of the concept of *summum bonum* in the *Critique of Practical Reason*, part I, book II ('Dialectic of pure practical reason').
37 'Theory and practice', 82–3.
38 Nietzsche: '"That is beautiful", said Kant, "which gives us pleasure *without interest*". Without interest! Compare with this definition one framed by a genuine "spectator" and artist – Stendhal, who once called the beautiful *une promesse de bonheur*. At any rate he *rejected* and repudiated the one point about the aesthetic condition which Kant had stressed: *le désintéressement*. Who is right, Kant or Stendhal?' ('Genealogy of Morals', third essay, §6, *Basic Writings of Nietzsche*, ed. Walter Kaufman, New York, Modern Library, 1968, 540).

CHAPTER 4 ARISTOTLE'S CONCEPT OF PRUDENCE

1 See John McDowell, 'Virtue and reason', *The Monist*, 62 (3), 331. Cf. 345–6: Cognitivism holds that the rationality of virtue is 'recognizable only from within the practice'; whereas non-cognitivism insists upon demonstration from 'a neutral external standpoint'.
2 Aristotle, *Nicomachean Ethics*, 1143a25–30; trans. Martin Ostwald, Indianapolis, Bobbs-Merrill, 1965, 165. (All page references to the *Ethics* are to the Ostwald translation.)
3 Eric Voegelin, 'What is right by nature?', in *Anamnesis*, ed. Gerhart Niemeyer, Notre Dame, University of Notre Dame Press, 1978, 69–70.

4 *Nicomachean Ethics*, 1143a12–16; 164–5.

5 ibid., 165, n. 47 (Ostwald's note).

6 ibid., 311 (glossary): 'In its most rudimentary sense, *pathos* is the opposite of *praxis*, "action", and denotes anything which befalls a person or which he experiences.'

7 To pursue this a bit further, we might find it instructive to consider how natural it is for us in (contemporary) English to use the expression 'to feel with' another, and conversely, to what extent we are at a loss for expressions that convey sympathy in the sense of 'judging with' another. ('Conscience' and 'consciousness', according to their original etymology, implied 'knowing with', but these terms have been thoroughly subjectivized.) An aphorism of Nietzsche's reads: 'Fellowship in joy, and not sympathy in sorrow, makes people friends' (*Human, All-too-Human*, vol. I, no. 499). A term such as 'fellowship' is required to communicate the idea of 'judgment in sympathy'. Sympathy itself, on the other hand, connotes participation in suffering, and thus is enmeshed in the purely passive associations of the word 'suffer', such as is preserved in more antiquated English usages (e.g. 'suffer them to come'). Such passive connotations oppose the notion of 'judging-with', which implies 'acting-with'. Naturally, one should tread carefully when making appeal to arguments from etymology, yet it is intriguing to pursue the question of how human capacities are conceptualized within a given language-world, whether in terms of active or passive dispositions.

8 *Nicomachean Ethics*, 1095a1–5; 5–6.

9 ibid., 1095a5–8; 6 (Ostwald uses 'emotion' to translate *pathos*).

10 ibid., 1156a32–4; 219.

11 Hans-Georg Gadamer, *Truth and Method*, New York, Seabury Press, 1975, 288.

12 ibid., 289.

13 Gadamer, 'Hermeneutics and social science', *Cultural Hermeneutics*, 2 (4), 316.

14 *Truth and Method*, 288.

15 For further examination of this problem, see the section on 'Friendship versus love' in chapter 6 of this study.

16 *Nicomachean Ethics*, 1159b25–1160a10 (VIII.9); 231.

17 ibid., 1160a28–30; 232.

18 ibid., 256, n. 17 (Ostwald's note); 309 (glossary).

19 ibid., 1167a22–30; 256.

20 ibid., 1167b2–4; 257.

21 ibid., 1167b5–11; 257.

22 ibid., 1171a16–18; 269.

CHAPTER 5   JUDGMENT AND RHETORIC

1 Hans-Georg Gadamer, 'On the scope and function of hermeneutic reflection', in *Philosophical Hermeneutics*, ed. D. E. Linge, Berkeley, University of California Press, 1976, 21–6 ('Rhetoric and hermeneutics').

2 ibid., 21.

3 ibid., 22.

4 ibid., 24.

5 Giambattista Vico, *On the Study Methods of our Time*, trans. Elio Gianturco, Indianapolis, Bobbs-Merrill, 1965, 41. For discussion of the concept of 'topics', see Jürgen Habermas, 'The classical doctrine of politics in relation to social philosophy', in *Theory and Practice*, trans. J. Viertel, London, Heinemann, 41–81; and Wilhelm Hennis, 'Topics and political science', *Graduate Faculty Philosophy Journal*, 7 (1), 35–77.

6 All references in brackets in this section are to the *Rhetoric*. The translation used is that of W. Rhys Roberts, in *The Works of Aristotle*, vol. XI, ed. W. D. Ross, Oxford, Clarendon Press, 1924.

7 *Politics*, 1281b; *The Politics of Aristotle*, ed. Ernest Barker, Oxford, Clarendon Press, 1958, 123.

8 ibid., 1282a; 125.

9 ibid., 126.

10 *Nicomachean Ethics*, 1141b7–14; Ostwald trans., 157.

11 ibid., 1143a7–10; 164.

12 ibid., 164, n. 45 (Ostwald's note).

13 ibid., 1141b14–18; 157.

14 ibid., 1141a22–6; 156.

15 ibid., 1142a32–3; 161.

16 ibid., 1142b3–5; 162.

17 ibid., 1142b32–5; 163.

18 Gadamer, *Truth and Method*, New York, Seabury Press, 1975, 287.

19 ibid., 525, n. 225.

20 *Nicomachean Ethics*, 1142b27–33; 163.

21 ibid., 1140a25–30; 152.

22 ibid., 1140b5–10; 153.

23 ibid., 1094a1–5; 3.

24 ibid., 1094a22–25; 4.

25 One reason why Aristotle might have been inclined to regard rhetoric instrumentally is that he may not have sufficiently liberated himself from the understanding of language adumbrated by Plato. Leo Strauss suggests another, possibly more authentic, explanation for why Aristotle's provision of a philosophical rhetoric seems intended more as an instrument of

policy than as an affirmation of the mediacy of rhetoric: one cannot reason with everyone. One can reason only with gentlemen. The Many are not gentlemen. In situations where the Many are bent upon an unwise course of action, the wise statesman must have recourse to a form of persuasion that is closer to compulsion than to reason. A philosophical rhetoric supplies the principles of this form of persuasion, to ensure that wisdom is capable of making its voice heard. In short, politics is only partially discursive, and the philosophical (as opposed to sophistic) study of rhetoric makes allowance for this fact. (In fact, Strauss argues in chapter 3 of *The Political Philosophy of Hobbes* that Aristotle's *Rhetoric* was one of the main sources of inspiration for Hobbes' philosophical anthropology.) With the affirmation of deliberation and rhetoric, on the other hand, one tends to portray politics as fully discursive, which in turn assumes that all men are amenable to reason (a post-Enlightenment assumption). See Strauss, *The City and Man*, Chicago, University of Chicago Press, Midway Reprint, 1977, 22–3, 123, 127, 233.

    This reading of the classical argument poses a serious challenge to the concerns of modern hermeneuticists, to which challenge we may reply as follows: the forgoing line of argument assumes an access to wisdom that is antecedent to the effort of joint deliberation. But the judging of particulars with a view to policy affecting all is a matter to which deliberation is in a constitutive rather than external relation. Here wisdom cannot be removed from participation with others in deliberating about common ends. Furthermore, Aristotle himself in at least one place (*Politics*, III. 11) seems to admit this primacy of deliberation-in-common. But this different focus on the problem of rhetoric does not necessarily exclude classical insights into the limits of rational persuasion.

26 Arendt, *The Human Condition*, Chicago, University of Chicago Press, 1958, 26.

27 The section reference corresponds to the original numbering of the *Critique*. The following page citation refers to the Meredith translation, part I ('Critique of aesthetic judgment') or part II ('Critique of teleological judgment').

28 These terms are borrowed from Charles Taylor, who employed them in lectures (at Oxford) on Plato's conception of rhetoric.

CHAPTER 6   WITH SYMPATHY AND DETACHMENT: HORIZONS OF A COMPREHENSIVE PERSPECTIVE

1 I am conscious that the desire to do justice to both Kant and Aristotle entails the risk of doing justice to neither. Hence the force of Nietzsche's anti-Hegelian counterblast 'against mediators': 'Those who wish to be mediators between two resolute thinkers are marked as mediocre: they lack the eyes to see the unparalleled' ('The Gay Science', no. 228, *Basic Writings of Nietzsche*, ed. Walter Kaufman, New York, Modern Library, 1968, 173).

2 The term 'theory' is perhaps misleading here. Indeed it seems strange to speak of a *theory* of political judgment since this really amounts to theorizing about the limitations of theory. Therefore when I speak of a theory of judgment, I mean no more than reasoned reflection about the faculty of judgment.

3 Sheldon Wolin, review of Richard Sennett, *The Fall of Public Man*, in *New York Review of Books*, 14 April 1977, 24 (6), 19.

4 Blaise Pascal, *Pensées*, no. 114, trans. W. F. Trotter, New York, E. P. Dutton, 1958.

5 *Nicomachean Ethics*, 1094b27–1095a10; Ostwald trans., 5–6.

6 *Critique of Judgment*, §26; Meredith trans., 1: 99.

7 *Nicomachean Ethics*, 1142b3–6 (Book VI, chapter 9); 162.

8 Vico, *On the Study Methods of Our Time*, trans. Elio Gianturco, Indianapolis, Bobbs-Merrill, 1965, 35; quoted in Jürgen Habermas, 'The classical doctrine of politics in relation to social philosophy', *Theory and Practice*, trans. J. Viertel, London, Heinemann, 45.

9 Cf. Habermas, ibid., 75–6.

10 Among contemporary theorists, the concern with prudence has been a hallmark of the political philosophy of Michael Oakeshott. For a definition of prudential judgment, see Oakeshott's essay on 'Learning and teaching', in R. S. Peters (ed.), *The Concept of Education*, London, Routledge & Kegan Paul, 1967, esp. 167–8. Important discussions of prudential judgment are also presented in Sheldon Wolin, 'Political theory as a vocation', *American Political Science Review*, vol. 63, 1062–82; and Roberto M. Unger, *Knowledge and Politics*, New York, Free Press, 1975, 253–9 (chapter 6: 'Theory and prudence').

11 A theory of taste need not be formal; indeed, it is precisely on these grounds that Gadamer criticizes Kant's theory of taste. For a brief treatment of theories of taste, see Ernst Vollrath, 'That all governments rest on opinion', *Social Research*, 43 (1), 46–61. Vollrath considers the connection

between opinion, power, and taste in the thought of Montesquieu, Hume, and Madison.

12 Stanley Rosen, 'Return to the origin', *International Philosophical Quarterly*, 16 (2), 169.

13 ibid., 156–64.

14 See Thucydides, *History of the Peloponnesian War*, trans. Rex Warner, Harmondsworth, Penguin, 1954, 324.

15 Hegel, *Philosophy of Right*, para. 118, trans. T. M. Knox, Oxford, Clarendon Press, 1967, 80.

16 See Arendt, *Lectures on Kant's Political Philosophy*, ed. R. Beiner, Chicago, University of Chicago Press, 1982, 77; and commentary, ibid., 126–7.

17 It should be recalled that Kant defines determinant judgment as that where the universal (the rule, principle, or law) is given for the subsumption of the particular. Kant defines reflective judgment as that where only the particular is given and the universal has to be found for it (*Critique of Judgment*, introduction, IV; 1: 18). In what follows, unless otherwise specified, judgment will be intended in the narrow sense of strictly reflective judgment, and not in the broad sense, which of course includes determinant judgment.

18 This point is very vividly confirmed in Stuart Hampshire's essay 'Morality and pessimism', in Hampshire (ed.), *Public and Private Morality*, Cambridge, Cambridge University Press, 1978, 1–22; see also the critique of utilitarianism in Bernard Williams' essay 'Politics and moral character', in the same volume, 55–73.

19 Cf. Leo Strauss, *Natural Right and History*, Chicago, University of Chicago Press, 1953, 156–64. It may be argued that Aquinas' account of prudence, as compared with Aristotle's account of *phronesis*, is closer to 'determinant' than to 'reflective' judgment (that is, the ends are fixed, not 'dialectically' mediated by deliberation upon means). Consider, in particular, the definition of *synderesis* ('conscience') in *Summa Theologicæ*, 2a2æ47, 6 (cf. 2a2æ47, 15). *Synderesis* is not a concept that is to be found in Aristotle. But on this point certain ambiguities are present on both sides, the side of Aquinas as well as that of Aristotle.

Reflection on Thomist political science suggests the following thought: the ultimate implication of a theory of judgment is that there can be no political science in the full and strict sense; and conversely, the ultimate implication of a rigorous and self-conscious political science is that the exercise of judgment, in a reflective as opposed to a determinant sense, is superfluous. A science of politics is a theoretical ordering of ends and means (although political science in the modern sense, guided by the methodology of Max Weber, restricts itself to analysis of means, and categorically refuses to judge ends). The assertion of the primacy of judgment in politics implies that there cannot be a science of politics, except in the sense of a second-order political science which demonstrates the limitations of a first-order science of politics. Aristotle's meta-reflection on political *episteme* in the *Ethics* corresponds to the latter, second-order, political science.

20 See Kant, 'An answer to the question: "What is Enlightenment?"', *Kant's Political Writings*, ed. H. Reiss, Cambridge, Cambridge University Press, 1971, 54–60.

21 *Critique of Judgment*, § 32; 1: 138.

22 The fact that Kant does discuss moral pedagogy (in the moral catechism of *The Doctrine of Virtue* and the 'Methodology of pure practical reason' in the *Critique of Practical Reason*) does not, to my mind, negate the claim that Kant does not, and cannot, offer a concept of moral education and a concept of moral wisdom. It is true that Kant recognizes that a child (a pre-moral subject) can be initiated into the moral life by a form of pedagogy (a 'moral catechism'). But this is different from recognizing differential moral capacities, embodied in fixed moral 'habits' (what Aristotle refers to by the term *hexis*), so that one moral subject may rightfully instruct another moral subject. The latter cannot be given a coherent account within the terms of Kant's moral philosophy. But to show this would require a detailed account of why the discussion of moral taste in the *Anthropology* and the *Critique of Judgment* conflicts with the theoretical basis of Kant's moral philosophy.

23 Hence Kant defines taste as 'the faculty of estimating what makes our feeling in a given representation universally communicable *without the mediation of a concept*' (*Critique of Judgment*, § 40; 1: 153; italics mine).

24 This rendering of Kant is advanced, and the doctrine thus imputed to Kant subjected to penetrating critique, by Hubert Dreyfus in *What Computers Can't Do*, New York, Harper & Row, 1972, esp. 68–9, 90, 158, 160, and 240n.

25 Cf. Gadamer, *Truth and Method*, New York, Seabury Press, 1975, 30, 37, and 503, n. 68.

26 Arendt, *Eichmann in Jerusalem: A Report on the Banality of Evil*, revised and enlarged edn, New York, Viking Press, 1965, 166–7 (italics mine).

27 Maurice Merleau-Ponty, *Humanism and Terror*, Boston, Beacon Press, 1969, xxiv–xxv (italics mine).

28 ibid., 166–7.

29 In addition to *Eichmann in Jerusalem*, see Arendt, *Origins of Totalitarianism*, three vols, 4th edn, New York, Harcourt Brace Jovanovich, 1968; 'Understanding and politics', *Partisan Review*, 20 (4), 377–92; 'Organized

guilt and universal responsibility', *Jewish Frontier*, vol. v, 19–23; and 'Personal responsibility under dictatorship', *The Listener*, 6 August 1964, vol. 72, 185–7, 205.

30 H. H. Gerth and C. Wright Mills (eds), *From Max Weber*, New York, Oxford University Press, 1958, 128. It may be objected that what I describe as 'tragic' are merely obvious facts – namely, the inherent limitations of political practice and judgment – and that to lament the 'tragedy' of these limitations must amount to some misguided form of sentimentality or pusillanimity. The answer to this seems to me to run as follows: if one regards politics as a kind of rubbish-bin to which one consigns all the nastier bits of human relationships (as theorists inspired by Hobbes do), then of course one will find nothing at all tragic about it. But if one sees political life (as I do) as something fundamentally expressive of man's humanity, then the recognition of hard and intractable limits to political practice and judgment will indeed appear tragic.

31 Arendt, 'Truth and politics', in *Between Past and Future: Eight Exercises in Political Thought*, enlarged edn, New York, Viking Press, 1968, 262.

32 ibid.

33 Arendt, *The Human Condition*, Chicago, University of Chicago Press, 1958, 235, n. 75. Cf. Judith Shklar: 'Political philosophy is tragic thought. Without a dramatic sense of fate and mutability no rational intelligence would turn to this hideous subject' ('Hannah Arendt's triumph', *The New Republic*, 27 December 1975).

34 Arendt, *The Human Condition*, 243.

35 See the section on 'Aesthetic judgment and moral respect' in chapter 3 above.

36 Arendt, 'On humanity in dark times: thoughts about Lessing', in *Men in Dark Times*, Harmondsworth, Penguin, 1968, 33. Cf. Max Weber: 'the ultimate and most sublime values have retreated from public life . . . into the brotherliness of direct and personal human relations' ('Science as a vocation', in Gerth and Mills (eds), *From Max Weber*, 155).

37 Arendt, *Men in Dark Times*, 31–2.

38 Arendt, *The Human Condition*, 53.

39 Arendt, *Men in Dark Times*, 33.

40 ibid., 37–8 (italics mine).

41 Philip Roth, 'The new Jewish stereotypes', in M. Selzer (ed.), *Zionism Reconsidered*, New York, Macmillan, 1970, 114–15.

42 '"Eichmann in Jerusalem": An exchange of letters', *Encounter*, 22 (1), 51, 54. (The Scholem–Arendt exchange is reprinted in Arendt, *The Jew as Pariah*, ed. R. H. Feldman, New York, Grove Press, 1978, 240–51.)

43 *Encounter*, 22 (1), 52, 54.

44 Arendt, *On Revolution*, New York, Viking Press, 1963, 81.

45 Daniel Bell, 'The alphabet of justice', *Partisan Review*, Fall 1963, 30 (3), 417–29.

46 ibid., 429.

47 'Arguments: more on Eichmann', *Partisan Review*, Spring 1964, 31 (2), 253–83.

48 See Arendt, *Eichmann in Jerusalem*, 296: sympathy with the wrongdoer 'may kindle a spirit of forgiveness'; yet forgiveness follows judgment, it does not displace it. 'Justice, but not mercy, is a matter of judgment.'

49 'Arguments', 268–9.

50 Arendt, *The Human Condition*, 242.

51 ibid., 51–2. See the section on 'Judgment and friendship' in chapter 4.

52 Alasdair MacIntyre, *After Virtue*, Notre Dame, University of Notre Dame Press, 1981, 141, 143–5. In speaking of 'the large and unAristotelian preoccupation with rules of modern moral philosophers', MacIntyre refers specifically to Rawls and Nozick, who offer 'rule-specified concepts of justice'. There is little mention of rules in Aristotle's *Ethics* because judgment, *phronesis*, has an indispensable role in the life of the virtuous man which it could not have in the life of the rule-abiding man. Preoccupation with law reflects an understanding of morality in terms of rules. Kant, pre-eminently, conceives of all moral life in terms of rule-governed activity. Therefore he turns to reflective judgments of taste to situate those forms of human experience that are non-rule-governed. This results in a disjunction of morality and judgment, whereby moral life is aligned with law, which is governed by rules. This Kantian subordination of moral judgment to moral rules informs the conception of moral theory represented by Rawls and Nozick.

53 Rawls, *A Theory of Justice*, London, Oxford University Press, 1973, 395–9.

54 See ibid., 30–3.

55 Walter Benjamin, 'The storyteller', in *Illuminations*, ed. Hannah Arendt, trans. Harry Zohn, New York, Schocken Books, 1969, 83–4. Cf. MacIntyre, *After Virtue*, chapter 15 ('The virtues, the unity of a human life and the concept of a tradition'), which explores the idea of a human life as 'enacted narrative': 'man is . . . essentially a story-telling animal' (201).

CHAPTER 7 TOWARDS A THEORY OF POLITICAL JUDGMENT

1 Although this illustration may appear fairly straightforward, even the most simple aesthetic judgment – 'This is a beautiful rose' – presents very complicated logical problems. To use the terms introduced in P. T. Geach's essay 'Good and evil' (*Analysis*, vol. 18, 103–12), it is not clear

whether the term 'beautiful' in the above example is an 'attributive' or a 'predicative' adjective (meaning by attributive that the meaning of beautiful is logically inseparable from the noun to which it is applied in the particular case, and therefore will vary relative to the various particular nouns of which it is predicated). Kant clearly believed that beautiful was *not* an attributive adjective, for he conceived of aesthetic judgment as a formal, non-cognitive faculty for representing pleasure: 'To deem something good, I must always know what sort of a thing the object is intended to be, i.e., I must have a concept of it. That is not necessary to enable me to see beauty in a thing. Flowers, free patterns, lines aimlessly intertwining – technically termed foliage, – have no signification, depend upon no definite concept, and yet please' (*Critique of Judgment*, §4; 1: 46). But surely there are cases where we would feel unqualified to render an aesthetic judgment without knowing something about the object to which we were ascribing the predicate beauty, and that knowledge thus influencing (in a perfectly legitimate way) whether or not we did in fact apply the predicate. (For instance, someone who has studied art history is capable of more subtle discriminations in virtue of being able to deliberate about whether or not a work falls under a certain class, where the ordinary person would fail to recognize certain features of the work for want of the terms with which to describe or characterize those features.) On the other hand, it is quite possible to conceive of aesthetic judgments that can be rendered with confidence without claiming any knowledge whatsoever concerning the objects judged. Thus it could be held (as Kant must have) that knowing that something is a rose has nothing at all to do with arriving at the judgment that it is beautiful. (Suppose I were transported to a strange planet; I might be quite capable of saying that something was beautiful without being able to determine whether it was 'animal, mineral, or vegetable'. But I could *not* say that the thing was 'good' without knowing more about that which was being judged.)

2 For discussion of some examples of practical judgment, see Hans-Georg Gadamer, 'Theory, technology, practice: the task of the science of man', *Social Research*, 44 (3), 529–61, esp. 548–52, on medical practice, and 556–8, on assimilation of research information and use of a word index; and Stuart Hampshire, 'Public and private morality', in Hampshire (ed.), *Public and Private Morality*, Cambridge, Cambridge University Press, 1978, 23–53, esp. 23–31, on perceptual judgment, and 31–4, on linguistic translation. Other examples are explored in Michael Oakeshott, *Rationalism in Politics*, London, Methuen, 1962.

3 See Michael Polanyi, *Personal Knowledge*, London, Routledge & Kegan Paul, 1962.

4 This 'reflective' dimension to determinant judgment is also noted by Arendt. See *The Life of the Mind*, vol. 1 (*Thinking*), ed. Mary McCarthy, New York, Harcourt Brace Jovanovich, 1978, 69.

5 See Stanley Cavell, 'The availability of Wittgenstein's later philosophy', in *Must We Mean What We Say?*, Cambridge, Cambridge University Press, 1976, esp. 47–52.

6 See Hubert L. Dreyfus, *What Computers Can't Do*, New York, Harper & Row, 1972; rev. edn, 1979. For specific analysis of the chess case, see Dreyfus' article, 'Phenomenology and artificial intelligence', in James M. Edie (ed.), *Phenomenology in America*, Chicago, Quadrangle Books, 1967, 31–47.

7 See Arendt, *The Life of the Mind*, vol. 2 (*Willing*), ed. Mary McCarthy, New York, Harcourt Brace Jovanovich, 1978, 217.

8 Cf. Julius Kovesi, *Moral Notions*, London, Routledge & Kegan Paul, 1967, 10. See also Thomas Kuhn, 'Objectivity, value judgment, and theory choice', in *The Essential Tension*, Chicago, University of Chicago Press, 1977, 320–39; Gadamer sees a reflection of his own concerns in Kuhn's work in the philosophy of science: see 'Discussion on "Hermeneutics and social science"', *Cultural Hermeneutics*, 2 (4), 336. For discussion of the notion of 'hard cases', as applied to legal judgment, see Ronald Dworkin, 'Hard cases' and 'Can rights be controversial?', in *Taking Rights Seriously*, London, Duckworth, 1978, 81–130 and 279–90 respectively.

9 Kant, *Critique of Judgment*, §31; Meredith trans., 1: 136.

10 Michael Polanyi, *The Tacit Dimension*, London, Routledge & Kegan Paul, 1967, 4.

11 ibid., 77–8.

12 ibid., 87.

13 See Arendt, *The Origins of Totalitarianism*, vol. 2 (*Imperialism*), 3rd edn, New York, Harcourt Brace Jovanovich, 1973, 109–11.

14 As Shaftesbury has written: historical truth is 'itself a part of moral truth. To be a judge in one, requires a judgment in the other' (*Characteristics*, Indianapolis, Bobbs-Merrill, 1964, vol. 1, 97).

15 Ludwig Wittgenstein, *Philosophical Investigations*, 3rd edn, New York, Macmillan, 1968, para. 242, 88.

16 This question of fundamental dispute over how to apply shared concepts directs us to the 'essentially contested concepts' literature, a way of looking at political concepts which was initiated by W. B. Gallie ('Essentially contested concepts', in M. Black (ed.), *The Importance of Language*, Englewood Cliffs, N.J., Prentice-Hall, 1962, 121–46), and which is best epitomized in William Connolly, *The Terms of Political Discourse*, Lexington, Mass., D. C. Heath, 1974.

17 The question here is not whether there is some ascertainable moral-political framework that will guarantee a resolution in all cases; but rather, whether there is, in principle, any limit to the possibility of overcoming incommensurability. Our contention is that there is no such limit: at no point are we justified in terminating an unresolved argument, for it always remains open to us to persevere with it still further. The next stage of argument may yet bring an enlargement of moral vision to one of the contending parties, allowing this contender to integrate the perspective of the other into his own in a relation of part to whole (as Aristotle does for democratic and oligarchic conceptions of justice in the *Politics*, book III, chapter 9). Therefore at any point there remains the possibility, though not the guarantee, of resolving deep conflict (not necessarily in the sense that one of the parties to the conflict will feel compelled to yield, but in the sense that sustained communication may eventually give rise to an asymmetry of moral perception – such that the insight of one of the contestants dialectically surpasses that of the other). Confronted with apparent stalemate, there is no need to give in to moral or intellectual 'pluralism', for it always remains open to us to say 'Press on with the argument'.

   In order to weigh truth claims, one need not require translation of the competing claims into a neutral language of description in which the claims are straightforwardly commensurable. Instead, one can formulate, say, moral truth in terms of counterfactual claims to more or less comprehensive moral *intuition*. Here one specifies (by counterfactual supposition) that, presented with two available (conflicting) alternatives, an ideally endowed being with full access to the moral vision of each of the protagonists would choose one of the two contradictories, or would locate a third position which did full justice to each of the two rejected, or superseded, claims. Or, adopting Habermas' formulation of the consensus theory of truth, we may simply ask (without methodically restricting, in advance, the scope of the argument): under ideal conditions of purely rational communication, in whose favour would the argument, in the very final resort, be decided?

18 Cf. John McDowell, 'Virtue and reason', *The Monist*, 62 (3), 347–8: 'It is sometimes complained that Aristotle does not attempt to outline a decision procedure for questions about how to behave. But we have good reason to be suspicious of the assumption that there must be something to be found along the route he does not follow.'

19 Obviously, there are situations in which the community to which we address our judgment is a community of one (or rather, of two-in-one, for, as Arendt teaches, thinking is not a monologue, but rather a dialogue with

oneself). But this still presupposes the possibility of explaining or giving an account of the judgment to another, even if we would not expect the other to arrive at the same judgment, or even to be vexed by the kinds of questions which prompted us to judge in the first place. (For example, I decide never again to eat meat, for moral reasons, and I am able to make my moral commitment intelligible to someone for whom the question of vegetarianism has never even arisen, and whom I would neither expect to join me in my resolution nor fault for not so doing.)

20 See Hans-Georg Gadamer, 'On the scope and function of hermeneutical reflection', in *Philosophical Hermeneutics*, ed. D. E. Linge, Berkeley, University of California Press, 1976, 34–5: 'Tradition is no proof and validation of something, in any case not where validation is demanded by reflection. But the point is this: where does reflection demand it? Everywhere? I would object to such an answer on the grounds of the finitude of human existence and the essential particularity of reflection.' According to Gadamer, Habermas employs a pre-phenomenological concept of reflection that involves objectifying one's relation to what is reflected upon, whereas Gadamer himself claims to have learned from Husserl and Heidegger 'to see through the false objectification inherent in the idealist concept of reflection'.

21 H. H. Gerth and C. Wright Mills (eds), *From Max Weber*, New York, Oxford University Press, 1958, 128.

CHAPTER 8 CLOSING REFLECTIONS

1 Hobbes, *Leviathan*, part I, chapter 8, ed. Michael Oakeshott, Oxford, Basil Blackwell, 1960, 43.

2 Norman Jacobson discusses three exemplary observers of political affairs: Albert Camus (in his writings on Algeria), George Orwell (on the Spanish Civil War), and Hannah Arendt (on totalitarianism). Jacobson writes: 'each builds his thought around political events experienced as you and I experience only our profoundest loves and despairs in our private lives' (*Pride and Solace*, Berkeley, University of California Press, 1978, 131).

3 For the notion of 'exemplary validity', see Kant, *Critique of Judgment*, § 22; Meredith trans., I: 84; § 59; I: 221; *Critique of Pure Reason*, B172–B173, trans. Norman Kemp Smith, London, Macmillan, 1963, 177–8; and Arendt, *Lectures on Kant's Political Philosophy*, ed. R. Beiner, Chicago, University of Chicago Press, 1982, 76–7, 79–80, and 84–5.

Bibliography

Aquinas, St Thomas, 'Treatise on prudence and justice', in *Summa Theologiæ*, second part of second part, questions 47–62, London, Eyre & Spottiswoode, 1974–5, vols 36–7.

Arendt, Hannah, *Between Past and Future: Eight Exercises in Political Thought*, enlarged edn, New York, Viking Press, 1968.

Arendt, Hannah, *Eichmann in Jerusalem: A Report on the Banality of Evil*, revised and enlarged edn, New York, Viking Press, 1965.

Arendt, Hannah, 'Freedom and politics', in A. Hunold (ed.), *Freedom and Serfdom: An Anthology of Western Thought*, Dordrecht, D. Reidel, 1961, 191–217.

Arendt, Hannah, *The Human Condition*, Chicago, University of Chicago Press, 1958.

Arendt, Hannah, *The Jew as Pariah: Jewish Identity and Politics in the Modern Age*, ed. R. H. Feldman, New York, Grove Press, 1978.

Arendt, Hannah, *Lectures on Kant's Political Philosophy*, ed. R. Beiner, Chicago, University of Chicago Press, 1982.

Arendt, Hannah, *The Life of the Mind*, vol. 1: *Thinking*, vol. 2: *Willing*, ed. M. McCarthy, New York, Harcourt Brace Jovanovich, 1978.

Arendt, Hannah, 'On humanity in dark times: thoughts on Lessing', in Arendt, *Men in Dark Times*, Harmondsworth, Penguin, 1973, 11–38.

Arendt, Hannah, *On Revolution*, 2nd rev. edn, New York, Viking Press, 1965.

Arendt, Hannah, *The Origins of Totalitarianism*, 3 vols, 4th edn, New York, Harcourt Brace, 1968.

Arendt, Hannah, 'Personal responsibility under dictatorship', *The Listener*, 6 August 1964, vol. 72, 185–7, 205.

Arendt, Hannah, 'Thinking and moral considerations: a lecture', *Social Research*, 38 (3), 417–46.

Arendt, Hannah, 'Understanding and politics', *Partisan Review*, 20 (4), 377–92.

'Arguments: more on Eichmann', *Partisan Review*, Spring 1964, 31 (2), 253–83.

Aristotle, *Nicomachean Ethics*, trans. M. Ostwald, Indianapolis, Bobbs-Merrill, 1965.

Aristotle, *The Politics of Aristotle*, ed. E. Barker, Oxford, Clarendon Press, 1958.

Aristotle, *Rhetoric*, trans. W. R. Roberts, in *The Works of Aristotle*, ed. W. D. Ross, vol. 11, Oxford, Clarendon Press, 1924.

Aubenque, Pierre, 'La prudence chez Kant', *Revue de métaphysique et morale*, vol. 80, 1975, 156–82.

Bell, Daniel, 'The alphabet of justice', *Partisan Review*, Fall 1963, 30 (3), 417–29.

Benjamin, Walter, 'The storyteller', in Benjamin, *Illuminations*, ed. H. Arendt, trans. H. Zohn, Fontana, 1973, 83–109.

Burke, Edmund, *A Philosophical Inquiry into the Origin of Our Ideas of the Sublime and Beautiful*, New York, P. F. Collier & Son, 1909.

Cavell, Stanley, *Must We Mean What We Say?*, Cambridge, Cambridge University Press, 1976.

Connolly, William, *The Terms of Political Discourse*, Lexington, D. C. Heath, 1974.

'Discussion on "Hermeneutics and social science"', *Cultural Hermeneutics*, 2 (4), 331–6.

Dreyfus, Hubert L., 'Phenomenology and artificial intelligence', in J. M. Edie (ed.), *Phenomenology in America*, Chicago, Quadrangle Books, 1967, 31–47.

Dreyfus, Hubert L., *What Computers Can't Do*, rev. edn, New York, Harper & Row, 1979.

Dworkin, Ronald, *Taking Rights Seriously*, London, Duckworth, 1978.

Gadamer, Hans-Georg, 'Hermeneutics and social science', *Cultural Hermeneutics*, 2 (4), 307–16.

Gadamer, Hans-Georg, *Philosophical Hermeneutics*, ed. D. E. Linge, Berkeley, University of California Press, 1976.

Gadamer, Hans-Georg, 'Practical philosophy as a model of the human sciences', *Research in Phenomenology*, vol. 9, 74–85.

Gadamer, Hans-Georg, 'Theory, technology, practice: the task of the science of man', *Social Research*, 44 (3), 529–61.

Gadamer, Hans-Georg, *Truth and Method*, New York, Seabury Press, 1975.

Gallie, W. B., 'Essentially contested concepts', in M. Black (ed.), *The Importance of Language*, Englewood Cliffs, N.J., Prentice-Hall, 1962, 121–46.

Geach, P. T., 'Good and evil', *Analysis*, vol. 18, 103–12.

Godwin, William, *Enquiry Concerning Political Justice*, ed. I. Kramnick, Harmondsworth, Penguin, 1976, book II, chapter 6.

The Great Ideas: A Syntopicon, vol. 2, chapter 41: 'Judgment', 835–42, and vol. 3, chapter 73: 'Prudence', 472–9, Chicago, University of Chicago, 1952.

Habermas, Jürgen, *Communication and the Evolution of Society*, Boston, Beacon Press, 1979.

Habermas, Jürgen, 'Hannah Arendt's communications concept of power', *Social Research*, 44 (1), 3–24.

Habermas, Jürgen, *Knowledge and Human Interests*, trans. J. J. Shapiro, Boston, Beacon Press, 1971.

Habermas, Jürgen, *Legitimation Crisis*, London, Heinemann, 1976.

Habermas, Jürgen, 'On systematically distorted communication', *Inquiry*, 1970, vol. 13, 205–18.

Habermas, Jürgen, 'On the German-Jewish heritage', *Telos*, vol. 44, 127–31.

Habermas, Jürgen, 'Some distinctions in universal pragmatics', *Theory and Society*, 1976, vol. 3, 155–67.

Habermas, Jürgen, *Theory and Practice*, trans. J. Viertel, London, Heinemann, 1974.

Habermas, Jürgen, 'Towards a theory of communicative competence', *Inquiry*, 1970, vol. 13, 360–75.

Hampshire, Stuart (ed.), *Public and Private Morality*, Cambridge, Cambridge University Press, 1978.

Hegel, G. W. F., *Philosophy of Right*, trans. T. M. Knox, Oxford, Clarendon Press, 1967.

Heidegger, Martin, *Kant and the Problem of Metaphysics*, trans. J. S. Churchill, Bloomington, Indiana University Press, 1962.

Heidegger, Martin, 'The origin of the work of art', in Heidegger, *Poetry, Language, Thought*, trans. A. Hofstadter, New York, Harper & Row, 1975, 15–87.

Hennis, Wilhelm, 'Topics and political science', *Graduate Faculty Philosophy Journal*, 7 (1), 35–77.

Hobbes, Thomas, *Leviathan*, ed. M. Oakeshott, Oxford, Basil Blackwell, 1960, part I, chapters 6–8.

Hume, David, *Of the Standard of Taste, and Other Essays*, ed. J. W. Lenz, Indianapolis, Bobbs-Merrill, 1965.

Jacobson, Norman, *Pride and Solace*, Berkeley, University of California Press, 1978.

Kant, Immanuel, *Anthropology from a Pragmatic Point of View*, trans. M. J. Gregor, The Hague, Martinus Nijhoff, 1974.

Kant, Immanuel, *The Critique of Judgement*, trans. J. C. Meredith, Oxford, Clarendon Press, 1952.

Kant, Immanuel, *Critique of Practical Reason and Other Works on the Theory of Ethics*, trans. T. K. Abbott, London, Longmans, 1909.

Kant, Immanuel, *Critique of Pure Reason*, trans. N. K. Smith, New York, St Martin's Press, 1963.

Kant, Immanuel, *The Doctrine of Virtue*, trans. M. J. Gregor, New York, Harper & Row, 1964.

Kant, Immanuel, *Foundations of the Metaphysics of Morals*, trans. L. W. Beck, Indianapolis, Bobbs-Merrill, 1959.

Kant, Immanuel, *Kant's Political Writings*, ed. H. Reiss, trans. H. B. Nisbet, Cambridge, Cambridge University Press, 1971.

Kant, Immanuel, *Observations on the Feeling of the Beautiful and Sublime*, trans. J. T. Goldthwait, Berkeley, University of California Press, 1960.

Kovesi, Julius, *Moral Notions*, London, Routledge & Kegan Paul, 1967.

Kuhn, Thomas, 'Objectivity, value judgment, and theory choice', in Kuhn, *The Essential Tension*, Chicago, University of Chicago Press, 1977, 320–39.

Lessing, Gotthold Ephraim, *Nathan the Wise*, trans. W. F. C. Ade, New York, Barron's Educational Series, 1972.

Locke, John, *An Essay Concerning Human Understanding*, ed. A. C. Fraser, 2 vols, New York, Dover, 1959, book II, chap. XI; book IV, chap. XIV.

Lukes, Steven, 'Of gods and demons: Habermas and practical reason', in J. B. Thompson and D. Held (eds), *Habermas: Critical Debates*, London, Macmillan, 1982, 134–48.

McCarthy, Thomas, 'A theory of communicative competence', in P. Connerton (ed.), *Critical Sociology*, Harmondsworth, Penguin, 1976, 470–97.

McDowell, John, 'Virtue and reason', *The Monist*, 62 (3), 331–50.

MacIntyre, Alasdair, *After Virtue*, Notre Dame, University of Notre Dame Press, 1981.

Merleau-Ponty, Maurice, *Humanism and Terror*, trans. J. O'Neill, Boston, Beacon Press, 1969.

Nietzsche, Friedrich, *Basic Writings of Nietzsche*, trans. and ed. W. Kaufmann, New York, Modern Library, 1968.

Oakeshott, Michael, 'Learning and teaching', in R. S. Peters (ed.), *The Concept of Education*, London, Routledge & Kegan Paul, 1967.

Oakeshott, Michael, *Rationalism in Politics and Other Essays*, London, Methuen, 1962.

Parekh, Bhikhu, 'The nature of political philosophy', in P. King and B. C. Parekh (eds), *Politics and Experience*, Cambridge, Cambridge University Press, 1968.

Plato, *The Dialogues of Plato*, trans. B. Jowett, 2 vols, New York, Random House, 1937.

Polanyi, Michael, *Personal Knowledge*, London, Routledge & Kegan Paul, 1962.

Polanyi, Michael, *The Tacit Dimension*, Garden City, N.Y., Anchor Books, 1967.

Rawls, John, *A Theory of Justice*, London, Oxford University Press, 1973.

Rorty, Richard, *Philosophy and the Mirror of Nature*, Princeton, Princeton University Press, 1979.

Rosen, Stanley, 'Return to the origin: reflections on Plato and contemporary philosophy', *International Philosophical Quarterly*, 16 (2), 151–77.

Rotenstreich, Nathan, 'Sublimity and terror', *Idealistic Studies*, 3 (3), 238–51.

Sandel, Michael, *Liberalism and the Limits of Justice*, Cambridge, Cambridge University Press, 1982.

Schiller, Friedrich, *On the Aesthetic Education of Man*, trans. R. Snell, New York, Ungar, 1965.

Selzer, M. (ed.), *Zionism Reconsidered*, New York, Macmillan, 1970.

Shaftesbury, Anthony, Earl of, *Characteristics*, Indianapolis, Bobbs-Merrill, 1964.

Shklar, Judith, 'Hannah Arendt's triumph', *The New Republic*, 27 December 1975.

The Socialist Register, nos 10 and 11, 1973–4.

Spinoza, Benedict de, 'Theologico-political treatise', chapter XX, and 'A political treatise', chapter III, in *The Chief Works of Benedict de Spinoza*, vol. I, trans. R. H. M. Elwes, New York, Dover, 1951.

Strauss, Leo, *The City and Man*, Chicago, University of Chicago Press, Midway Reprint, 1977.

Strauss, Leo, *Natural Right and History*, Chicago, University of Chicago Press, 1953.

Strauss, Leo, *The Political Philosophy of Hobbes: Its Basis and Its Genesis*, trans. E. M. Sinclair, Chicago, University of Chicago Press, 1952.

Taylor, Charles, 'Interpretation and the sciences of Man', *Review of Metaphysics*, 25 (3), 3–51.

Taylor, Charles, 'The opening arguments of the *Phenomenology*', in A. MacIntyre (ed.), *Hegel*, New York, Anchor, 1972, 151–87.

Thucydides, *History of the Peloponnesian War*, trans. R. Warner, Harmondsworth, Penguin, 1954.

Unger, Roberto Mangabeira, *Knowledge and Politics*, New York, Free Press, 1975.

Vico, Giambattista, *On the Study Methods of Our Time*, trans. E. Gianturco, Indianapolis, Bobbs-Merrill, 1965.

Voegelin, Eric, 'What is right by nature?', in Voegelin, *Anamnesis*, trans. and ed. G. Niemeyer, Notre Dame, University of Notre Dame, 1978, 55–70.

Vollrath, Ernst, 'That all governments rest on opinion', *Social Research*, 43 (1), 46–61.

Weber, Max, *From Max Weber*, ed. H. H. Gerth and C. W. Mills, New York, Oxford University Press, 1958.

Wittgenstein, Ludwig, *Philosophical Investigations*, 3rd edn, New York, Macmillan, 1968.

Wolin, Sheldon, 'Political theory as a vocation', *American Political Science Review*, vol. 63, 1062–82.

Index